T0360480

ROUTLEDGE LIBRARY EDITIONS:
LABOUR ECONOMICS

Volume 6

FLEXIBILITY, MOBILITY AND THE LABOUR MARKET

FLEXIBILITY, MOBILITY AND THE LABOUR MARKET

GEORGE S. CALLAGHAN

LONDON AND NEW YORK

First published in 1997 by Ashgate Publishing Ltd

This edition first published in 2019
by Routledge
2 Park Square, Milton Park, Abingdon, Oxon OX14 4RN

and by Routledge
52 Vanderbilt Avenue, New York, NY 10017

Routledge is an imprint of the Taylor & Francis Group, an informa business

© 1997 George S. Callaghan

All rights reserved. No part of this book may be reprinted or reproduced or utilised in any form or by any electronic, mechanical, or other means, now known or hereafter invented, including photocopying and recording, or in any information storage or retrieval system, without permission in writing from the publishers.

Trademark notice: Product or corporate names may be trademarks or registered trademarks, and are used only for identification and explanation without intent to infringe.

British Library Cataloguing in Publication Data
A catalogue record for this book is available from the British Library

ISBN: 978-0-367-02458-1 (Set)
ISBN: 978-0-429-02526-6 (Set) (ebk)
ISBN: 978-0-367-07548-4 (Volume 6) (hbk)
ISBN: 978-0-429-02134-3 (Volume 6) (ebk)

Publisher's Note
The publisher has gone to great lengths to ensure the quality of this reprint but points out that some imperfections in the original copies may be apparent.

Disclaimer
The publisher has made every effort to trace copyright holders and would welcome correspondence from those they have been unable to trace.

Flexibility, Mobility and the Labour Market

GEORGE S. CALLAGHAN

Ashgate

Aldershot • Brookfield USA • Singapore • Sydney

© George S. Callaghan 1997

All rights reserved. No part of this publication may be reproduced, stored in a retrieval system, or transmitted in any form or by any means, electronic, mechanical, photocopying, recording or otherwise without the prior permission of the publisher.

Published by
Ashgate Publishing Ltd
Gower House
Croft Road
Aldershot
Hants GU11 3HR
England

Ashgate Publishing Company
Old Post Road
Brookfield
Vermont 05036
USA

British Library Cataloguing in Publication Data

Callaghan, George S.
Flexibility, mobility and the labour market
1. Labour market 2. Labour mobility
I. Title
331.1'2

Library of Congress Catalog Card Number: 97-72669

ISBN 1 85972 604 6

Printed and bound by Athenaeum Press, Ltd.,
Gateshead, Tyne & Wear.

Contents

List of tables vii
List of figures ix
Acknowledgments xi
Preface xiii

Chapter 1 Introduction: Flexibility in labour markets 1

Chapter 2 The nature of labour markets 9

2.1 Introduction 9
2.2 Free market approach to labour markets 9
2.3 Segmented labour market theory 15
2.4 Conclusion 20

Chapter 3 Studying labour markets and labour forces 21

3.1 Introduction 21
3.2 Changes in employment 21
3.3 Occupational and industrial mobility 24
3.4 Bristol's economy 25
3.5 Qualitative methodology - micro social studies 26
3.6 The research settings - Bristol Insurance and Bristol Laminated 32
3.7 The interviews 33
3.8 Data analysis 37
3.9 Conclusion 39

Chapter 4	**Recruitment of labour**	41
4.1	Introduction	41
4.2	Recruitment methods	42
4.3	The recruitment process	51
4.4	The rationale behind using networks	67
4.5	Advantages of networks	72
4.6	Formal vs informal: a contrasting rationale	80
4.7	Conclusion	86
Chapter 5	**Labour and skill**	89
5.1	Introduction	89
5.2	The conceptualisation of skill	90
5.3	Construction of a skilled job	100
5.4	Perceptions of skills	112
5.5	The acquisition of skills	133
5.6	Conclusion	140
Chapter 6	**Work and workers**	143
6.1	Introduction	143
6.2	Perceptions of work and workers	144
6.3	Occupational hierarchy and ambition	165
6.4	Conclusion	185
Chapter 7	**Conclusions: Prospects for the future**	189
7.1	Introduction	189
7.2	Analytical material	190
7.3	Theoretical reflections	192
7.4	Labour market policy	194
Appendices		197
Bibliography		203
Index		229

List of tables

3.1	Bristol % change	23
3.2	GB % change	23
3.3	Changes of employer and industry	24
4.1	Successful method of engagement (%)	48
4.2	How employees first heard about job (%)	49
4.3	Recruitment channels favoured by employers (%)	50
4.4	Bristol Insurance, summary table of how respondents first heard about job	52
4.5	Bristol Insurance, the extent of use of family and friendship networks	53
4.6	Bristol Insurance, respondents who commented on meritocratic nature of recruitment process	58
4.7	Bristol Laminated, summary table of how respondents first heard about job	61
4.8	Bristol Laminated, the extent of use of family and friendship networks	61
4.9	Bristol Laminated, reciprocal help	66
4.10	Bristol Insurance, advantages of family and friendship networks	72
4.11	Bristol Laminated, advantages of family and friendship networks	75
5.1	Bristol Insurance, classifications of a skilled job	100
5.2	Bristol Laminated, classifications of a skilled job	105
5.3	Bristol Insurance, breakdown of social skills	113
5.4	Bristol Insurance, breakdown of technical skills	118
5.5	Bristol Laminated, breakdown of own skills and skills necessary for factory work	122
5.6	Bristol Insurance, how skills are acquired	133
5.7	Bristol Laminated, how skills are acquired	137

6.1a	Bristol Insurance, perceptions of factory workers	144
6.1b	Bristol Insurance, perceptions of factory work and working process	145
6.2	Bristol Insurance, perceptions of office work and workers	149
6.3	Bristol Laminated, perceptions of office work and workers	157
6.4	Bristol Laminated, perceptions of factory work and workers	158
6.5	Bristol Insurance, references to stratification	168
6.6	Bristol Insurance, references to ambition	174
6.7	Bristol Laminated, references to stratification	179
6.8	Bristol Laminated, references to ambition	181

List of figures

2.1	Profit maximising level of employment	11
2.2	Labour supply	12
2.3	Effects of basic minimum wage	12
3.1	Changes in employment	22
3.2	Breakdown of changes	22
3.3	Changes of employer and occupation	25

Acknowledgments

My primary acknowledgement must go to those workers and managers at Bristol Insurance and Bristol Laminated, who gave up their time to talk to me. I would also like to thank colleagues at The University of the West of England, Bristol - Jeffrey Weeks, Marion Jackson and Colwyn Jones, whose comments, advice and guidance have been invaluable. There are others at Bristol I would like to thank, particularly Simon Thompson, Ian Welsh, Rosemary MacKeknie, Arthur Baxter and Richard O'Doherty, whose patience and thoughtful comments have been vital throughout. My gratitude extends to many others but, in addition to my family, I would like to thank my friend and flatmate Steve Cramer, for being so helpful for so long and, finally, both Anne-Marie O'Hara, without whom I would never have started this work, and Eileen Campbell, without whom I would never have finished it. Finally thanks to the Centre for Social and Economic Research at the Faculty of Economics and Social Science, The University of West of England, for providing me with a postgraduate student bursary with which to complete the Doctoral dissertation upon which this book is based, and most especially Christine Hunt, for providing the assistance and resources to enable publication.

Preface

The central problematic of this text deals with the concept of flexibility and the related potential for mobility between industrial sectors. Throughout the 1980s and into the 1990s the concept of flexibility gained popularity amongst academics and policy makers alike. It seemed to offer a catch all solution to the problems of deindustrialization and the labour market - for an economy to succeed in an increasingly competitive international global economy it had to respond quickly to changes in demand. The free market and the price mechanism were viewed as the most efficient and effective channels of communication between economic agents which would allow supply and demand in various markets to settle at equilibrium. The consequent policy focus was on creating the conditions within which the market could operate most effectively and concentrated on supply side policies - such as making the factors of production more responsive. Within the labour market this meant aiming for a flexible labour force and numerous deregulating acts were passed to remove what were seen as "barriers" and "rigidities" to the price mechanism.

While there are many characteristics to flexibility, with the academic literature especially focused on what have become known as the "flexible firm" and "flexible specialisation", this research concentrates on a related but underdeveloped function of flexibility - the potential for industrial and occupational mobility. Evidence from Employment Department publications and White Papers is used to demonstrate that this was an important part of the government's aims - to ensure that people in declining industries had the motivation and incentive to move to where the work is, both in terms of geographical location and industry.

This book sets out to investigate this "mobility" aspect of flexibility using a qualitative case study approach, which examines the views and values of employees from a large factory (Bristol Laminated) and a large office (Bristol Insurance). The objective is to gain an understanding of any barriers to mobility which may be perceived by those who inhabit firms at opposite ends industrial restructuring and, by so doing, determine a more accurate picture of the potential for workers to be flexible in this way - to shift between declining and expanding industries and occupations.

Attention is focused in three main areas - methods of recruitment; perceptions and understanding of skill and perceptions of each other and each others work. By building up an understanding of the social, historical and institutional processes which shape the meanings and motivations articulated by respondents on these issues it is possible to gauge the extent to which the labour market is competitive in the neo-classical sense, or whether the labour market is more accurately conceptualised as consisting of what the classical economists and later segmented labour market theorists described as non-competing industrial groups.

Turning to sources, the secondary material used is fully referenced throughout with a detailed bibliography at the end. The primary material, drawn from transcriptions of taped semi-structured interviews, is cited by reference to a number and the name of the firm. The Appendix contains a more detailed list of the job functions of each numbered respondent but, for anonymity, real names are not used.

1 Introduction: Flexibility in labour markets

> ... 1979 saw a change of emphasis in economic policy, with the election of a government committed to strengthening the role of market forces. Indeed, a competitive, efficient and *flexible* labour market is the overarching aim of the government's labour market policies. (Beatson, 1995: executive summary, emphasis in original)

> Flexible labour markets play a key part in a competitive economy. They allow employers to deploy their workforce in the most efficient way. They allow workers to make the most of their skills and experience. And they bring supply and demand for labour into balance. (Department of Trade and Industry, 1994: 50)

These extracts from Government sources illustrate the central importance of flexible labour markets to Government economic policy. This policy has developed within the context of severe macroeconomic shifts in demand for labour, in particular the shift from manufacturing to service work. From 1979 to 1993 employment in the services sector increased from 58.5% of all UK employees or some thirteen and a quarter million people to 72.8% or some fifteen million people. Over this same period employment in manufacturing fell from 31.4% of those in employment, representing around seven million employees' to 20.4%, or around four million (Employment Department Group, 1994), a trend which is seen as continuing (Skills and Enterprise Network, 1993). The Employment Department, in the White Paper '*Training for Employment*' (1988a) commented of this economic restructuring:

> In nearly all advanced industrial economies, there has recently been a declining trend in the number of jobs in manufacturing, especially in unskilled occupations. The recent vacancy survey commissioned by the Department of Employment suggested that currently only 17% of vacancies are for unskilled manual jobs. The prospect is of increasing demand for skilled workers, and

continuing growth in the commercial and service sectors. (Employment Department, 1988a: 15)

This restructuring of the economy has caused immense upheaval in the world of work, with shifting demands for labour and consequent changes in employment opportunities, making (as the above statistics illustrate) the position of those in manufacturing particularly vulnerable. These changes have occurred not just in the United Kingdom but have been common across the industrialised (Western) world (OECD, 1989; OECD, 1994). This shift from manufacturing to service sector employment has been accompanied by a resurgence in neo-classical 'monetarist' economics, evident through the election of Margaret Thatcher in the United Kingdom in 1979 and of Ronald Reagan in America in 1980. These elections ushered in an ideology which looked favourably upon the free market and sought to introduce (or extend) the rigour and discipline of competition to all aspects of economic and social life. Recent commentators have written of this:

> The search for flexibility was also associated with moves at a more macro level to change the nature of the employment relationship, in fact to deregulate labour markets so that they resembled the labour markets of neo-classical theory. (Rubery and Wilkinson, 1994: 5)

Since 1979, then, the role of market forces has been emphasised above all others and the policies flowing from such an ideological outlook were focused particularly in the field of employment, where the aim has been to sweep away what were seen as regulatory and legislative restrictive practices. As Margaret Thatcher and Nigel Lawson commented in their separate memoirs:

> ... the 'supply side' reforms were highly successful. These were the changes which made for greater efficiency and flexibility and so enabled British business to meet the demands of foreign and domestic markets... Trade union reform was crucial. The most important changes were those made between 1982 and 1984 but the process continued right up until I left office... These reductions in trade union power, together with the reinforcements of individual trade unionist's rights and responsibilities, were crucial to a properly functioning labour market, in which restrictive practices were overcome and unit labour costs kept down below the levels they would otherwise have reached. The abolition of that monument to modern Luddism - the National Dock Labour Scheme - was another blow to restrictive practices. (Thatcher, 1993: 669)

> In a market economy and a free society it is plainly a matter for business and industry itself to determine rates of pay, which in turn in the long run determine the level of employment; and the responsibility of government is essentially to provide the right overall economic climate. But there were some specific areas in which government action was needed, and to a considerable

> (although incomplete) extent that action was taken. One such area was that of the long-established statutory Wages Councils, which set minimum pay rates in certain low-pay industries. These were not, as I would have liked, abolished; but their powers were greatly limited and (outside agriculture) those under twenty-one were removed from their scope altogether. (Lawson, 1992: 432, 433)

Anything which was perceived as standing in the way of market forces, such as Trade Unions and Wages Councils, were to be removed.[1] In addition, Welfare benefits, which were seen as a disincentive to look for work, also came under attack early in the first Thatcher administration, with benefit calculations being changed to increase in line only with prices and not, as was previously the case, with earnings (Johnson, 1991). Through deregulation the labour market was to become more flexible and more responsive to market forces as exercised through the price mechanism. Throughout the 1980s, then, the concept of flexibility emerged to sum up at once both the nature of change in the labour market which had been caused by economic restructuring and the change in the nature of labour market participants and their work which would allow economies to capitalise on such restructuring. As Beatson (1995) has commented:

> Flexibility is not an easy concept to define and measure. It is, however, concerned with the markets ability to adapt and respond to changing conditions. (Beatson, 1995: Executive Summary)

Despite the ambiguity surrounding the concept of flexibility the centrality of market forces is clear, as is the importance of creating the conditions in which the market can operate efficiently. The subsequent flexibility debate has manifested itself with different features of flexibility, in particular around discussions of the 'flexible firm' and 'flexible specialisation', which deal respectively with changes to the organisation of the workforce and with changes to the nature of the production process.

Turning firstly to the 'flexible firm', this was popularised by a brief but influential paper by Atkinson (1984), 'Manpower strategies for flexible organisations', where the recommendation for management was to develop a 'flexible firm' which can rapidly vary the number, type and working time of employees to meet changing market conditions and capitalise on changing technologies. The responsiveness of output is, in large part, seen as related to workers offering two main kinds of flexibility: functional and numerical. 'Functional' flexibility refers to a situation where traditional lines of occupational demarcation are removed and a group of core workers is created who are 'multi-skilled' with the ability to 'multi-task', these workers are likely to be in secure full

---

[1]For more detail on the Employment Acts which focused on Trade Union reform see Deakin (1986) and Hendy (1993).

time employment. 'Numerical' flexibility, on the other hand, refers to a more peripheral group of workers, whose numbers may be increased or decreased according to short run changes in product demand. In addition, these workers are more likely to be on short term contracts and/or part time working arrangements. Atkinson went on to expand this model (Atkinson 1985a, 1985b; Atkinson and Gregory, 1986; Atkinson and Meager, 1986), further developing and recommending a labour market which is defined by dualism, with a 'core' group of stable employees being supplemented by a more insecure 'periphery' group. The continuing significance and strength of such an approach is evident not only from the Acts which have been passed relating to labour law (Deakin, 1986; Hendy, 1993) but also from a number of recent government publications aimed at employers and employees (Employment Department 1991, 1993a). For example, in *A guide to flexible working* the Employment Department recommends flexible working both for the employer and the employee:

> For the employer: flexible working arrangements can make a business more competitive and attractive to potential employees. It may help an employer meet production deadlines or provide a better service to customers. It may reduce a business's staff turnover and cut overheads. It may also attract a wider range of applicants for jobs.
>
> For the employee: many people, including those with domestic responsibilities, some people with disabilities and some older workers, have long recognised the advantages that flexible working can offer them. In the 1990s other people, who have traditionally worked a set 35 - or 40 - hour week on their employer's premises, are becoming aware of these advantages. (Employment Department, 1993a: 3,4)

The flexible firm theories have, however, come in for some criticism (Pollert, 1988a, 1988b, 1991; Marginson, 1991; Elger, 1991; Curry, 1993). The main thrust of the criticism has been not on a denial of changed working practices *per se* but of the overwhelming emphasis given to the supposedly radical disjuncture associated with these changes. These authors do not deny or criticise change for its own sake, rather they argue that commentary and analysis should be placed in historical, political and social context. Thus changes in working practices should not be seen as a 'natural' development but instead as part of a continuing process of negotiation between those involved in the labour process. Such a process is characterised not by 'natural' development down any one route but by continuous communication, involving both co-operation and confrontation and leading to a constantly shifting consensus.

The second major feature of the flexibility debate has become known as 'flexible specialisation' (Piore and Sabel, 1984; Piore, 1986a, 1986b; Sabel and Zeitlin, 1985; Murray, 1987; Tolliday and Zeitlin, 1987). This movement towards 'flexible specialisation' was seen as being caused by two factors: changing (and more specialised) consumer demand, and advances in technology which allowed small batch production to meet niche market demand. These two factors were seen as facilitating a move away from 'Fordist' mass production, where automation and mechanisation combined to produce low per unit cost output for a standardised mass market, and towards 'post-Fordist' specialised production with the use of craft skills to meet the demand for changing, and more eclectic, consumer tastes (Urry, 1988). Flexible specialisation was seen as offering a system which would satisfy changing patterns of consumption, capitalise on changing technology and assure sustained economic growth. The response from academics, however, has been mixed, ranging from the explicitly critical (Williams et al, 1987; Pollert, 1988b, 1991; Smith, 1991) through the critical acceptance of the French regulationists who describe the emerging regime as 'neo- Fordism' and see it as including either the potential for increased worker involvement or increased capitalist control (Palloix, 1976; Aglietta, 1979; Lipietz, 1987), to writers who are more positive about the perceived changes and recommend policies which would bring about, or speed up, the move towards flexible specialisation (Piore and Sabel, 1984; Hirst and Zeitlin, 1988, 1989; Scott, 1988; Zeitlin, 1988; Murray, 1989a, 1989b). Criticisms of the flexible specialisation school have included allegations that they are, in terms of industry and area, empirically selective (Williams et al, 1987; Hyman, 1988; Pollert, 1988b, 1991; Amin, 1991; Curry, 1993); that there is a false dichotomy between mass and specialised markets, suggesting that during the period of 'Fordism' there still existed small scale production demanding craft skills and also asserting that mass, 'Fordist', methods of production to meet the mass market demands are still prevalent in markets such as motor vehicles and consumer electronics (Williams et al, 1987); and on the extent to which these new flexible specialisation methods of production will, apriori, feed through into better conditions, and more control, for workers (Elger, 1987; Rubery et al, 1987; Kelley, 1989).

Pollert (1988b) argues that flexibility in general and the flexible firm and flexible specialisation in particular is rooted solidly in a pro-market ideology:

> ... there is a much wider ideological message of social integration. The 'core' and 'periphery' model is one of organisational balance, labour process flexibility in the one supplemented by labour market flexibility in the other. The 'flexible specialisation' analysis is likewise based on dual labour market analysis as a model of dynamic equilibrium. It rejects an analysis of capitalism as a system based on contradictory class interests, and wholeheartedly supports market regeneration. It poses a new equation of sectoral and productive balance, which is healthier for markets.... The convergence between these perspectives, and the neo-classical revival of the enterprise economy, individualised competition and policies of employment deregulation and attacks on trade unionism lead one to question why such a broad ideological consensus should have developed. Capitalist crisis, and the lack of control by nation states over the system may predispose the relinquishing of policies of control, towards an emphasis on the primacy of 'markets', raising economic flexibility to be the panacea. (Pollert, 1988b: 68, 71)

The theme, therefore, running through the two characteristics of flexibility which have received most attention from academics - the flexible firm and flexible specialisation - is of the equilibrating power of the market and the need to remove rigidities (in the nature of working practices or method of production) in order for the market to function effectively. There is an additional aspect of flexibility, however, which has received less attention from academics - this the need for occupational and industrial mobility.

The Government have argued that if the labour market is to operate flexibly the workforce must not only accept different working patterns and routines but must be mobile in response to changing labour market demands, both in terms of moving to where the work is and in doing work in different industries and occupations. That this is an important policy priority for the Government is clear from extracts from Employment Department publications on labour market flexibility:

> In a flexible labour market, labour should be mobile. Labour mobility has a number of dimensions. It can be thought of as the degree to which people are prepared to move, in response to labour market phenomena, between jobs, industries, occupations and localities. (Beatson, 1995: 54)

> (labour mobility)... describes the movement of workers to different jobs, occupations and geographical areas according to changing economic conditions. It can refer to the level of movement within the same company, between firms or industries and between different local labour markets. (Watson, 1994: 240)

In addition, the Government commented in an Employment Department White Paper entitled *Employment for the 1990s* that:

> The demands of the 1990s, with more intense international competition and a more rapid pace of change, will highlight the need for a better trained and more flexible labour force. The fact is that in spite of many improvements we are not, even now, training enough of the kinds of people we need... The aim must be a system which enables individuals to build on their skills and experience throughout working life; meets the needs of individuals and employers; and allows mobility between jobs, between education and training opportunities, and between industries and occupations. (Employment Department, 1988b: 28, 32)

The aim, then, is for workers who are employed in industries typified by low demand (or rapid technological change) to 're-skill' (throughout their working lives) and move to other jobs in other occupations or other areas. It is difficult, however, to measure the extent of such mobility, as there have been very few studies of industrial/occupational mobility. In one of the few statistical studies (from the Labour Force Survey and detailed in chapter three) there is evidence that around one sixth of job changes involve a change between manufacturing and service sectors and around one eighth a shift from manual to non-manual work. It is this gap in the research which this work aims to partially fill - to complement the picture of industrial restructuring and industrial/occupational mobility emerging from quantitative work with qualitative material. Using case study evidence from two firms at opposite ends of the industrial spectrum - an insurance office (Bristol Insurance) and a laminating factory (Bristol Laminated) - analysis is undertaken in order to determine the probability of such mobility and the extent of any barriers which may stand in the way of movement. It is argued that by choosing firms which are on contrasting sides of industrial restructuring it will be possible to more fully understand the social, historical and institutional forces which shape difference and by so doing build up a more accurate understanding of the nature and functioning of labour markets - are, for example, labour markets characterised by competition or non-competition and, if the latter what are the forces which serve to create such bounded labour markets. The focus of the study was on two industrial groupings but the workers interviewed in these firms also tended fell into two occupational groupings - manual and non-manual - so the findings reflect not only industrial differences but also, to an extent, occupational differences.

To turn briefly to the detail of the case studies, attention was focused on three areas: recruitment, skills and perceptions of the work and workers in each sector. Looking firstly at recruitment, central to increasing flexibility and ensuring the 'efficient' workings of the market, is the deliberate construction of a labour market where information on employment opportunities is open to all and where the most able and efficient candidate will get the job. In such an environment informal recruitment channels (i.e. personal contacts) are seen as barriers and rigidities which stand in the way of flexibility and whose influence must be reduced and eventually removed (Skills and Enterprise Network, 1993). Given, therefore, the central importance of recruitment practices to creating a free and flexible labour market one of the major themes of inquiry was the nature of and attitude to different recruitment channels in and among case study respondents. Is it is the case, for example, that respondents view and value, understand and use recruitment channels differently, and if so, what are the implications for flexibility and occupational mobility? Furthermore, if there are competing views on recruitment and contrasting methods of recruitment, to what extent do these serve to create bounded labour markets and, furthermore, are there any identifiable processes at work in the creation of such non-competitive work groups which may inform the macro picture?

Moving on to skill perceptions, this is an area where the government's focus on flexibility is also strongly evident (Benn and Fairley, 1986; Finn, 1987; Skills and Enterprise Network, 1993) and, given this, a second theme of inquiry was into how case study respondents comprehend skill. To what extent, for example, do respondents in Bristol Insurance and Bristol Laminated conceive and conceptualise skills differently? And if there is a dissimilarity in the assessment of and approach to skills conceptualisation does this represent a rigidity, a barrier to mobility and flexibility and, if so, does this provide evidence of the existence of particular processes which shape views and values reflected at a macro level?

In addition to questions on recruitment and skill, a third area was covered, which sought to investigate how respondents perceived each other and each others work. Questions were asked and data gathered on the general views and values respondents held of each other, with the aim of isolating common or competing conceptions. For example, is it the case that factory workers hold a shared view of office work and workers (and vice versa for office workers) and, if the opinions of the two sets of case study respondents differ, what are the causes of these differences and how do such differences reflect on the construction of the macro labour market?

To turn to the structure of the text, this introduction is followed by a review of recent literature on the nature of labour markets. This theoretically contextualising literature review is followed by a chapter which uses statistical data to set the context of the local and national labour markets and which details and explains the research methodology. Chapters four, five and six concentrate on the analysis of the empirical material. Chapters four and five deal respectively with recruitment and skill and, given the body of secondary work dealing specifically with both these issues, the analysis of the empirical material is preceded in each case with a survey of secondary research. The theoretical material is dealt with slightly differently in chapter six, where, because of the more general nature of inquiry (into perceptions of work and workers), there was no one encompassing theoretical theme and, consequently, secondary work and theory is integrated with the empirical analysis on a topic by topic basis. The final chapter draws out where the case study material is innovative, gives a brief summary of the findings and analyses how these affect the contemporary theoretical debate surrounding flexibility, mobility and labour market deregulation.

2 The nature of labour markets

2.1 Introduction

The whole of the advantages and disadvantages of the different employments of labour and stock must, in the same neighbourhood, be either equal or continually tending to equality. If in the same neighbourhood, there was any employment evidently either more or less advantageous than the rest, so many people would crowd into it in the one case, and so many would desert it in the other, that its advantages would soon return to the level of other employments. (Smith, (1776), 1892: 76, 77)

What Adam Smith was describing here represents an early articulation of the power of supply and demand to bring the labour market into equilibrium. This belief in the market mechanism was build upon by the later neo-classical theorists who saw price as the communicating agent which would bring supply and demand into balance. This chapter sets out to describe and analyse neo-classical labour market theory and examine how the work of such theorists combined with the outlook of leading government advisers and politicians to shape the deregulating and pro free market policy agenda of the UK in the 1980s. This is followed by an analysis of the critiques of such theoretical conceptualisations with particular emphasis on the work of segmented labour market (SLM) theorists.

2.2 Free market approach to labour markets

In the field of mainstream economics the prevailing labour market theory has been that of neo-classical theorists. This school of thought shared a continuity with classical economics linked to a common utilitarian approach and became strongly associated with marginalist theory (Hicks, 1932, 1963; Stigler, 1941). In the field of labour markets the most important development of this school has been related to marginal productivity theory, which, it is argued, controls the demand for labour. Under this theory demand for labour is derived demand, that is labour is not demanded for its own sake but for the contribution it makes to the production of goods and services. The essential assumptions of marginal productivity theory are that firms are price takers both in product and factor markets; factors of production are mobile and firms are profit maximisers. Given these assumptions firms will continue to employ units of its variable factors of production (labour) until the last unit hired adds as just as much to revenue as to cost. Hicks (1932) wrote of this theory:

> It does summarise in a single convenient expression the complex causes which slowly mould the level of wages, and the prices of other factors of production. It is not true that a man's wage must always equal his marginal product, but if it does not, there is a danger of certain things happening. If his wage is below his marginal product, other employers will have an incentive to attract him away by offering him higher pay. They may desire to take him on so as to put him in the place of another man who is costing more; or because they are reorganising their businesses, and can thus put him in the place of some other more expensive factor; or because they are expanding their businesses. The statement that his wage is less than his marginal product means simply that these things can be done profitably. Similarly, if his wage is more than his marginal product, his own employer has an incentive to dismiss him. This may take place because it is cheaper to use some other method of production, which dispenses with his services; or because the whole business in which he works ceases to pay. But dismissal may not be feasible at once; it may have to wait until machinery comes to be replaced; yet an incentive to dismissal exists, and again that is what is meant by the marginal productivity proposition. Stated in these terms, the theory seems both simple and impossible to controvert. It is an absolutely necessary foundation for sound economic reasoning about wages. (Hicks, 1932: 87, 88)

Any difference, therefore, between wages and productivity will lead to a change in the number of workers employed. Algebraically marginal productivity theory is written as:

$$MCl = MRPl$$

Where:

MCl - The marginal cost (or supply) of labour is equal to the additional cost of employing an extra worker and, given that under perfect competition the firm is a price taker, this is equal to the wage. Under such conditions the supply of labour is perfectly elastic.

MRPl - The marginal revenue product of labour represents the extra revenue a firm gains from employing an additional unit of labour and is calculated by multiplying the extra amount produced (MPP or marginal physical product of labour) by the extra revenue gained from selling an additional unit of output (MR or marginal revenue).

A diagrammatic example is shown in figure 2.1, where the number of workers a profit maximising firm would employ is decided by the point of intersection between MCl and MRPl. The MRPl curve is downward sloping after point x illustrating the point at which diminishing returns set in (defined as the point at which the extra output from additional units of a variable factor added to a fixed factor diminish). Given these assumptions this firm would employ Qe workers at wage Wm.

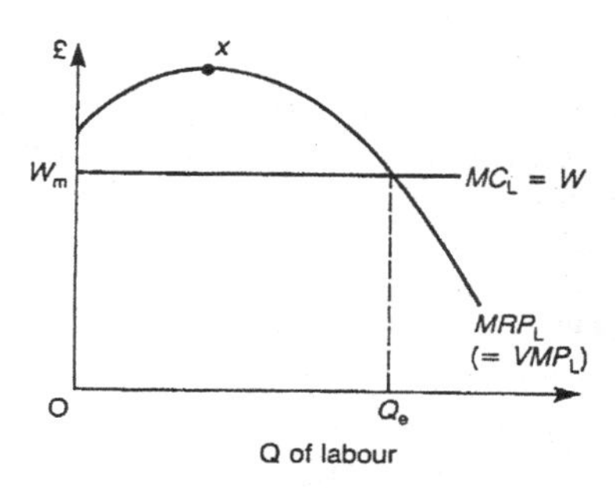

Figure 2.1 Profit maximising level of employment

Source: Sloman, 1991: 277

Turning to the supply of labour, under neo-classical assumptions individuals are assumed to be utility maximising and work is seen as a disutility, with individuals substituting the utility of leisure for work. The result is that the marginal disutility of work (MDU) will increase the longer people work. This will tend to give an upward sloping supply curve as wages are increased in order to persuade people to forgo utility laden leisure (figure 2.2).

Under a competitive labour market the price mechanism would act as a communicating agent between individual buyers and sellers of labour. The forces of supply and demand would create a market in labour which would tend towards equilibrium. Anything which stands in the way of such market forces, such as an unwillingness to learn new skills or working practices which inhibit the development of new technology, tend to make supply and demand less responsive (i.e. inelastic) and the labour market less competitive and more inefficient. Neo-classical theory would recommend that such tendencies are minimised so the responsiveness (elasticity) of supply and demand are maximised.

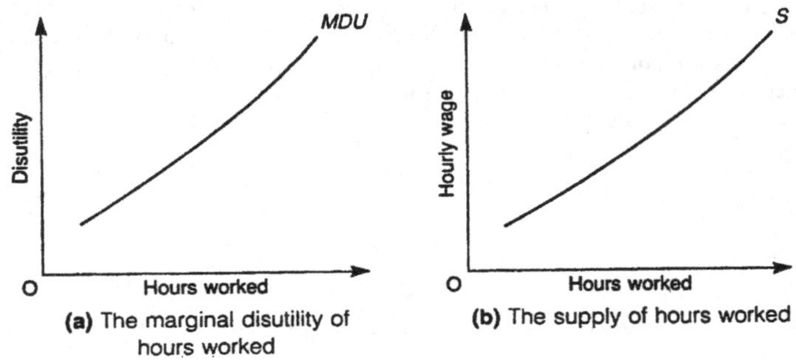

Source: Sloman, 1991: 270

Figure 2.2 Labour supply

This neo-classical conceptualisation of the labour market strongly informed the Conservative Government of the 1980s with its emphasis on supply side policies aimed at removing rigidities and creating an atmosphere conducive to the efficient functioning of the price mechanism. For example, the Government have argued that if wages are set above market clearing levels unemployment will result (figure 2.3). Here a minimum wage of OW1 is above the equilibrium wage level OW with the result that less people are employed - OL1 instead of OL.

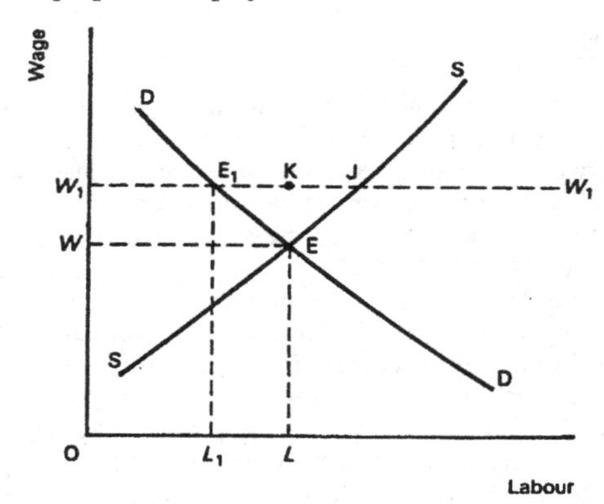

Source: Hardwick et al, 1990: 267

Figure 2.3 Effects of basic minimum wage

The market, therefore, should be left free to allow supply and demand to meet in equilibrium. Any organisation, institution, practice or habit which stands in the way of market forces must be removed. In the field of flexible labour markets this means not only should workers be more responsive to changing patterns of production and work organisation (i.e. the flexible firm and flexible specialisation) inside the firm, but that workers should be encouraged to respond quickly to changes in product demand by moving to the industries and towns where there is work. According to neo-classical theory increases in demand would be articulated through a higher price for labour (higher wage) and, consequently, supply would increase:

> One would expect, for example, that an increase in the relative demand for workers of a particular skill type would lead eventually to an outward shift in the relative supply curve of labour of that type, either because of changes in the education and training decisions of new entrants or through occupational mobility on the part of the existing work force. (Abraham, 1991: 474)

Wages are seen as playing an essential role in neo-classical labour market theory, influencing the actions of economic agents and bringing supply and demand into balance (MacDonald, 1988; Erikson 1991; Topel and Ward, 1992). For example, Topel and Ward (1992), in their (US) study into job mobility and the careers of young men, conclude that:

> ... we have shown that the job-changing activities of young workers are strongly consistent with matching models of on-the-job search: controlling for unobserved heterogeneity, the key element leading to the eventual durability of jobs is the wage, growth of which is largely an outcome of the search process itself. (Topel and Ward, 1992: 474)

The principal determinant, therefore, in labour supply decisions is seen to be the wage,[2] with workers moving in response to increased demand which is articulated through higher wages.

This belief of neo-classical labour market theorists in the efficiency of market forces and the importance of the price mechanism is closely linked with the work of right wing economists (Hayek, 1944, 1980, 1986) and intellectuals (Joseph, 1979). Hayek, for example, commented:

> I gradually found that the basic function of economics was to explain the process of how human activity adapted itself to data about which it had no information. Thus the whole economic order rested on the fact that by using prices as a guide, or as signals, we were led to serve the demands and enlist

---

[2]Allowance is made for other factors, for example in this study a variable is included to account for "unobserved heterogeneity".

> the powers and capacities of people of whom we knew nothing... It seems obvious, once it is stated, that the basic foundation of our civilisation and our wealth is a system of signals which informs us, however imperfectly, of the effects of millions of events which occur in the world, to which we have to adapt ourselves and about which we may have no direct information. (Hayek, 1986: 144)

This belief in the power of the marketplace was shared by the monetarists who, from 1979, had a strong influence on UK Government policy (Friedman, 1962; 1970; Walters, 1986). Ian Gilmour, writing of Britain under Thatcher, writes of monetarism:

> ... monetarists believe that a market economy is fundamentally self-regulating. Hence it should be left alone as much as possible, thereby enabling its inbuilt equilibrating mechanisms to do their work. Accordingly, the government should concern itself with its own finances... with removing rigidities and distortions in the market, with enlarging incentives and with improving and promoting the system of private enterprise and, of course, with controlling the money supply. (Gilmour, 1992: 12)

The influence of these right wing thinkers on public policy is evident from the memoirs of Nigel Lawson, Conservative Chancellor from 1983 to 1989, who commented of Margaret Thatcher that:

> (she) instinctively realised the need to regain the moral as well as the practical initiative from collectivism. In this she was strongly fortified by the writings of the economist and philosopher Friedrich Hayek... Hayek's development of the concept of a spontaneous market order provided a strong philosophical underpinning for the market... Economic planning was both impossible and unnecessary. Individual agents acting on incomplete information could none the less operate a market economy by means of the price mechanism. This was a much more efficient means of transmitting consumer wants and needs than the vast bureaucracies of Whitehall and the nationalized industries, as I had argued for nearly twenty years. (Lawson, 1992: 13, 14)

Throughout the 1980s, therefore, there has been a joining together, almost a symbiosis, between the theory of neo-classical and monetarist economists, right wing intellectuals and Conservative politicians. In the field of employment the labour market is to be viewed as much the same as any other market and the task of government is to remove barriers and rigidities which impede the ability of the market signalling system to function effectively and to create a balance between the supply and demand for labour. Thus with rigidities removed the labour market would be more flexible and workers would be more likely to move from sector to sector and town to town to meet demand. The next section turns to a discussion of the critiques of neo-classical theory.

2.3 Segmented labour market theory

> During the past twenty years economists dissatisfied with orthodox theory have proposed different explanations of how labour markets operate. Some of the alternatives simply extend orthodoxy to include the effects of various institutional factors; others have explicitly sought a new paradigm. All reject a predominately competitive analysis, insisting instead upon the fragmented nature of labour markets and the importance of institutional and social influences upon pay and employment. 'Labour market segmentation' provides a common label for these alternative approaches. (McNabb and Ryan, 1990: 151)

This quote, from McNabb and Ryan (1990), neatly sums up the common themes of segmented labour market (SLM) theorists, the most important of which are a recognition that neo-classical competitive labour market theory is inadequate, both in terms of description and analysis and a desire to recognise the importance of social, historical and institutional influences on labour market inequality, decisions and outcomes. This led to the recommendation by various SLM theorists for a variety of policies, on the demand side there have been calls for public employment, subsidy of wages and positive discrimination and on the supply side there have been calls for human capital investment programs in education, training and job search assistance to be deemphasised (Doeringer et al, 1972; Bluestone et al, 1973).

Central to the work of SLM theorists is a concern with inequality, in terms of wages, working conditions and employment opportunities amongst different occupational, industrial and demographic groups. This concern can be traced back to the writings of classical economists, in particular criticism of Smith's sources of wage inequality (Smith, (1776), 1892). Smith listed five sources of wage inequality: compensating differentials where non-pecuniary advantages of work make up for a shortfall of wages; human capital investments; barriers to entry, which may be institutions such as trade unions or certain views on class/status; transitory differentials and real differences in ability. It was the third of these, barriers to mobility, which were used by John Stuart Mill ((1848), 1976) and John Cairnes ((1874), 1974) in their criticism of Smith and which were stressed by the later SLM theorists. Mill ((1848), 1976) criticised Smith ((1776), 1892) for paying inadequate attention to the importance of 'social rank' in acting as a barrier to mobility, commenting that:

> So complete, indeed, has hitherto been the separation, so strongly marked the line of demarcation, between different grades of labourers, as to almost be equivalent to an hereditary distinction of caste, each employment being chiefly recruited from the children of those already employed in it, or in employments of the same rank with it in social estimation, or from children of persons who, if originally of a lower rank, have succeeded in raising themselves by their exertions. (Mill, (1848), 1976: 393)

Mill, therefore, stressed the importance of non-economic phenomena in shaping labour market inequality and acting as a barrier to mobility. Cairnes ((1874), 1974) further developed from this criticism the theory of non-competing groups:

> I attempt... to furnish help towards a more distinct apprehension of the limitations imposed by social circumstances on the free competition of labour than would be obtained from more general statements. As I have already said, I am far from contending for the existence of any hard lines of demarcation between any categories of persons in this country. No doubt the various ranks and classes fade into each other by imperceptible gradations, and individuals from all classes are constantly passing up or dropping down; but while this is so, it is nevertheless true that the average workman, from whatever rank he be taken, finds his power of competition limited for practical purposes to a certain range of occupations, so that, however high the rates of remuneration in those which lie beyond may rise, he is excluded from sharing them. We are thus compelled to recognise the existence of non-competing industrial groups as a feature of our social economy; and this is the fact which I desire here to insist upon. (Cairnes, (1874), 1974: 73, emphasis added)

Cairnes and Mill, therefore, recognised that there were powerful social forces which shaped the labour market into non-competing industrial groups. Cain (1976) wrote of this:

> In my view, the importance and prevalence of non-competing groups offer the single most basic criticism of the operations of the labour market and of the application of competitive assumptions by neo-classicalists. This criticism is fundamental to the SLM challenge. (Cain, 1976: 1224)

These non-competing groups were seen as being formed in a number of different ways - through the development of an official labour market institution such as a trade union and/or via the interaction of social forces (such as class) which served to create an occupationally and industrially stratified labour market. This theme of non-competition was taken up by the later institutionalists of the 1940s and 1950s in America, who developed the concepts of balkanised labour and structured labour markets (Kerr, 1954; Dunlop, 1957). Kerr, for example, wrote:

> Painters do not compete with bricklayers, or typists with accountants, or doctors with lawyers; nor individuals in Portland, Maine, with those in Portland, Oregon (except perhaps in certain professions). (...) The competitive market areas within which somewhat similar jobs, and within which somewhat similar employers try to fill somewhat similar jobs, are normally quite restricted. (Kerr 1954: 94)

Kerr conceptualised the labour market as a balkanised market: a market where different occupations inhabited different 'territories' and where the actions of workers and employers in these 'territories' were guided by institutional rules. These rules created certain barriers to entry which served to stratify the labour market. Dunlop (1957) built on this by analysing the labour market in terms of 'job clusters' and 'wage contours', a conceptualisation of the labour market as being constructed from various segments, split both vertically and horizontally.[3]

The intellectual heritage of both the earlier classical scholars and the later institutionalists were merged with the work coming out of studies into the persistence of poverty in urban USA in the 1960s (Doeringer and Piore, 1971)[4] and 'radical' theories of the stratification of the US working class (Gordon et al, 1982) to produce the broad approach summed up by the heading of segmented labour market theory. These authors sought to account for the persistence of poverty and unemployment amongst certain groups (particularly blacks in large American cities) by reference not only to economic but to social, historical, institutional and political forces which served to create two, essentially non-competitive, sectors: a core, primary workforce occupying relatively secure jobs with relatively good pay and conditions and a peripheral, secondary workforce with insecure jobs and relatively poor pay and conditions.[5] What brought these SLM theorists together was a shared recognition of the empirical implausibility of a perfectly competitive neo-classical labour market, where competitive markets equalised wages and a belief that the labour market itself was an important generator of economic inequality.

Despite these common themes the empirical work which comes under the broad banner of SLM theory has been varied, moving out from a duality between a core and periphery workforce to encompass studies investigating differences based on areas such as gender, race and skill. Turning to a brief overview of some of the empirical evidence of segmentation, firstly in the US and secondly in the UK One of the earliest US studies was that of Osterman (1975), who concluded from an analysis of pay that the occupational structure was split into two segments, primary and secondary, with returns to schooling and work experience proving significant only in the primary segment. Other studies into the existence of segmentation between primary and secondary sectors was done by Oster (1979) and Kaufman et al (1981), while Buchele (1981) used segmentation theory to argue that women are disadvantaged in terms of tenure, promotion and pay and Flanagan (1973) and

---

[3]For more recent institutionalist work see Solow (1990).

[4]For early references on dualism see Boeke (1953) and Averitt (1968).

[5]These authors share the use of dualism which Atkinson (1984) used to develop his flexible firm but while Atkinson saw a "core" and "periphery" workforce as a result of and response to increased competition and the market SLM theorists saw a dualistic labour market as a result of non-competitive markets which resulted in compounding labour market inequalities.

Leigh (1976) demonstrated that blacks suffer systematic discrimination in the labour market.

Moving to empirical work done in the UK, segmentationalist studies have included Bosanquet and Doeringer's (1973) investigation into the existence of internal labour markets in the UK, which concluded that the labour market is divided into primary and secondary segments; Barron and Norris's (1976) investigation into evidence of sexual divisions in the labour market, which found that women were relegated to the secondary labour market; Mayhew and Rosewell's (1979) study into labour market segmentation, which argued that while there was evidence for immobility between three segments[6] it was insufficient to support the case of SLM theorists and Ashton and McGuire's (1984) work into the youth labour market, which concluded that the labour market consisted of horizontal and vertical segments. Research from various academics associated with Cambridge University (the Cambridge School), shifted the emphasis to the importance of the supply side and highlighted the agency of workers themselves in shaping the structure of labour markets (Rubery, 1978; Rubery and Wilkinson, 1981; Burchell and Rubery, 1989). Burchell and Rubery's (1989), as part of the SCELI[7] project, investigated the existence of 'job clusters' in the Northampton labour market, and concluded that:

> The empirical investigation of the existence of labour market segments has revealed a structuring of the labour supply which appears likely to be relatively stable over time and which is associated with quite marked and interactive relationships between individual's past work history, their current labour market position and their attitudes towards their current jobs and expectations of the future. Simple models of segmentation, such as those that differentiate between casual secondary workers and stable primary workers, core and periphery employees or between male and female or black and white workers, have been found to be too crude to fit the complexities of labour market processes. (Burchell and Rubery, 1989: 42)

These authors pointed to an important criticism of segmentation theory, namely that the search for evidence of a strict dualistic formulation led to oversimplifications (McNabb and Ryan, 1990; Rubery and Wilkinson, 1994). Other critics of SLM include Psacharopoulos (1977) who has argued that these theories

---

[6]These segments were defined in a similar way to those used by Osterman (1975) in the U.S.: Segment I referred to the upper tier of the primary segment, II to the lower tier and III to the secondary split.

[7]SCELI: The Social Change and Economic Life Initiative was a major labour market research project funded by the Economic and Social Research Council, producing many publications - see Penn et al (1994) and Rubery and Wilkinson (1994).

are too descriptive; Apostle et al (1985) who has suggested that the definition of segments has been too weak and Carter (1982) who, while noting the richness of much of the data produced by SLM studies, has argued that SLM theories lack a rigid theoretical core. This belief that, despite some positive features, SLM theory has failed to displace neo-classical theory from its position of dominance in labour market theory, has also been articulated by Blaug (1976) and Cain (1976), with the latter writing:

> Unfortunately, the SLM theories are sketchy, vague, and diverse if not internally conflicting. Description, narratives and taxonomies crowd out model development. On the positive side the theories evolve from detailed data that are often richer in historical, institutional, and qualitative aspects than is customary among the econometrically-orientated orthodox theories. (Cain, 1976: 1221)

He goes on to conclude:

> My brief summary judgement of the SLM challenge is that it does not begin to offer a theory of the labour market that can replace neo-classical theory... The SLM economists' theoretical and methodological criticisms of the neo-classical theory are not substantial and are often misguided; nevertheless, a tradition of criticism of orthodox economics is sustained, and this is healthy. The main theoretical contributions, which amount to modifications and additions to orthodox theory, are (1) the ideas of the endogenous determination of attitudinal variables among workers, and (2) the historical and institutional dimensions of internal labour markets - which enrich our understanding of the economics of bureaucratic organisation. Their main contribution to the mixture of analysis and policy debates is their attention to class (or group) interests and behaviour, and to the historical basis for these collective actions, which often extend into the political market. (Cain, 1976: 1247, 1248)

Even staunch defenders of neo-classical labour market theory, therefore, note that SLM theory encourages the consideration of non-economic forces, such as the importance of historical, institutional and ideological phenomena and offer the potential to gather data which are rich in quality. Under SLM theory there is explicit recognition that attitudes and biases which may create inequality in the labour market, whether in the form of different wages or different employment opportunities, are seen, not as neo-classical theorists would argue, as exogenous, as outside the labour market, but rather are seen as endogenous, as being part of labour market decisions and outcomes. Cain (1991) later commented that SLM theory:

> Uses a research methodology that draws primarily upon historical, institutional and case study materials, the segmentation economists emphasize the roles of technology, the shaping of attitudes and preferences, and certain features of

> bureaucratic organisation - aspects of labour markets that neoclassical economists tend to place in the background. (Cain, 1991: 286)

It is such an outlook which informs the methodological approach and theoretical conceptualisation adopted in this work, with case study material being used to investigate the attitudes and preferences of workers from two firms on the opposite sides of industrial restructuring. The aim being to investigate the extent to which such attitudes and preferences
segment the labour market across industrial and occupational lines and the degree to which this may inhibit plans for retraining and making the labour market more flexible. As the next chapter goes on to argue it is such a qualitative approach, with its potential for gathering rich data, which offers the opportunity of gaining access into the mechanics of the labour market, into the meanings and motivations employees attach to concepts such as skill and to perceptions of each other. Such meanings and motivations often reflect underlying differences on certain issues, such as views on occupational status, which are influenced by perceptions of class or gender - social, historical and institutional perceptions whose strength serves to segment the labour market and create non-competing industrial groups.

2.4 Conclusion

This chapter opened with a description and explanation of what were summarised as pro-market labour market theories. These included neo-classical theory with its emphasis on marginal productivity theory; the economics of monetarism and the economic and ideological outlook of successive post 1979 Conservative Government's. It was argued that what bound these theoretical perspectives together was a belief in the primacy of market forces and the power of the price mechanism. In the world of work this meant viewing the labour market as the same as any other market and one which would, therefore, function more effectively and efficiently with all barriers and rigidities removed. The theoretical call for a competitive labour market was met by a government policy response of deregulation where labour was encouraged to respond to demand, to move to where the work was and to learn the skills necessary for employment in a changing industrial climate. This was contrasted with the segmented labour market critique of 'free' markets. Such an approach, it was shown, had historical roots in the classical economists' theory of non-competing industrial groups, which tended to emphasise the role of non-economic phenomena, such as class perceptions, in stratifying the labour market and in acting as a barrier to occupational and industrial mobility. This was built upon by later institutionalists and SLM theorists, who stressed the importance of social, historical and institutional factors in shaping labour market inequality. Finally it was argued that such a methodological and theoretical approach, with its emphasis on rich data and non-economic phenomena, was most appropriate in a case study investigation into the potential for mobility between industrial groups.

3 Studying labour markets and labour forces

3.1 Introduction

This chapter opens with an analysis of quantitative material illustrating the changing patterns of employment at a national and local level. This is followed by an examination of data on the degree of occupational and industrial mobility and a description of Bristol's economy. It is then argued that while quantitative material is useful for contextualising debate a fuller analysis of labour markets is possible by complementing statistical data with qualitative material. This is the methodological approach adopted in this research and there is a full discussion of this methodology from a theoretical perspective. Following this there is a discussion of the case study approach in general and a brief description of the case study firms. The final sections describe and examine the methods used for gathering and analysing data.

3.2 Changes in employment

From the 1970s changes in product demand and in methods of production led to a shift in patterns in employment, with less people employed in manufacturing work and more in service sector work. As figure 3.1 shows this pattern has occurred both at a Great Britain level and at the level of the Bristol economy. From 1981 to 1991 there was a 33% drop in the numbers employed in manufacturing in Bristol and an 18% increase in those working in service sector jobs. The similar figures for Great Britain are a 25% drop in manufacturing and a 17% increase in service sector jobs.

A more detailed analysis of this material shows that increases were concentrated in the financial services sector. As figure 3.2 shows from 1981 to 1991 both Britain and Bristol experienced employment decreases in primary, manufacturing and construction industries. In contrast there were large increases at Bristol and Great Britain levels in the numbers of people employed in financial services, with the number in the Bristol district increasing by 84% and that for Britain rising by 51%.

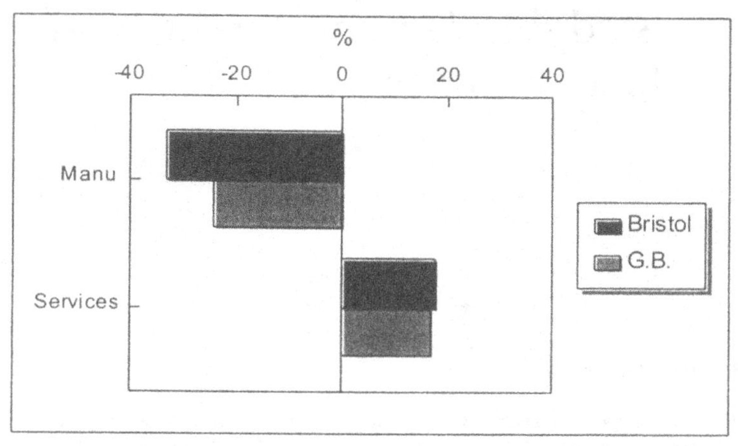

Source: Census of Employment

Figure 3.1 Changes in employment

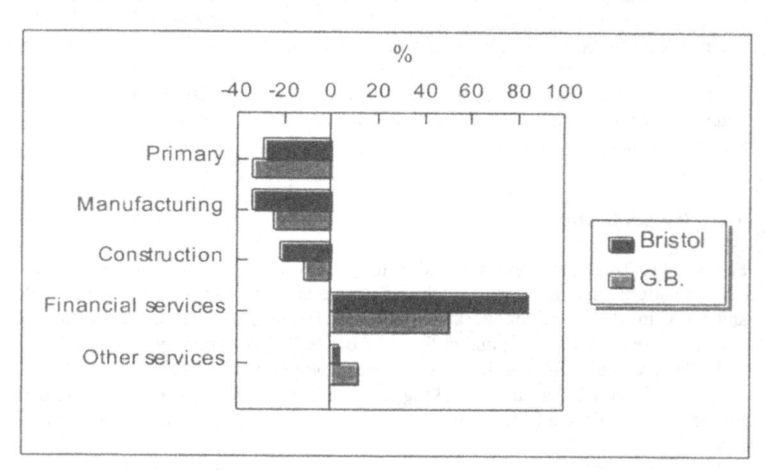

Source: Census of Employment

Figure 3.2 Breakdown of changes

As tables 3.1 and 3.2 show these shifting patterns of employment have been experienced both by men and women and by part time and full time workers. For example the number of male full time workers in financial services increased in Bristol between 1981 and 1991 from 13,200 to 21,200, a jump of 61% and the number of full time females in this category rose 9,500 to 19,100, an increase of 102%. Thus, while there were varying degrees of change, there was a decrease in the numbers working in manufacturing and an increase in the numbers employed in financial services for all categories of worker, both at the level of Great Britain and Bristol.

Table 3.1
Bristol % change

	F-T male	P-T male	F-T female	P-T female
Primary	-35	0	0	-33
Manufacturing	-32	0	-35	-41
Construction	-28	0	50	0
Financial Services	61	140	101	135
Other Services	-9	56	8	12
Total	-10	58	20	15

Source: 1987 LFS estimates

Table 3.2
GB % change

	F-T male	P-T male	F-T female	P-T female
Primary	-38.7	0.5	-12.7	-10.1
Manufacturing	-25.6	-19.5	-20.1	-28.5
Construction	-14.5	-8.4	19.9	16
Financial Services	38.8	72.9	60	68.2
Other Services	-2.1	44	11.6	26.6
Total	-11.5	36.8	8.8	22.5

Source: 1987 LFS estimates

3.3 Occupational and industrial mobility

As the above figures and tables have shown there have been shifts in employment between manufacturing and services. There is more doubt, however, about the numbers of people who have shifted from between manufacturing and services. As was argued in chapters one and two the ability and willingness for the supply of labour to respond to changes in demand is an important function of a flexible labour market. This has been one of the most important aims of various Government training policies - to train workers so they can fill gaps in the labour market (Employment Department, 1984, 1988b). This means not only planning training for 'new' entrants to the labour market but re-training those in areas, such as manufacturing and primary industries, where demand for workers is falling.

There have, however, been relatively few studies into analysing the numbers who have moved between industries and occupations. Table 3.3, below, details analysis from a Labour Force Survey (LFS) projects into labour mobility and shows that around 10% of people were with a different employer in 1987 than they were with in 1986 (Employment Gazette, 1991). This table also shows that 484,000 people were in a different industrial sector. Of these inter-sectoral shifts about 0.3 million occurred between manufacturing and services. Thus of the 1.8 million job changes about 16% involved a shift from manufacturing to services.

Table 3.3
Changes of employer and industry

	Numbers (000s)	Percentage
All persons	18,460	
With same employer	16,607	89.96
With different employer	1,836	9.95
Same activity heading	568	3.08
Diff activity heading, same industry division	347	1.88
Diff industry division, same industrial sector	408	2.21
Diff industrial section	484	2.62

Source: 1987 LFS estimates

Turning to occupational data, the LFS analysis found that around 8% of people who were in employment both in 1986 and 1987 had changed their occupation during the year (figure 3.3). A more detailed analysis shows that 0.2 million people changed from manual to non-manual work, showing that of the 1.6 million who had changed occupations 12% had moved from manual to non-manual.

Thus while there is relatively little data on occupational and industrial mobility what there is shows that there is some movement between manufacturing and service work - one sixth of job changes involve a move from manufacturing to service sector and one eighth involve a move from manual to non-manual work. Similar proportions are cited by Beatson (1995). This quantitative material is used to contextualise the case study material which follows.

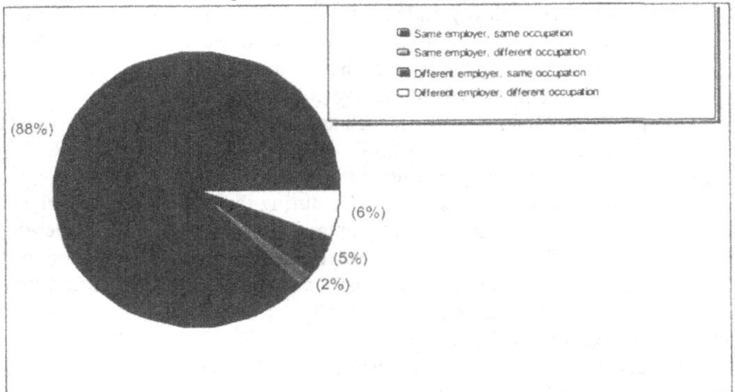

Source: 1987 LFS estimates

Figure 3.3 Changes of employer and occupation

3.4 Bristol's economy

Bristol has a economy whose early prosperity was based on the 'triangular' colonial trade, involving the exchange of British manufactured goods, West African slaves and commodities (sugar, rum and tobacco) from the Americas. The large port which developed as a result of this trade stimulated the growth of shipbuilding and helped make Bristol, by 1800, a national centre for the refining and distilling of sugar, a regional centre for the manufacture of glass and known for its iron foundries, high quality brass manufacture and production of lead shot. This local industry supported a population of between 60,000 - 70,000 in 1801, second only to London. From this base the economy specialised in the nineteenth century in industries such as confectionary, tobacco and paper and packaging (Alford, 1976), and, in the twentieth century, moved to expanding manufacturing sectors such as aerospace and (in the post war period) to office work (Boddy et al, 1986).

Throughout the 1980s Bristol experienced large job losses in the traditional paper and packaging and food, drink and tobacco sectors - Imperial Tobacco, a company with a long historical association with the city, closed its last cigarette making factory in the city at Hartcliffe in 1992. The decline in manufacturing throughout the 1980s was not, however, uniform, and those firms who were defence dependent, such as British Aerospace and Rolls Royce, located just outside the city boundary in the district of Northavon, increased their levels of employment throughout this period. Increased industrial activity in this northern fringe is also evident through the setting up in the past few years of new manufacturing plants by firms such as Hewlett Packard and Dupont. Development on the north of the city has been helped by good transport links with the close proximity of both the M4 and M5 and the Parkway railway station, with fast and frequent inter-city services to London. Such travel links have also aided the development of the financial services industry, which, as is shown in table 3.1 above, saw the biggest change in employment in Bristol during the 1980s.. Over this period Bristol attracted many inward-moving firms, such as Lloyds Bank whose new headquarters is situated on the city centre waterfront. Such movement has made Bristol the largest financial sector in England after London.

Unemployment in Bristol was around 7% during the late 1980s and early 1990s, but this relatively low figure disguises areas of deprivation and prosperity - for example some wards in the city centre have unemployment rates of around 20% while more prosperous suburban areas have rates as low as 4%. During this time there was also said to be a skills mismatch between the skills of the unemployed and the demands of the labour market, with skill shortages being reported for clerical and secretarial staff, software specialists, accountants, scientific/engineering professionals, mechanical/electrical engineers, carpenters, bricklayers and mechanics (Training Agency, 1989; Griffin et al, 1992).

The Bristol economy, which sets the economic context for the case study work, is relatively prosperous and, to an extent, can be seen as a microcosm of the changing patterns of demand and production which have affected the national economy - not only did Bristol industrialise just before the country as a whole but Bristol was quick to move into service sector work and saw a jump in financial sector employment which outstripped the national increase. I would argue that this 'typicality', in the sense of similar trends to the national picture, make Bristol a suitable setting for a qualitative study into the potential for mobility between industrial sectors.

3.5 Qualitative methodology - micro social studies

The statistics point to changes in the pattern of employment, with more people employed in service sector work and less in manufacturing, and they also show that there is some movement between the two sectors. While this quantitative data sets a useful context a qualitative approach is necessary to go a little deeper - What are the opinions of the labour market participants who make up the statistics? What do they think of mobility? More broadly, what do they think of the work and workers in other industrial sectors? It is such questions where a qualitative approach offers the opportunity to flesh out and explain the movements and tendencies shown in quantitative data. By examining workers from a laminating firm located firmly in the declining manufacturing sector and an insurance company in the expanding financial services sector it is possible to compare the views and values of employees at opposite ends of industrial restructuring and by so doing more clearly identify and isolate the social, historical and institutional forces which influence the level of industrial or occupational mobility.

To turn to the theoretical rationale for a qualitative approach, two authors working in this field have commented:

> I believe in the seeming paradox that it is through micro-social approaches that we will learn most about the macro-order, for it is these approaches which through their unashamed empiricism afford us a glimpse of the reality about which we speak. Certainly, we will not get a grasp of whatever is the whole of the matter by a microscopic recording of face-to-face interaction. However, it may be enough to begin with if we can - for the first time - hear the macro-order tick. (Knorr-Cetina, 1981b: 41, 42, emphasis in original)

> The dynamics as well as the statics of the larger social world ultimately depend upon its only living elements, people in micro-situations. Structural aggregates of micro-situations in time and space are on another level of analysis, and play a part in social causation only as they bear upon people's situational motivations. It is within micro-situations that we find both the glue and the transforming energies of these structures. Any other view of them remains metaphorical. (Collins, 1981: 105)

These two quotes argue for the importance of small scale research studies in any attempt to more fully understand the nature and structure of larger orders. It is such an approach to methodology, described by Knorr-Cetina (1981b) as 'micro-social', which has been followed in this research. It is argued that such a micro-level approach, where the views and values of a small number of respondents are recorded and analysed, produces data which are both rich and reflexive, allowing the identification and investigation of the processes which shape such views and values and by so doing inform conceptualisations of the macro-order. As Knorr-Cetina writes:

> The macro emerges from such work not as the sum of unintended consequences of micro-episodes nor as their aggregate or network of interrelations, but rather as a summary representation actively constructed and pursued within micro-situations. (Knorr-Cetina, 1981b, 34, emphasis added)

The emphasis is, therefore, on examining micro results in order to identify processes which construct difference and which may inform macro level conceptualisations. So, for example, in chapter six data from both Bristol Insurance and Bristol Laminated make explicit reference to class and the importance of occupation and certain attitudes to one's class position. What this data shows is that respondents are both influenced by and influence such class perceptions, that the micro actively makes and is made by the macro. Evidence of barriers to flexibility and of non-competitive work groups thereby informs macro level conceptualisation by giving a clearer insight into such processes and phenomena at a micro level. It is, then, with this object in mind that a micro level qualitative methodology is followed - not to argue that because these were the results in Bristol Insurance and Bristol Laminated that they are necessarily typical of manufacturing/ service divide, but to argue that the processes which shape different perceptions and attitudes are common amongst working communities and that the most appropriate methodology, which would facilitate the examination and further understanding of such processes, is a qualitative micro-level approach. To work one's way in and through the complex combination of competing and contending motivations which underlies such processes requires an approach which respects the influence of a number of macro views on the individual (social, political and historical as well as economic) and, perhaps more importantly, the importance of the agency of the individual in using such views to suit and shape the attitudinal contours of each workplace community. As Turner (1988) comments:

> One of the major virtues of qualitative research is that it does not try to reduce the world to a few simple categories, but offers instead theoretical accounts which are multi-faceted. This quality makes it more likely that they will offer to the reader and the practitioner an adequately complex map of the portion of the social world which is under investigation. (Turner, 1988: 119)

Qualitative methodology, then, is seen to be characterised by a number of advantages: theory is grounded in empirical reality (Schutz, 1964; Glaser and Strauss, 1967; Turner, 1981); the data is 'rich' in quality (Mitchell, 1983; Rose, 1991); the importance of human agency and of respondents to create their own frames of reference is recognised (Schutz, 1964; Bresnen, 1988; Crompton and Jones, 1988); 'flexibility' in research approaches is offered (Bryman, 1988a; Allan, 1991); the analysis of processes is encouraged (Knorr-Cetina, 1981b; Allan, 1991) and the potential for interaction is emphasised (Knorr-Cetina, 1981b; Allan, 1991). Despite these advantages, however, a number of criticisms have been levelled at qualitative methodology (Bryman, 1988a; Allan, 1991). Both Bryman (1988a) and Allan (1991) cite a common criticism that qualitative research is 'impressionistic' and 'anecdotal', Bryman writes:

> There is a tendency towards an anecdotal approach to the use of 'data' in relation to conclusions or explanations in qualitative research. Brief conversations, snippets from unstructured interviews, or examples of a particular activity are used to provide evidence for a particular contention. (Bryman, 1988a: 77)

Allan (1991), while recognising the potential for qualitative methods to suffer from such criticisms, argues that such features are characteristic of such methods and, if the correct approach is used, need not weaken the analysis and conclusions. He writes:

> Inevitably, then, in the early phase of qualitative research good practice is for the research to be impressionistic - this is one of its hallmarks.... However this does not mean that 'anything goes' and that rigour has no part to play in qualitative methods. While the researcher will certainly want to keep an open mind and be reflective about the processes and action being observed or discussed, at the same time the collection of data and the testing of ideas need to become as systematic as possible. (Allan, 1991: 180, 181)

Here, then, the response to such criticisms is that they misunderstand the nature of qualitative research. Firstly, it is the 'anecdotal', the narrative, which is of central interest to the investigator as it is just this material which potentially offers the richness and depth which characterises good qualitative research. Secondly, the methodology is potentially 'rigorous', not in the quantitative sense of statistical 'rigour', but in the sense of analytical rigour, of a consistent and systematic approach to the collection and analysis of data. A second criticism of qualitative methods is that they are 'non-verifiable':

> ... concerns also surface when we are confronted with the spectacle of divergencies of opinion between two ethnographers of the same social context. If the aim is to see through the eyes of those whom one studies, the expectation of some consistency of findings is not unreasonable. (Bryman, 1988a: 74, 75)

Bryman (1988a) then goes on to cite the two 'classic' example of non-verification: Lewis's (1951) re-study of a Mexican village which had been studied by Redfield (1930) and Freeman's (1983) re-study of Mead's (1928) work on the anthropology of child rearing in Samoa. For example, he writes of the work on the Mexican village of Tepoztlan:

> Redfield found the village to be harmonious, well integrated, and free of divisions, and its inhabitants were seen as contented. Lewis's re-study seventeen years later portrays a village in which conflict, divisions, individualism and a 'pervading quality of fear, envy, and distrust in interpersonal relations' were rife. (Bryman, 1988a: 75)

The responses to the failure of attempted replication studies have ranged from the importance of differences in the time of the research to the exact geographical location of the research. One of the most common reasons cited for 'failure' to verify is the role played by the researchers' own values and agenda to the subject under study. So, for example, two researchers may take to the same topic different assumptions and make different interpretations of the same phenomena. To return again to Bryman (1988a), who cites Redfield's reply to Lewis:

> Lewis is especially interested in the problems of economic need and of personal disharmony and unhappiness, topics which I did not investigate... I think we must recognise that the personal and cultural values of the investigator influence the content and description of the community. (Redfield, 1955: 136; from Bryman, 1988a: 75)

While it is obviously the case that the orientations which the researcher brings to the project will colour the design, implementation and analysis of the data arising from the project I would argue that this is the case with all research (both quantitative and qualitative) and that it, again, misunderstands the nature of qualitative research (Knorr-Cetina, 1981b; Turner, 1981). Turning to the first point, Knorr-Cetina writes:

> Social situations may not have a natural beginning and an end, thus forcing the researcher to choose an arbitrary cutting point. When a short segment of conversation is carved out of an encounter between two or more persons for microscopic analysis, the situated character of the organizational properties of the talk, and certainly the content of the utterances, may be lost. Furthermore, it is clear that members themselves selectively organize and draw upon their 'environment'. Though much of the physical setting of an encounter may be potentially available for attention, most of it will remain unnoticed. Furthermore, circumstances of action which transcend the immediate situation are continually called upon by social actors. For example, while recent micro-sociological studies of scientific work consistently confirm the circumstances of laboratory action to be of crucial relevance in the process of knowledge production, they also illustrate that it is not their (physical) presence but their availability in the sense of an awareness of a phenomenon which makes it contextually relevant. In addition, actors can be seen to consciously manipulate contextual limitations and to increase their contextual knowledge or attention, if needed. (Knorr-Cetina, 1981b: 11, emphasis in original)[8]

What Knorr-Cetina (1981b) found in her study was that the research agenda and procedures of physical scientists is also characterised by personal orientations. This is perhaps most obvious when she writes that her 'actors' have the ability to 'consciously manipulate contextual limitations'. The second point is that the desire to 'verify' the exact findings of a qualitative research project misunderstands the nature of such an approach, which has at its core an appreciation of the agency of those studied and the dynamic and continually negotiated contours of their

---

[8]For more on the construction and contextual nature of science see Knorr-Cetina (1981b).

environment. Thus to expect to get exactly the same responses over time or in different locations misses the point: it is the processes which lead to the identification of interconnections (or differences) which are important. As Allan (1991) writes 'qualitative methods can be replicable in purpose if not in detailed procedures' (Allan, 1991: 183, emphasis added).

The method chosen as the most appropriate to complement the quantitative picture of the labour market and investigate the potential for mobility was that of the comparative case study (Gallie, 1978; Rose, 1991). Two firms on the 'opposite' sides of economic restructuring, a large office and a large factory, were chosen in order to facilitate a process of comparing and contrasting the views and values of respondents on certain themes with the aim of extracting and examining data which would demonstrate the extent of difference (or similarity) between (and possibly among) different working communities. The value of comparing case study firms on the 'extremes' of the industrial spectrum is that any information gathered and analysed is likely to demonstrate the dimensions of difference and the magnitude of the problems facing mobility. The aim was not to argue that these results are statistically representative of offices or factories and therefore generalisable to the macro, but to isolate and investigate common and conflicting themes and processes (such as social, historical and institutional forces) which create and recreate difference (or similarity) and, further, to argue that it is the results of the analyses of these themes and the functioning of these processes, as forces and flows which shape labour markets, which reflect upon and allow a clearer conceptualisation of the complexity of the macro order.

A common criticism of case studies is that they are not representative, but as Mitchell (1983) and Yin (1984) argue, this is based on a misunderstanding of the nature of case study analysis. Any statements referring to the macro reflect not the statistical representativeness of the 'sample' but the underlying theoretical rationale for the choice of case studies, with the aim as Eckstein (1975) points out, of choosing case study firms in order to:

> ... deliberately used to stimulate the imagination towards discerning important general problems and possible theoretical solutions... (Eckstein, 1975: 104, from Mitchell, 1982: 196)

Thus I would argue that by choosing a large office and large factory one has the opportunity for a detailed comparative study. Mitchell (1983) characterises a case study as:

> ... a detailed examination of an event (or series of related events) which the analyst believes exhibits (or exhibit) the operation of some identified general theoretical principle... (Mitchell, 1983: 192)

Here I would suggest that my 'general theoretical principle' is the extent to which labour markets are competitive or non-competitive and that by examining in detail attitudes and values (my 'events') of workers from a factory and office on issues crucial to mobility it will be possible to understand more fully the nature of the macro labour market. As Mitchell writes in his conclusion:

> The rich detail which emerges from the intimate knowledge the analyst must acquire in a case study provides the optimum conditions for the acquisition of those illuminating insights which make formerly opaque connections suddenly pellucid. (Mitchell, 1983: 207)

The aim, then, of case studies, is not to make valid statistical inferences but to use the analysis of micro data to investigate, inform, expand and explain general theories (Yin, 1984). The next section describes the two case study firms and the qualitative interviewing which took place in these firms.

3.6 The research settings - Bristol Insurance and Bristol Laminated

Interviews were conducted in two case study firms - a large insurance company and a large manufacturing company, both located in Bristol. In order to preserve anonymity, neither the real names of the companies nor the real names of any of the people interviewed are used. However, a brief description of both companies will help to contextualise later analysis. Starting with Bristol Insurance, this is a major site of a relatively large and profitable national and international insurance and finance company, employing over 2000 people and with around £10 billion of funds (1993) under management. The company's association with Bristol dates back to the early nineteenth century and the Bristol site, presently employing over 900 people, is the location of the administrative headquarters, which opened in 1975. This site contains the administrative functions of accounting, internal audit and national accounts as well as more research orientated functions such as corporate communications and marketing, a situation which has led to it being known as the 'paper factory' within the company. The majority of the Bristol workforce are, therefore, involved in insurance administration and work an average of 35 hours from Monday to Friday but with flexi-time around the 'core' times of 10am-12am and 2pm-4pm. The office environment is relatively modern and on-site services such as a licensed restaurant and canteens are provided.

Moving on to Bristol Laminated, this firm was recently acquired by a larger international manufacturing company to form a holding company which has interests in printing and packaging, coated industrial films, tissue, building and engineering. The holding company is involved in markets in Western Europe, the Far East, USA and Australia, has sales of over £2 billion (1995) and employs over 25,000 people worldwide. The original group's association with Bristol dates back to the middle of the nineteenth century and the Bristol operation employs over 500 people concentrating on complex coating, laminating and packaging processes. The factory is split into 2 sites, one (smaller site) dealing mainly with printing and the other with the packaging and laminating. The workforce are unionised and work on large (but relatively quiet) machines in 3/4 person teams and on a continuous shift system from Monday at 6am to Friday at 10pm.

My access to Bristol Insurance was through a contact (what Hammersley and Atkinson (1983) call 'informal sponsorship') and access to Bristol Laminated was achieved speculatively. In total 28 workers and managers were interviewed in a semi-structured manner, 18 in Bristol Insurance and 10 in Bristol Laminated.[9] The original intention had been to interview 10 people in each research setting, with interviewees from across the occupational spectrum. However, given that access to Bristol Insurance was through a manager in the marketing division the original interviews were all in this section. In order, therefore, to broaden the occupational spectrum of those employed in the office, I returned to interview employees in the largest, administration, section. All of the interviews were used in the final analysis. The interviews were semi-structured, lasted from one and half to two hours and were taped. In addition to recording the interviews a research diary was kept which noted additional points about the personalities of those interviewed, the setting of the interview and any comments made when the tape recorder was switched off. This number and type of interviews produced a large quantity of rich data and the next sub-section goes on to briefly describe the priorities, processes and practical problems associated with the collection of this qualitative data, before going on to discuss the analysis of the material.

3.7 The interviews

The aim of the interviews was to gather data on respondents' views and values on three key issues relating to the potential for industrial mobility: methods of recruitment, perceptions of skill and perceptions of each other and each others type of work. The aim was to conduct a series of interviews which, while allowing respondents the freedom to expand on any particular topic, retained certain themes common to all the interviews. In the first two interviews I used a quite detailed questionnaire but it quickly became apparent that such an approach stifled confidence and self expression, and this was changed to an aide-memoir (Bresnen, 1988) which listed the main themes.[10] Thus while not every interviewee was asked exactly the same questions, the same themes (recruitment channels, skill perceptions and perceptions of each other and of each others work) were covered. In addition, if some interviewees were more animated and articulate on certain themes (for example some gave considerable time to the relationship between physical strength and gender), the interviews followed this lead. One of the most positive features of such a method, allowing respondents the freedom to influence the research agenda, also presents the researcher with a problem - how to maintain certain 'boundaries' to the interview which facilitates wide ranging discussion while

---

[9]See Appendices 1 and 2 for fuller details of interviewees.

[10]See Appendix 3 for further details.

continually focusing on certain themes. Jones (1991), cites Lummis (1987) on this:

> The art of good interviewing lies in being able to keep most of the interview conversational while following various digressions, remembering which questions the flow of information has answered and yet being prepared to question more deeply and precisely when necessary. (Lummis, 1987: 62, from Jones, 1991: 203)

The technique, then, is to remember points made or missed which one wishes to explore at a deeper level and to return to these later in the interview. Turning to the actual structure of the interviews, each started with an explanation of the aims of the research project, the idea being that interviewees would be more relaxed and positive if they understood the purpose of the research (Whyte, 1982; Buchanan et al, 1988; Jones, 1991). The next step was to ensure confidentiality and then go on to ask interviewees what they thought of the problematic under study, whether they thought it mattered if people found difficulty moving between different industries and occupations. The aim here was immediately to 'empower' the interviewee, to make each person feel part of the project and to be conscious of the fact that while their views and values would both be reflected in and influence the research they would remain anonymous. Following this discussion of the broad aims of the research my first question tended to relate to the job done by those interviewed, I found that interviewees were eager to discuss their own job and that this served to set them at their ease and create a confident and comfortable atmosphere for the remainder of the interview. The initial aim, then, was trying to create an atmosphere of confidence and trust which would facilitate animated and creative dialogue. Another tactic I employed was to vary my style of dress depending on the research environment, thus a shirt and tie was worn in the Bristol Insurance but not Bristol Laminated. The effectiveness of such a tactic is demonstrated by the comments one respondent from Bristol Laminated made in discussions on the differences between office and factory workers:

> I'm a blue collar worker, I'm not a white collar worker. I'm not the type of person what could get a job in a office. (Why not?) For the simple fact... that it's not in me, I would get bored out of my brain. More so than I do at the moment. (What's boring about it?) The pressures on me are the pressures I can handle but the pressures of being in a situation with my type of education and also losing it (your temper) a little bit you would be a little bit embarrassed. And also the way I am and the way I talk and the type of person I am I would find it hard to get on and work with people who're better educated and who talk differently. You don't put me down cause I'm as good as anyone else but I'd find that I'd get a little bit, how can you say, a little bit uppity. You know what I mean. I'm not being funny, you've been to Polytechnic but *you don't talk much different from what I do*. Talking to you now I haven't got any problems, but *if you were la di da and all suited up* and that I would be a lot more uncomfortable than what I am now. (BL 10)

This extract provides a good example of the impact made by the dress and manner of the researcher, with this respondent (even though I came from an institute of higher education), not feeling threatened or 'uncomfortable'. The importance of image in general and dress in particular has been noted by other researchers (Patrick, 1973; Hammersley and Atkinson, 1983; Crompton and Jones, 1988; Jones, 1991). Some researchers have gone to considerable lengths to 'fit in'. Patrick (1973), for example, in his study of a Glasgow gang noted that:

> Clothes were another major difficulty. I was already aware of the importance attached to them by gang members in the school and so, after discussion with Tim, I bought... a midnight-blue suit, with a twelve-inch middle vent, three-inch flaps over the side pockets and a light blue handkerchief with a white polka dot (to match my tie) in the top pocket... Even here I made two mistakes. Firstly, I bought the suit outright with cash instead of paying it up, thus attracting both attention to myself in the shop and disbelief in the gang when I innocently mentioned the fact. Secondly, during my first night out with the gang, I fastened the middle button of my jacket as I was accustomed to. Tim was quick to spot the mistake. The boys in the gang fastened only the top button; with this arrangement they can stand with their hands in their trouser pockets and their jackets buttoned - ra gallous wae. (Patrick, 1973: 13,15)

It is clearly important, therefore, for the researcher to adopt a manner and attitude which aims to create an atmosphere of confidence and trust. An additional element of this process of creating an atmosphere which is conducive to communication is the establishment of an informal contract, whereby the interviewer listens attentively to whatever the interviewee is saying, even if it is not within the 'direct' focus of the research. Crompton and Jones (1988) argue that a researcher needs to offer something in exchange for access, writing 'For respondents, you... need to offer a listening ear.' (Crompton and Jones, 1988: 70). To give an example, having covered the main themes in one interview at Bristol Insurance I turned the tape recorder off and the interviewee lit up a cigarette and asked why I had not enquired about sexual harassment. While I had covered some issues relating to 'gender' (mainly connected to skill perceptions) it had not been my intention to ask any explicit questions about sexual harassment. However, once it became clear this respondent wished to discuss this issue, I asked her about sexual harassment and made notes on her replies. What this makes clear is that such interviewing is a two way process. There is, or at least should be, a dialogue, a necessary communication, a process by which both parties 'gain' something - the researcher obtains data (hopefully) rich in quality and the interviewee is given the opportunity of expressing their opinions in an uncritical environment.

The process is not, however, without some drawbacks. The first is that if, as was the case with my research, interviews are conducted over a period of time, future respondents will have had an opportunity to discuss with previous respondents their experiences and these discussions may influence the expectations and answers of those awaiting interview. As an interviewer I found that I became suspicious that detailed prior discussion had taken place when respondents gave very rapid replies to lines of enquiry which were met in the majority of cases by thoughtful pauses. I responded to this by asking the same question in a number of different ways and/or coming back to this area later in the interview. It would, obviously, be difficult to ensure that each interviewee was ignorant of the research topic until the time of interview but even if people were somehow persuaded or pressurised into keeping lines of enquiry confidential this very secrecy may affect the attitudes and answers of those not yet interviewed. The approach I adopted was to recognise that such prior discussions were bound to take place and make every effort to keep the interview varied while maintaining consistency through covering the same themes. The second drawback I found to be connected to the use of a tape recorder. Jones (1991), wrote of using this method of recording responses:

> I always ask people if they mind being taped and people quickly forget that the tape is there. (Jones, 1991: 206)

I found that in my work this was not the case and that, often, if interviewees thought they were straying into a 'sensitive' area (most commonly connected to gender issues), they would glance (almost unconsciously) at the tape recorder before giving a curt response, attaching a caveat or, in some cases, asking for the tape recorder to be switched off. A senior personnel manager from Bristol Insurance, for example, gave the following comment when discussing the importance of the type of dress which was worn in the office:

> Ehm, *don't take to much notice of the fact that it's on the tape*, I am disappointed with the standard of dress in this organisation, ehm you might call me middle aged or Victorian in my outlook but to me there is an acceptable sense in dress for the office. *It's not a sexist comment*, I think generally the men are pretty well conformists, I think there's a lot to be desired with the clothes that some of the females wear, some are extremely smart and should be complimented, you go to the other extreme, I personally don't believe that jeans should be allowed in an office. (BI 1)

The relationship between dress and occupation and the possible association with social class are discussed in the later analytic chapters. What is relevant here is that this respondent felt that his comments relating to dress were of a contentious nature and related to what was regarded as a 'sensitive' subject area - gender. The sensitivity of these two areas is shown by the attachment of two caveats, one relating to the comments being recorded and the other to it 'not (being) a sexist comment'. In another interview the respondent was discussing the race of some of her previous work colleagues and asked for the tape recorder to be switched off. There is clearly no simple solution to these problems: one has to balance the enormous practical advantages of having a concrete verbatim account to return to during analysis while admitting the possibility that the presence of a tape recorder may reduce the reflexivity of the respondent. I adopted the tactic, used by others, of making explicit my willingness to turn the tape recorder off whenever the interviewee wished and to combine the recording with a research diary which covered points made off tape (Burgess, 1982; Hammersley and Atkinson, 1983). Qualitative interviewing, then, while requiring considerable concentration, has the potential to produce rich data containing the views and values, the meanings and motivations and the perceptions and priorities of interviewees. The next step was to decide what to do with the data, and in particular how to analyse it, and this is considered in the next section.

3.8 Data analysis

Following the collection of the data on tape the next task was to transcribe the material, this was done on a partial transcription basis. It would, perhaps, have been preferable to fully transcribe the tapes, but given limited resources and the fact that I could return to the tapes at any time (which I frequently did) I felt that a partial transcription would suffice (Hammersley and Atkinson, 1983). The objective was to analyse systematically each tape and extract all relevant data, which would then be entered into a separate computer file for each interviewee, in order to let the common themes, definitions and issues emerge from the data. This, perhaps, was the most challenging task. As Allan (1991) writes:

> ... ultimately the success or otherwise of your thesis is likely to rest on how well you analyse your qualitative data. Be warned: this is not an easy task. You should certainly not underestimate the amount of time analysis takes. It is likely to be a long and often difficult process. Putting things simply, the main task is to categorize the varied data you have so that links can be made between them which explain the events which are the focus of the thesis. (Allan, 1991: 183, 184)

The data which emerged fell broadly into three areas: recruitment, skills and perceptions of each other and of each others work. In any such exercise there is bound to be some overlap but the aim was to split data into the three emergent categories and then further subdivide these categories by issue and by firm. So, for example, replies relating to recruitment channels were split (by firm) into formal/informal and then this was further subdivided into help from family and/or friends. This approach to analysing material is similar to the grounded theory approach which grew out of the work of Glaser and Strauss (1967). Allan (1991) writes of this approach:

> (it is) a process by which analytical categories can be developed inductively from the data through careful scrutiny of all the different interview or observational accounts gathered in the fieldwork. The essence of the approach involves 'stripping' particular episodes of action/speech into their essential component elements. Other episodes in the fieldnotes are then scrutinised to

see if they contain similar or different elements. Where there is similarity and overlap, modified categorizations can then be generated which encompass and 'bridge' a wider range of phenomena... (Allan, 1991: 186)

Like the grounded theory approach, therefore, my method places emphasis on the primacy of empirical data in shaping the important analytical categories, with any theoretical implications or conclusions being literally 'grounded' in empirical data (Turner, 1981; 1983; 1988). The data is presented both in tables and through selective quotes. The tabular data, in which each respondent is allocated a label, gives an indication of the frequency of the most common themes. Thus, for example, if Bristol Insurance 1 (BI 1) linked formal recruitment, ambition and meritocracy with office work and workers it would be possible to go through the tables and 'map' a 'path' of these replies for this particular interviewee. It is not the case, however, that every table will contain every respondent. The tables reflect the issues which arose in each interview and while every interview covered the same themes (recruitment channels, skill perceptions and perceptions of each other) some interviewees went into more detail on some of these themes than others. So, for example, in the chapter which deals with recruitment, while all 18 interviewees at Bristol Insurance were asked questions covering the broad theme of recruitment, only 4 discussed the advantages of informal recruitment, thus in this table only 4 respondents are listed (table 4.10). This does not mean that the other 14 had nothing to say on this topic but rather reflects a different interview flow, with (perhaps) these interviewees saying more about skills or barriers. The tables, then, give a guide to the frequency with which certain issues arose, with the analysis of why certain issues were common emerging more clearly from the quotes. The tables are accompanied by selected quotes which place the themes highlighted in the tables in the context and language of the interviewees, thus allowing insights into and interpretation of the meanings and motivations underlying the views and values articulated during the interviews.

This method of presenting 'strips' of interview material has been used by a number of other authors writing in the field of labour markets: Bakke (1940) in a study to discover the readjustment problems faced by unemployed American workers and their families; Scott et al (1956) writing of the relations between technical change and the social structure of a large UK steelworks; Young and Wilmott (1957) on family and kinship in east London; Beynon and Blackburn (1972) in a study of work perceptions in a food processing factory; Wedderburn and Crompton (1972) on workers attitudes to changing technology; Cockburn (1983) in a study into printers and their work; Jenkins (1982, 1986) into the role of race perceptions on recruitment; Crompton and Jones (1984) in their research into the 'proletarianisation' of office work and Curran (1985, 1988) in studies on the role of gender on recruitment. While these studies differed in the exact type of qualitative approach (structured/unstructured interviews with/without participant observation) they all used quotes to illustrate, explain and further explore the main themes emerging from the research.

3.9 Conclusion

This chapter opened with an account of the changing patterns of employment which have been experienced at both Bristol and Great Britain levels and at the limited information on mobility. This quantitative material was used to set the context for my investigation and it was argued that to go beyond the picture portrayed by statistics and look at what employees themselves thought of mobility it was necessary to use a qualitative methodology. Following an examination of the theoretical rationale for using such a methodology, where reference was made to Knorr-Cetina assertion that the tick of the macro-order may be heard at the micro level, it was suggested that by investigating an office and factory, two firms on the extremities of industrial restructuring, it would be possible to obtain a realistic impression and understanding of the magnitude of the problems facing any simple 'retraining' response to industrial restructuring. The next three chapters move on to present and analyse the results of my case study investigations in Bristol Insurance and Bristol Laminated, which show work groups populated by people with contrasting views and values, contrasts which, it is argued, indicate the existence of processes which create non-competitive work groups whose existence and persistence works strongly against any simple concept of labour market flexibility.

4 Recruitment of labour

4.1 Introduction

> Helping people keep in touch with the labour market is essential. TEC's will want to work closely with the Employment Service so that their services for unemployed people complement each other. It is also important to make sure unemployed people are not excluded by negative attitudes and working practices, such as the use of informal networks in recruitment, which act to prevent their return to the labour market. (Skills and Enterprise Network, 1993: 43)

This extract from the work of a branch of the Department of Employment illustrates the importance of recruitment practices to the government's attempts to increase labour market flexibility and describes the role of informal recruitment networks as 'negative working practices', as a rigidity which must be reduced and removed. It is the role of different recruitment processes in Bristol Insurance and Bristol Laminated which is the central interest of this chapter. As other studies have shown (Hedges, 1983; IFF, 1988; SCELI, 1992; Hales, 1993; Atkinson et al, 1994) informal methods are used more often in manual than in non-manual jobs, implying that manual factory workers are more likely than non-manual office workers to hear jobs through 'word of mouth'. This clearly has relevance to the underlying problematic of the research, because if it is the case, for example, that respondents view and value, understand and use recruitment channels differently, there may be important implications for flexibility and occupational mobility. Furthermore, if there are differences these may serve to create bounded labour markets, analysis of which may shed some light on the processes which create of such non-competitive work groups and which in turn may inform the macro picture. The focus of this chapter, therefore, is on the recruitment channels used by Bristol Insurance and Bristol Laminated, with particular emphasis on the role of informal channels, which other studies have shown to be an important discriminator between manual factory workers and non-manual office workers.

This chapter is split into three main sections. The first broad section relates to the nature and extent of use of informal methods and opens with an examination of secondary data from America and Britain. It is noted that while network analysis has an established research history much of the work done has focused on blue collar industries or on specific issues, such as the relationship between networks and sexist or racist recruitment practices, and that there has been very little work done comparing and contrasting the role of informal networks between offices and factories. The second main section investigates the rationale for the use of family and friendship networks in Bristol Insurance and Bristol Laminated and the third section moves onto an examination of why informal recruitment networks are concentrated in manual blue collar jobs and industries.

4.2 Recruitment methods

This section has two main, interlinked, aims, firstly to investigate secondary material for evidence of the extent and role of informal methods in recruitment and secondly to examine this material for reference to the particular significance of this recruitment channel to manual blue collar work. Turning firstly to the general importance of family and friendship networks, Marshall gave the following comments at the end of the last century:

> The advantages which those born in one of the higher grades of society have over those born in a lower, consist in a great measure of the better introductions and the better start in life which they receive from their parents... in the large majority of cases the son follows the father's calling. In the old fashioned domestic industries this was almost a universal rule; and, even under modern conditions, the father has often great facilities for introducing his son to his own trade. Employers and their foremen generally give to a lad whose father they already know and trust, a preference over one for whom they would have to incur the entire responsibility. And in many trades a lad, even after he has got entrance to the works, is not very likely to make good progress and obtain a secure footing, unless he is able to work by the side of his father, or some friend of his father's, who will take the trouble to teach him and to let him do work that requires careful supervision, but has an educational value. (Marshall, (1890), 1970: 468)

This quote offers a relatively early recognition of the importance of informal recruitment channels to successfully obtaining employment. The context within which such practices are discussed also point to an association between family and friendship networks and manufacturing work. This is evident from the way Marshall writes of 'trades', 'foremen' and 'works', words which set the comments firmly in a manual, manufacturing context. The growing importance of informal methods of recruitment was noted in much of the work of later classical American labour market studies. For example Rees (1966) wrote:

> We may divide information networks in the labour market into two groups: formal and informal. The formal networks include the state employment services, private fee-charging employment agencies, newspaper advertisements, union hiring halls, and school or college placement bureaus. The informal sources include referrals from employees, other employers, and miscellaneous sources, and walk ins or hiring at the gate... The literature stresses the great importance of the informal channels, and our study of the Chicago labour market offers additional support for this emphasis. In the four white-collar occupations under study, informal sources account for about half of all hires; in the eight blue-collar occupations, informal sources account for more than four-fifths of all hires. (Rees, 1966: 559)

The findings of this study clearly demonstrate both the significance of informal methods and their particular importance to blue-collar workers. These findings were supported by other early American studies, for example Myers and Shultz's (1951) study into the mobility of displaced textile workers; Reynolds' (1951) study into New Haven manual workers and Sheppard and Belitsky's (1966) study into Erie manual workers. The findings of these studies are usefully summarised by Parnes (1954):

> The patterns followed by workers in seeking jobs are apparently ingrained. When Reynolds asked a sample of employed manual workers how they would go about getting a job if they were out of work, the responses followed rather closely the pattern of their past behaviour.[11] A third reported that they would canvass their acquaintances and relatives, a fifth said they would try gate applications, and one in seven indicated he would go to a previous employer. The remaining third were equally divided between those who would register with the public employment office, those who would consult advertisements, and those who would rely on union or other contacts. (Parnes, 1954: 163)

These American studies, therefore, found that between 50% and 70% of blue collar workers had used informal methods to find employment. The actual mechanics of such networks is illustrated in data from an earlier study from Bakke (1940), who quoted an interview with a worker who had just found a job following a prolonged period of unemployment:

> The only thing that will get you into a job is to know somebody. Now you take the way I got this job. You know I had a friend who was a friend of his wife's, and that friend got busy on the wife and slowly she worked around so

---

[11]Reynolds (1951) conducted a study of manual workers in New Haven and found that 28% of sample found their present job through friends or relatives and 20% by direct application at the gate. Myers and Schultz (1951), in their study of displaced textile workers found the figures to be 36% and 14% respectively.

> at last one day he called me up and told me he had a job, but even now he won't give me the real day job. That's what I'd like to have. I just have to be satisfied with a night job. But I know right well that if I had somebody that was close to him, I could get him to give me a day job. Do you know what this here depression has done to men? It's made them realise more and more how important it is to have somebody on the inside... (Bakke, 1940: 226)

This quote illustrates two important points. Firstly, it offers a clear example of the relative strength of different network connections. This respondent understands that while his connection to the employer can get him a job it is not strong enough to get him the day job he really wants. His present connection to his employer, through a friend of a friend is, he believes, too distant to apply sufficient pressure to allow him access to the sought after job. The second point emerging here is early evidence of the particular importance of such informal methods in times of recession, a finding which this has been supported by more contemporary studies (Marsden, 1982; Jenkins et al, 1983; Grieco, 1987; Atkinson et al, 1994).

Informal networks were also seen to be important in the (relatively few) U.S. studies into informal recruitment practices in white collar jobs, but these tended to concentrate on recruitment to professional, academic jobs (Caplow and McGee, 1958; Brown, 1967).[12] The results of studies which compared white and blue collar occupations (Rees, 1966; Corcoran et al, 1980a) have found that informal methods are most common amongst semi and unskilled manual workers in blue collar occupations. For example Corcoran et al (1980a), in their analysis of data from the 11th wave of the Panel Study of Income Dynamics,[13] found that:

> White men in blue-collar occupations were more likely than other white men to hear about their job from a friend, to know someone on the job, and to be helped by someone. (Corcoran, 1980a: 35)

Turning to data for the UK, research carried out in the 1950s and 1960s, again mainly in manual occupations, pointed to the prevalence of informal recruitment mechanisms (Scott et al, 1956; Young and Wilmott, 1957; Kahn, 1964; Wedderburn 1965; Tunstall, 1969). Scott et al's research into the relationship between a steel plant and the local community found that an employee of the firm had an average of 2.6 relatives who worked with them in the same plant and 4.1 relatives who had worked there at some time in the past, while Wedderburn's research on redundancy amongst railwaymen found that 64% asked friends and

---

[12]Caplow and McGee (1958) found that 40% of assistant professors and 61% of associate and full professors had contact with the relevant department before being appointed.

[13]This is an ongoing longitudinal study of more than 5,000 American families which begun in 1968. For more information on this see Corcoran et al (1980a).

acquaintances if any there were any vacancies or to put a 'word in'. Young and Wilmott (1957), in their research into family and kinship relations in East London, found that the strength of family reputations and ties was such that a sponsor could get relations a job even after they had left the firm:

> Mr Meadows' father, for instance, worked for a large motor transport undertaking for 25 years until he retired, and in all that time 'he had never bothered and he never complained'. When Mr Meadows lost his own job as a furniture craftsman in a firm no longer able to compete with mass production, his father suggested he try transport: 'He recommended me to go for it and said it was a good job if you're prepared to work hard. I went to see the Personnel Officer at Head Office and he said 'nothing doing.' I said then I'd come because my father had asked me to call. He said 'Oh, yes. Who's that, your father?' and I said 'Mr Meadows'. He said 'Oh, yes, I know Mr Meadows. He used to work here, didn't he? Hang on a minute.' He went out and in a few minutes he came back and said, 'Yes, Meadows, we can fix you up'. (Young and Wilmott, 1957: 73)

These in-depth studies were followed by others in the 1970s and 1980s, which continued to emphasise the important role of networks. Again, however, the focus was mainly on manual work in primary or secondary industries: for example Hill's (1976) work on dock workers; Hedges and Beynon's (1982) work on the steel industry; Manwaring's (1984) study into the recruitment practices of manufacturing firms in Birmingham, West London and South Wales;[14] Bresnen et al's (1985) work into recruitment in the construction industry; Lee's (1985) study into the employment prospects of redundant steelworkers in Wales; Dick and Morgan's (1987) study into the recruitment practices of a textile mill in Yorkshire; Grieco's (1987) work into the role of family based recruitment in the fish industry in Aberdeen, tobacco workers in Basildon and steel workers in Corby and Thompson's (1988) work into factory culture and skills amongst Coventry car workers.

The nature and extent of the role of the family was evident in the work of Dick and Morgan (1987) who, in their research, found that of sixty nine members of an established family network all but six were originally introduced to the firm via their family connections. The authors also found that help often extended beyond the immediate workplace into the community to include areas such as child minding for a network member who was working:

> ... one woman we talked to, who worked a full day shift, would look after her daughter's children after she had come home from work in order to allow her daughter to work a short evening shift. Kinship support could also help men.

---

[14]This study does cover routine white collar workers but only those who work in the offices of manufacturing firms.

One woman, for example, stayed with her cousin's ill wife at night, while he did a night shift. (Dick and Morgan, 1987: 235)

The importance of family connections also emerges powerfully from Grieco, whose research into the fish industry in Aberdeen found that 14 out of a workforce sample of 15 considered themselves as having married within 'the fish' and, as the following extract, illustrates, believed this to be customary practice:

I used to work with his (talking of her husband) sister before we even knew one another. She and me were pals. Then after we were married, I just carried on working alongside her. I reckon we worked our way round every fish house in Aberdeen at one time or another. Aye, and we work together still. (Aberdeen fish worker, Grieco, 1987: 21)

Grieco, from the three studies undertaken, arrives at the following conclusion:

... there is substantial evidence of the continued role of kin networks in the social organisation of employment in the contemporary period. Family relationships are relevant to the employment chances of the individual in a wide spread of geographical and occupational sectors. Kinship networks operate in modern western society as both employment information systems and employment sponsorship systems. Kinship remains of relevance to occupational choice and functioning in modern industrial society. (Grieco, 1987: 180)

The importance of family and friends to the recruitment process was also identified by Manwaring (1984), who developed the concept of extended internal labour markets (EILM) to describe and analyse recruitment through this channel. Manwaring writes:

This term is used to describe recruitment through existing employees of the firm. The knowledge of vacancies available to employees of a firm is extended beyond the firm, through social networks, to friends and relatives of the present workforce within the local community. (Manwaring, 1984: 161)

Thus Manwaring makes explicit the link between social factors, such as the community outside of the workplace, and channels of recruitment. In his empirical work into the existence of EILM's amongst manual and routine non-manual workers in the 25 largest manufacturing firms in Birmingham, West London and South Wales he found that 'friends and relatives' were the most commonly used recruitment channel for manual workers and local advertising for routine non-manual workers, results which support earlier work pointing to a blue collar manual/white collar non-manual split. While Manwaring's work provides strong evidence for the importance of informal networks, his structuring of labour markets is problematic. He argues for the existence of three major types of extended internal labour market: Type A: the 'structured' EILM; Type B: the 'unstructured' EILM and Type C: the 'unstable' EILM. Central to this typology is Manwaring's definition of a stable community, which is based on a geographically specific definition of spatiality. He writes:

> Because most of those working in a firm in manual and lower white-collar jobs live locally this also implies that the labour market is closed spatially; i.e. that knowledge of job opportunities will be confined to local areas. (Manwaring, 1984: 162)

and later:

> From the point of view of the employer, the most important factors are: whether the community from which candidates are recruited is able to supply the relevant skills. The local community is more likely to be able to satisfy this requirement if members of the community have lived in the area for a long time. This is termed an area's social stability. If there is high social stability, social networks can be well established and employment at a firm may stretch across generations. (Manwaring, 1984: 170)

I would argue, however, that Manwaring is placing too much emphasis on the necessity for geographical proximity between members of a social network in order to construct a 'stable' community made up of strong social connections. The labour market for the firm Manwaring was commenting on was certainly closed, indeed in this instance it may even have been closed spatially, but there is no automatic link between spatial closeness and tightness of a social network. As Grieco's (1987) research into kinship migration from Peterhead to Corby demonstrated, it is possible for strong and influential kinship networks to exist even though the members of such networks live apart. Grieco writes of this:

> ... low frequency of physical contact cannot be taken as evidence of either weakness of tie or low information transfer. (Grieco, 1987: 42)

Grieco's work illustrated that a strong network existed even over distance[15] with workers not only providing information on employment opportunities but also giving accommodation upon arrival in Corby. In short, Manwaring has highlighted what may well be a sufficient criterion for a strong network to exist, namely close geographical proximity, but it is not a necessary condition.

---

[15]These ties over space are known as "invisible colleges", the strength of which is measured by the degree of reciprocity which exists between network members (Grieco, 1987). This measurement contrasts with that of Hill (1976) and Granovetter (1973) who have argued that the strength of a tie is determined by the amount of regular physical contact.

The evidence detailed above illustrates that family and friendship networks play an important role in the process of recruitment. The focus of much of this data, however, has mainly been on manual workers in primary industries or secondary manufacturing firms. Network analysis has expanded, but there have been few comparative case studies of the recruitment process of non-manual offices workers and manual factory workers. The detailed network based research has mainly developed into researching specific issues such as the relationship between networks and the reproduction of a working environment influenced by race (Jenkins, 1985, 1986); the relationship between network based recruitment and discrimination in favour of men (Curran, 1985; Campbell, 1988); the increased influence of networks in times of recession (Wood, 1986; Jenkins et al, 1983; Dawes, 1993; Atkinson et al, 1994) and the relationship between network based recruitment and the 'underclass' (Morris and Irwin, 1992). Comparative studies of alternative recruitment channels have mainly taken place at a macro level, through large scale surveys (Courtenay and Hedges, 1977; Hedges, 1983; LMQ, 1984; IFF, 1988; SCELI, 1992; Hales, 1993). Table 4.1 provides a useful example of such a survey and its findings:

Table 4.1
Successful method of engagement (%)

	Manual workers			Non-manual workers		
	1973	1977	1982	1973	1977	1982
Job Centre	21	22	31	7	11	21
Advertisement	35	22	16	45	42	35
Informal	43	52	49	25	29	33
Other	0	4	4	0	6	4
Base - 100%	1700	1581	3602	6718	868	2147

Source: Labour market quarterly review (Feb 1984)
Informal methods include personal contacts, recommendations from existing employees, direct applications and mailing lists.

What emerges from these data is a continuous association between manual workers and informal recruitment channels, with around 50% of manual workers successfully obtaining employment through such a channel compared to around 30% of non-manual workers. Table 4.2 (see over), based on data collected during the recent extensive research project entitled Social Change in Economic Life Initiative (SCELI 1992), provides more detailed information on how employees first heard about their jobs. Again, the greater reliance of those classed in manual skilled and unskilled occupations on informal recruitment channels (particularly family and friends) compared to those in clerical occupations is quite clear, with around 60% of skilled and unskilled manual workers hearing about their first job through an informal channel compared with around 40% of those in clerical occupations. It is interesting to note that the data from SCELI (table 4.2), which concentrated on asking employees how they first got their job tends to give greater emphasis to the role of informal channels than surveys which concentrate on the management perspective (table 4.1). This difference is even more marked in comparison with a recent (IFF 1988) survey of recruitment channels favoured by employers (shown in table 4.3).

Table 4.2
How employees first heard about job (%)

Channel	Service	Clerical	Tech/supp	Skilled	Nonskilled
Family	6.1	11.3	12.9	16.9	16.5
Friends	16.3	15.3	19.1	25.6	27.5
Approach employer	10.7	10.8	13.3	13.3	13.7
Employer approach	8.4	5.3	3.7	5.8	5.9
Informal total	**41.5**	**42.7**	**49.0**	**60.8**	**63.6**
Job Centre	3.1	10.2	9.4	7.8	11.6
Private emp agency	2.5	5.0	1.6	0.5	0.8
Advert local news	20.9	26.1	22.4	18.6	15.4
Advert nat news	14.6	4.1	7.4	2.7	2.1
Careers office	6.2	5.3	3.6	3.9	1.5
Formal total	**47.3**	**50.7**	**44.4**	**33.5**	**31.4**
Other	11.2	6.6	6.6	5.7	5.0

Source: SCELI (1992) Total sample 3832

Table 4.3
Recruitment channels favoured by employers (%)

Recruit-ment Channel	All	Mgt/ prof	Non -mgt	Clerical	Retail/ Catering	Skilled Manual	Unskilled Manual
Job Centre	54	29	57	45	64	53	62
Careers Service	4	3	4	7	3	4	4
Private agency	6	5	12	17	1	2	4
Local papers	36	35	36	47	33	34	31
National papers	4	15	3	5	2	3	2
Trade press	6	31	3	5	2	3	2
Notice board	9	6	9	4	18	4	3
Informal	42	34	43	30	51	45	39
Other	6	0	8	7	6	4	4

Source: IFF (1988) Vacancy and recruitment survey

The first point to note about these data is that while the most favoured management channel for both manual and non-manual jobs was the job centre (formal) and the second most favoured for non-manual workers remained formal (local papers), for manual workers the second most favoured were the informal channels. Again, therefore, there is seen to be a difference between these two sets of workers with respect to informal channels. Compared to both tables 4.1 and 4.2, however, particular channels, most obviously Job Centres, are seen to play a greater role in recruitment. This may be because employers feel they are under a certain obligation to notify government offices (Wood, 1982; Beardsworth et al, 1981) and so perhaps overestimate the 'official' (formal) channel and underestimate the unofficial (informal) channel. Wood (1982) writing on this point comments:

> Several personnel managers who reported vacancies to the job centre did so as a matter of routine and/or obligation (perceived sometimes as a legal one),

even though they did not actually recruit from them or expect to attract candidates from them. (Wood, 1982: 110)

Wood, making a distinction between nominal and effective channels, found that although 59% of the British firms covered in his study always reported their vacancies to government employment agencies only 8% claimed that this was a successful recruitment channel. Manwaring (1984) makes a similar distinction between frequency of use of different channels and the significance of use (in the sense of actually recruiting through such a channel). He writes of this:

> This (distinction) is especially important in the case of the Job Centre which is typically ranked higher in terms of frequency than significance; employers may feel that they ought to notify the Job Centre but would not actually employ someone sent from the Job Centre. Conversely, the informal channels are often ranked as more important in terms of significance than frequency. (Manwaring, 1984: 163, emphasis added)

In summary, there is considerable secondary evidence on the importance of informal recruitment channels in general and kin/friendship networks in particular. Large scale secondary survey evidence has been used to illustrate the importance of such networks as a discriminator between manual and non-manual jobs. This is not to argue that informal networks have no role in non-manual clerical employment, rather that such methods are more characteristic of blue collar manual work. This conclusion has been supported by numerous smaller scale investigations but, as has been argued earlier, these studies have concentrated on primary and manufacturing manual firms and industries with little comparative case study work taking place between non-manual white and manual blue collar workers. The data gathered from Bristol Insurance and Bristol Laminated goes some way to providing such information, and it to these data that we now turn.

4.3 The recruitment process

Bristol Insurance

This section introduces and analyses primary data on the recruitment methods and experiences of respondents from Bristol Insurance. What emerges from the data is that the majority of those interviewed got their jobs through formal methods, such as press advertisements or recruitment agencies, but that family and friendship networks still played a role in the recruitment process, often providing 'low level' information on employment opportunities.

Turning firstly to the summary picture of how respondents heard about their own jobs, table 4.4 details the responses given in discussion of recruitment.

Of the 18 people interviewed at Bristol Insurance 9 cited formal channels, 1 an informal channel, 1 a mixture of both (BI 18) and 7 did not discuss their own recruitment channel. Of the 7 who are listed as 'did not discuss', this is not because recruitment as a theme was not covered but because (as the later table 4.5 shows) the discussion surrounding recruitment amongst the managers tended to focus on which channels they used in recruiting new staff, rather than how they themselves were recruited. Of those who did discuss their own recruitment channel the emphasis was on formal channels, with sources ranging from advertisements in the local press to private employment agencies and, for higher graded staff, trade papers. One of the respondents (BI 5) who gave an informal channel had obtained his job at Bristol Insurance through writing a speculative letter, while the other respondent who had utilised an informal channel (BI 18) had combined information

Table 4.4
Bristol Insurance, summary table of how respondents first heard about job

	Formal			Informal	Did not discuss	Total
	Advert in trade press	Advert in local press	Private emp agency			
Managerial grade	bi3			bi5	bi1; bi2; bi6; bi8; bi9; bi10; bi11	9
Supervisory grade	bi7	bi12; bi4	bi13; bi15			5
Clerical grades		bi14; bi16; bi17; bi18		bi 18		4
Response Total	10			2	7	*19*\18

Note: response total (in italics) may be more than number of respondents due to multiple replies

from his sister (an employee with Bristol Insurance) with information from the local paper. At one level this evidence supports the findings of larger recruitment studies (Hedges, 1983; LMQ 1984; IFF, 1988; SCELI, 1992) which showed that formal channels predominate in non-manual, particularly clerical, jobs. As is shown in table 4.5, however, further analysis of the data indicates that while the majority of the respondents interviewed believed formal channels transferred *decisive* information on employment opportunities, there is evidence which points to the existence of family and friendship networks which provide information and advice which is *incrementally* influential in employment choice and success.

Table 4.5
Bristol Insurance, the extent of use of family and friendship networks

	Personally used information networks to:			Perceives role for networks in giving info on co.	Knows of family connections in BI	Denies any n-w in BI	Total
	Recruit	Obtain info on job	Obtain /give info on co.				
Managerial grade	bi 9 bi 10 bi11			b2 bi3 bi6	bi1 bi5 bi6	bi8 bi2	9
Supervisory grade			bi4	bi7 bi14	bi4 bi15	bi12 bi13 bi 15	5
Clerical grade		bi16 bi18	bi18		bi 16 bi 18	bi14 bi17	4
Response totals	7			5	7	7	*26*\18

Note: response total (in italics) may be more than number of respondents due to multiple replies.

Table 4.5 illustrates the summary picture relating to the existence and use of family and friendship networks at Bristol Insurance. This table shows that information providing family and friendship networks do exist at Bristol Insurance: eight of the managers, three of the supervisors and two of the clerks had either used, perceived a use for or knew of family connections inside Bristol Insurance. In total over half of the 10 who had given a formal channel as the source of their own job had either supplemented this with information from an informal source or knew of kinship relations within Bristol Insurance. I would argue that this evidence suggests that family and friendship networks still play a role in non-manual white collar recruitment, but that the transmission and effect of this information is difficult to detect. Furthermore, I would suggest that this difficulty may lead to underestimations of the significance of informal networks in large (particularly employer based) questionnaire type surveys. Turning to an analysis of the primary data itself, table 4.5 shows that 3 of the managers had recently recruited staff through 'word of mouth' recruitment channels. Comments included:

A girl who worked for me, *that was word of mouth actually*, because the girl who was leaving knew someone who knew Anna. (BI 9)

A number of people in marketing, our marketing organisation is only seven years old and when I joined it eh we took on people from the Polytechnic and one of the girls who was taken on said '*Actually, I've got a friend*' and so that friend was interviewed. She hadn't actually written and applied for jobs, she was asked to send in her C.V. and things and then she was interviewed and given a job. That happens I think probably fairly frequently. (BI 10)

The two cases cited above refer to the use of friendship networks, involving friends of present or past employees. The mechanism by which they work is through trusting someone already 'inside' the network. The nature of this assistance comes through more clearly from comments made by a Bristol Insurance clerk who was given information from a primary kin relation:

Q: How did you get your job here?
(laugh) *Through my sister* (laugh) Ehm I knew that Bristol Insurance were going down to Clevedon and I live in Yate which is about 4 or 5 miles away and I thought it'd be a great opportunity to get down there. My sister was employed to go down to Clevedon, she was *in* about four or five months before I was, and I knew from what she was saying that they encourage promotion... and being local... (What did your sister say?) Well it was in all the local papers and obviously my sister did mention it as well. But *I don't think that because she is in here I got the job because of that*. It was just I heard more about the job because she was here. I could see, *rather than just read* the advert in the paper which obviously they try and glorify it up a bit and say this is a brilliant job and all that. *She could tell me there's bad points about it*, obviously even though she'd been here five months, there's bad points about any job. But ehm she was pleased with it and I felt that I would be, and I am. (BI 18)

Three key points emerge from this response. Firstly it demonstrates how the process of obtaining a job involves a mixture of information sources, with this respondent finding out about the vacancy both through a formal channel (local newspapers) and an informal channel (his sister). He believes, however, that the information provided by his sister gave him a more realistic picture of what the job entailed, information which not only influenced his decision to apply but which, through shaping his employment expectations, may well have influenced the outcome of the job interview. The second point is the sensitivity which surrounds the use of family and friendship networks. This is evident from the laugh before and after the first admission that he had got his job '*through his sister*', an admission which is contradicted later in the same quotation: 'But *I don't think that because she is in here I got the job because of that*'. Here the initially powerful role of a family member in giving employment aid is weakened to 'just' providing information. The third point concerns the type of the information which covers both the specifics of the job and the general nature of Bristol Insurance as an employer. It is this low level, general information, which, I would argue, may have an incremental importance in shaping employment opportunities. Five other respondents (three managers and two supervisors) while not identifying nepotism with Bristol Insurance, believed that information of a general nature flowed between network members. Typical comments were:

> Recruitment through friends and family I would guess happens more, rather than being 'there's a job here so just you apply for it', it's probably more yeah *they're a good company* to work for why don't you have a go. Slightly different, it's a general application rather than a specific job. (BI 3)

> ... I think on the whole, when all's said and done *Bristol Insurance's a good company to work for* and I think most staff here would agree that, at whatever level and therefore if you happen to know that your brother, sister, cousin, aunty is looking for a job you might say *'Well Bristol Insurance is nice, come and apply'*. (BI 6)

> ... a company like Bristol Insurance which is a big employer in Bristol, it's not necessarily somebody coming on and saying there's a job in such and such an area, it's actually that people who know people working in Bristol Insurance are *more aware of the name* when it comes up in a job ad. (BI 7)

There is a clear and important role here for family networks, but, as is more obvious from Bristol Laminated data (analysed in the next section), the nature of the assistance is not so much obtaining and passing on information which pertains to a particular job or of putting a strong 'word in' for a friend or family member, but rather on passing general information on the quality of the company as an employer - 'they're a good company'. I would argue that although this assistance is relatively weak, by communicating an image of a positive and non-threatening workplace, it plays an important part in the process of employment decision making and employment outcomes. The general, even vague, nature of information offered by such a network is evident from another set of comments, where a respondent, while recognising that information on the reputation of the company might flow between friends, denies that friends and relatives help each other obtain employment with Bristol Insurance:

> Q: How often have you heard of people getting jobs through friends and relatives?
> *Not here...* I'm not saying that someone wouldn't say *it's a good company* why don't you apply for an interview but I don't think anyone who is a manager here would try to influence recruitment, normally it would be done through Human Resources... not me saying I've got a mate I'd like him to come and work for this group. (BI 2)

This illustrates the different ways in which information networks can be interpreted. There is an apparent contradiction between the denial that people are recruited to Bristol Insurance through family and friends: '*Not here...*' and the acknowledgement that someone would pass on sufficient information to persuade a friend/relative to apply for an interview. This contradiction illustrates both the complexity and sensitivity surrounding the use of family and friendship networks. The denial that this type of recruitment process is followed in Bristol Insurance could be based on a desire to play down the importance of any 'nepotistic' recruitment practices and by so doing emphasise the essentially meritocratic nature of recruitment at Bristol Insurance, which relies on the 'Human Resources' department. It could also, however, demonstrate that information networks operate on a number of different levels, and that this respondent associates family and friendship information networks with the more powerful process of helping a particular friend/relative to get a particular job and consequently passing on information on the reputation of the company might be considered as 'common' knowledge, and not as conveying privileged information. Comments from another respondent, of supervisory grade, illustrate how information flows between network members and provide a good example of the nature and extent of family connections inside Bristol Insurance:

> Q: Have you ever heard of people getting their jobs through family or friends: Yes, there's *quite a lot of family that work here*. Ehm, not allowed in the same department. But I know one women who works in personnel whose daughter works in annuities, ehm one of receptionists, her husband is manager of one of the other departments. There's *quite a lot of family connections*. Ehm one of my friends who I worked with in travel (previous occupation) she works here, pure coincidence, and then we were saying what a great job it is to another friend and they applied, so they now work here. So now there's three of us who worked for the same (travel) agency. One of those people who were here before, one of the people who worked for an agency, she knows somebody who works for Wessex Water who works here, which is (Wessex Water) that building there (pointing out the window and across the road) who also knows four other people who used to work for Wessex Water who now work here... *Reputation of the company* gets around, rather than specific vacancies. I saw an advert for Bristol Insurance and I knew the name of Bristol Insurance. It wasn't an advert for a job that I could do or wanted to do but I thought 'ah they're recruiting and *that's a company that I know of*'... but I knew the company via when I worked in travel somebody who I knew husband worked here, as it turned out he was chief executive of one of the subsidiaries, but I didn't know that, I just knew he worked for Bristol Insurance and it sounded like *a pretty good company*, so that's how I came to apply. So *it was reputation* as opposed to a particular job. (BI 4)

Three important points emerge from this response. Firstly the actual mechanics of the functioning of networks is again evident: 'we were saying what a great job it is to another friend and they applied, so they now work here'. Secondly, the manner in which network information is helpful is evident, with this respondent initially seeing an advert (formal channel) for a job that she could neither 'do or wanted to do' but applied for because of positive information on Bristol Insurance which was obtained through a friendship network (a friend's husband). Thirdly, there is comprehensive evidence of the nature and extent of friendship and family networks. Eight family/friendship connections are described, and these range from mother/ daughter and husband/wife relationships to relatively complex friendship networks. Knowledge of family and friendship connections in Bristol Insurance was also evident from data from six other respondents (three managers, two clerks and one other supervisor grade). These data ranged from the quite detailed responses such as the one given above to more general perceptions of 'lots of family' being employed at Bristol Insurance. Examples include:

> There is an element of paternalism in the organisation, *we have sons, daughters...* (BI 1)

> ... I can think of *a lot of brothers and sisters* of people that work here. And a lot of people here are married to each other or are having relationships or whatever. (BI 6)

> You can try personnel but you'll see an *awful lot of sons, daughters, brothers* working here and I think that's part of the traditional attitude of this company... My *old boss' son* was looking for some job experience, asked here and a job very easily (appeared). (BI 5)

> I know of a guy whose quite high up in office services who's *got a son working here.* (BI16)

The picture which emerges is of a workplace where family and friendship networks are in existence and where information on employment is offered, with evidence ranging from general knowledge of such networks to specific instances where respondents believe family members have obtained a job for kin. Yet despite this the overall emphasis was on playing down the role of such informal networks and emphasising the formal, meritocratic nature of recruitment. For example, seven respondents (two managers, three supervisors and two clerks) denied the existence of family and friendship networks in Bristol Insurance. One respondent went as far as to name a close family connection yet still deny any role for family and friends:

> There *is a family who work here*, there is a mother, her son and daughter who work here. *But on the whole, no. I think it's just pure coincidence.* (BI 15)

It is interesting to note that of the seven respondents who denied the existence of family and friendship networks in Bristol Insurance five had obtained their own job with Bristol Insurance through formal channels, which may suggest these respondents associate Bristol Insurance with an 'open' and meritocratic recruitment process. This underlying belief in meritocracy would account for both these network denials and the fact that even those respondents with network experience or knowledge of family and friendship connections inside Bristol Insurance often underplayed the role of such networks (often relegated to providing only 'low level' information), preferring to emphasise the importance of formal channels, a preference which, I would argue, points to an identification with a meritocratic recruitment process. As table 4.6 shows, a total of five respondents stressed the existence or importance of meritocracy:

Table 4.6
Bristol Insurance, respondents who commented on meritocratic nature of recruitment process

Respondent	Keyphrase	Recruitment channel used
BI 1	'getting value for money' 'best person who comes in will get the job' '*procedure* is honest stage by stage'	Aware of the existence of family and friendship connections in BI
BI 2	'recruitment is done through Human Resources'	Perceived a role for networks in passing on general level information on BI
BI 13	'here you have to go through the *procedure*'	Got own job through formal channel - private employment agency, and denied existence of networks
BI 16	'have to have the right qualifications' 'have to get a job on your own *merits*'	Got own job through formal channel - local paper, but knew of family and friendship connections in BI
BI 18	'its up to you to *prove* yourself'	Got own job through both formal and informal channel - local paper and sister

A more detailed analysis, placing these keyphrases in context, demonstrates the depth of feeling underlying the perceived importance attached to a meritocratic recruitment procedure. Three of the respondents stressed the role of the Personnel Department to the 'fairness' of the recruitment process. Comments included:

> *There is an element of paternalism in the organisation*, we have sons, daughters... it has happened but it won't increase, it could decrease, I mean I think more in the future when people have got to be sure they're getting

value for money from who they recruit, whoever's *the best person* who comes in will get the job. The fact that their father might work here, well *in the past* it might have helped but I don't think it will in the future. But there are *some sort of family links* in the organisation... But we don't slip the net we make sure *the procedure is honest stage by stage.* (BI 1)

When I was at the temping agency it happened, one girl who worked in the office whose friend was looking for a job and she joined. It's all through word of mouth in that sort of environment but here *I think you have to go through the procedures*. (BI 13)

The stress is on a standard recruitment 'procedure'. The emphasis of meaning is on an orderly process, a systematic, almost legalistic approach to recruitment. The connections with formal legal processes are also evident, with this respondent arguing that the contemporary recruitment process is 'honest stage by stage'. Two of the five respondents were more explicit about the ultimate importance of relying on one's own merits,

Well it was in all the local papers and obviously my sister did mention it as well. But *I don't think that because she is in here I got the job because of that.* It was just I heard more about the job because she was here. (BI 18)

... I wouldn't think it would *sway Personnel that much* if I was to go down and say 'my sister's looking for a job'. I don't think they'd be particularly interested, she'd have to have the right qualifications and apply the same way as everybody else, so I wouldn't have thought through your family and friends, really no. *You have to get the job on your own merits*. (BI 16)

The first quotation is from a clerk who, although admitting to employment help from his sister, argues this is not the main reason he got the job. In discussions of previous employment this respondent noted how his brother had helped him to obtain employment in the post office but argued that at most all a relation could do was to arrange an interview, and then it was 'up to you to prove yourself.' This belief in one being judged on one's own abilities and merits is shared by the second respondent quoted above, with the emphasis being placed on a standard recruitment procedure where '*you have to get the job on your own merits*'. Here it is assumed one is rewarded because of qualities of goodness or excellence, which are particular to the individual and which have been earned. I would argue that the belief in meritocracy and the association of such a process with Bristol Insurance provides one reason for the emphasis on formal methods and the apparent reluctance of some respondents to fully articulate and elaborate on the role of family and friendship networks.

In summary, the case study data from Bristol Insurance showed that, amongst respondents who gave details of how they got their own job, the most common recruitment channels were formal (newspaper advertisements and private employment agencies) and that this supports the findings of larger scale survey work (Hedges, 1983; LMQ, 1984; IFF, 1988; SCELI 1992). It was argued, however, that not only did some managers and supervisors use networks to obtain information on potential employees, but that many of those who said they got their own job through a formal channel still used family and friends to obtain information, and therefore that, to an extent, large scale questionnaire surveys may underestimate the role of family and friendship networks. Thus, it was suggested that although the most commonly articulated recruitment channels at Bristol Insurance were formal, there was still a role for family and friendship networks in providing information which, in terms of determining employment outcomes, may be persuasive rather than decisive. While, therefore, informal connections may not be seen as the defining recruitment channel, there is evidence which shows that the merits of certain companies and types of work are discussed amongst family and friends and which suggests that while the importance of such discussions may be difficult to measure, even in white collar Bristol Insurance they play an important role in constructing the package of information which informs employment 'choice'. It was also argued that one reason for the focus on formal channels was the emphasis placed on the essentially meritocratic recruitment process of Bristol Insurance, a belief shared even by some respondents who had themselves used family and friendship networks to obtain information on employment with Bristol Insurance and others who were aware of close kin relations within Bristol Insurance. Having established that informal methods play a secondary (but potentially important) role in the recruitment process we turn to the data from Bristol Laminated where networks are seen to differ, both quantitatively and qualitatively, from those in Bristol Insurance

Bristol Laminated

This section moves on to a discussion and examination of data from Bristol Laminated, where it is found that all of the workers interviewed obtained their jobs through informal methods and that both of the managers interviewed had used such networks to recruit new employees. The difference from Bristol Insurance data was not only that informal methods were found to be more popular than formal, but also that the nature and use of networks was substantially different. Workers and managers in Bristol Laminated were seen to rely more strongly on intensive, high quality information assistance. While there was a certain awareness on the part of some of the respondents (mainly the Personnel Manager) of the potential sensitivity of such recruitment practices the common feeling emerging from the data was that utilising friendship and family networks to obtain employment is an ordinary and routine practice.

The summary picture is shown in Tables 4.7 and 4.8. Table 4.7 details how respondents first heard about their own job and illustrates that of the 10 respondents interviewed all 8 of the manual workers obtained their jobs through informal networks, with 5 obtaining assistance from family, 1 from family and friends and 2 from friends. Table 4.8 goes into more detail and shows that the two managers also used networks (for recruitment), thus showing that all 10 respondents from Bristol Laminated had made use of networks. The two managers used them to advertise vacancies and receive information on prospective employees while the workers utilised family and friendship connections to hear of jobs, obtain an application form, have a word 'put in', have a reference put in or some combination of these. The in-depth nature of this assistance contrasts strongly with the network help which emerged from Bristol Insurance data, where, instead of a friend or family member placing a particular individual in a particular job, network connections offered 'weaker', more 'general' information, commonly on the reputation of the company as an employer.

Table 4.7
Bristol Laminated, summary table of how respondents first heard about job

	Formal	Informal			Did not discuss	Total
		Family	Friends	Both		
Managers	0				bl 1; bl 6	2
Workers	0	bl 2; bl 8; bl 9; bl 10; bl 5	bl 3; bl 7	bl 4		8
Totals	0	8			2	10\10

Table 4.8
Bristol Laminated, the extent of use of family and friendship networks

	Nature of network use				
	Told/advertised vacancy through network	Obtained applic form	Put a 'word in'	Family reputation	Total
Managers	bl 1; bl 6				2
Workers	bl 2; bl 3; bl 4; bl 8; bl 9	bl 4; Bl 9	bl 4; bl 5; bl 7; bl 9	bl 8; bl 10	8
Response totals	7	2	4	2	*15*\10

Note: response total (in italics) may be more than number of respondents due to multiple replies

Turning to the comments given by interviewees, the personnel manager gave the following reply to a question on recruitment channels:

> *We do make use of word of mouth* but very recently we've been very aware of *equal opportunities*. And the result of that is that we've advertised more widely than we would *have done in the past*. So if I had, like I had recently some vacancies in the factories, normally I would have only advertised it here and the other factory, normally we would have got friends, neighbours... but this time we then went to the Job Centre and we spread that around Eastwood and down in town to make sure that we got quite a wide catchment. I had three vacancies and had 80 odd replies. (And who ended up filling the vacancies?) It's very interesting actually, it's one man who came from the job centre completely unknown to us, one man who came from the job centre *that's got a brother in our company here*, but came through the job centre anyway and *another friend of a manager out at the other factory* who again came through the job centre. So they were all registered at the job centre as looking for work. So they came two ways really, *they knew of the advert because their friend told them or their brother told them* but they also knew of it through the job centre. (BL 1)

The first point to note about this quotation is that while this personnel manager makes explicit reference to network based recruitment channels: '*We do make use of word of mouth*', she is aware that there is some sensitivity surrounding this practice. This is apparent from the pre-delicate hitch (Coxon and Davies, 1986) 'Ehm' which precedes the admission that such channels are used and by the detailed explanation that because of '*equal opportunities*' they advertise more widely than they '*have done in the past*'. This practice of pushing any potentially sensitive or unpleasant phenomena to the past was also evident in the last section, where the personnel manager from Bristol Insurance said of network based recruitment '... it has happened in the past but it won't increase.' (Bristol Insurance 1). The second point to note is the underlying strength of this network based recruitment process. This is evident from the fact that despite the wider advertising, two of the three workers recruited, although coming through the job centre, knew of the vacancy because '*their friend told them or their brother told them.*' This quotation also provides an example of the distinction Wood (1986) draws between nominal and effective recruitment channels and the similar distinction Manwaring (1984) draws between frequency of use of a channel and effectiveness of use. Although the Job Centre was the nominal channel of information on employment opportunities the effective channel was a friend or member of the family.

As table 4.8 shows, the ten respondents interviewed used a number of different forms of assistance: two workers received information only on job vacancies (BL 2 and BL 3); one used family reputation (BL 10); two relied on network connections putting a 'word in' (BL 5 and BL 7); one used a combination of being told of a vacancy and relying on family reputation (BL 8) and two used a combination of being told of a vacancy, obtaining an application form and having a word 'put in' (BL 4 and BL 9). Turning firstly to those who received only one form of assistance, two workers were told of vacancies through a network connection:

> Q: How did you get your job here?
> *Through a friend, I heard it through a friend* (He worked here?) A neighbour who worked here, well two neighbours actually. (BL 3)

> Q: How did you first find out about your job here?
> Well as I said I was working for St Anne's Board Mills and the wife's uncle worked here, he's been made redundant now. He knew that I was fed up with the continental shift[16] work and it *came up in conversation one evening* that at a date there could be an opening for me here. So that's the way I got in, I mean eh he found out that they were taking on half a dozen I came for an interview, got the job, started that way. (BL 2)

The first worker above relied on a friend while the second worker obtained assistance through a family relation. The description of how BL2 was helped illustrates that this type of help was in no way unusual, it simply '*came up in conversation*' that Bristol Laminated were taking on people. This advance advice and family connection enabled this respondent to obtain an interview and subsequent employment with Bristol Laminated. Another respondent benefited from being part of a family network, without even directly approaching kin for assistance:

> When I came here then, you could only get into Bristol Laminated then, if you knew someone. Funnily enough when I come to apply I did have a cousin here which I didn't know about, there were five Spence's in here so *as soon as they seen the name Spence I managed to get in*. (BL 10)

Here the importance simply of having a known 'name' was, this respondent felt, enough to ensure employment. Two other employees were helped by people putting a 'word in':

> Q: How did you get you job here?
> Ehm, *a friend of my father in law's*. (What did he do to get you in?) He put *a word in* with the personnel manager at the time. You were one foot in the door because you knew someone. (BL 5)

> Q: How did you find out about your job here?
> One of my drivers (previous employment was in the railways) used to live next door to one of the managers here and I was down at his house and he had

---

[16]This means that the shift patterns cover weekend working.

> a party in there and the hours (at the railway) were very unsociable at that time and I had to leave this party to go to work and he said *'Why don't you see if I can get you a job in our place*?' I said alright then. (BL 7)

The first worker was sponsored by a friend of the family's, pressure being applied to the personnel manager to ensure employment. The commonplace nature of assistance in finding a job through connections comes through, again, in the second quotation, where this respondent got a job simply by meeting one of the managers at a party. Turning to the three respondents who had received 'multiple' assistance, one worker got help both by being told of a job vacancy and through relying on family reputation:

> *That's how I got my job*, I had two brothers here at that time, they're both gone now, redundant, but I had two brothers working here and I was fed up with the Board Mills, I could see it was going to close down soon, things were getting really bad down there so I said are there any jobs going down there and they said 'yeah they're taking people on' so I phoned up the personnel and *happened to mention that I had two brothers working here* (laughs at this point) and they sent me a form and came for an interview and that was it. (BL 8)

This respondent first heard about his job from a primary kin relation (brother) and then used this family connection in his first contact with personnel. There is some evidence here that this respondent is aware of some sensitivity in using family connections to obtain or improve one's chances of employment. This is evident from the laughter which follows the admission that he '*happened*' to mention his brothers worked at Bristol Laminated. Assistance of a more systematic nature was offered to two other workers:

> Q: How did you find out about your job here?
> Basically I was on the milkround and started *asking people* if they knew of any jobs and luckily somebody worked here and they were taking on people at the time so *I got him to get me an application form*, chucked it in and I think I had two interviews and a medical to get through. (Did you use this person as a reference?) I did yeah, he put *in a good word* for me. And as it happens my wife's uncle worked here as well so he put in a reference for me as well. (BL 4)

> Q: How did you find out about your job here?
> *My brother told me about it*. (Did he put in a word for you?) Yeah, *he asked for me*. (Did they ask you about your brother at the interview?) Yeah, they ask you if you got any relatives here right, I've got two (Your brother and who else?) *An uncle of mine*... It was luck of the draw really, if you knew there were jobs going here you had to be here at the right time to get it. (Physically here?) Yeah, *my brother told me that jobs were going* I came straight down

here like. He gave me a form to fill in and I filled the form in and I brought it straight in here. (BL 9)

The commonplace nature of the assistance is again evident from the first quotation. This worker simply asked around different customers on his milkround, got an application form and got his sponsor to put in a reference. The tightness of the network is also shown by the fact that once this worker knew of a vacancy at Bristol Laminated he was able to call on the assistance of a relation to provide further assistance. The second quote provides further evidence of the systematic nature of some assistance, firstly this respondent's contact (brother) told him of a vacancy, then obtained an application form, then 'put a word in'. Thus this worker knew about the job before it was widely advertised, an experience which is supported by the findings of Manwaring (1984) who, in his study of recruitment in Birmingham, London and Wales found that '... personnel managers recall that friends and relatives are often first in the queue even though this channel is not explicitly being used.' (Manwaring, 1984: 163)

The strength of such network arrangements is illustrated by the fact that employment assistance was reciprocal for some respondents. Grieco (1987) argued that the degree of reciprocity, which could take place through proxies, was the most effective and accurate measure of the strength of a tie. Reciprocal assistance was seen as evidence of a strong tie because one was putting the family 'name' and reputation as workers on the line. The importance of family 'name' has also been noted by Marsden (1982) and Dick and Morgan (1987). Dick and Morgan (1987), for example, writing of the family network they found in a Yorkshire textile mill, commented that:

> The family reputation was seen as precious by its members and they stressed the need to keep it so. Interviews with network members and managers revealed that even though there were a number of different surnames within the group, the group was identified as a unified entity - the Gray family. Members of the group felt they shared the same principles as well as a family relationship. 'We were all brought up to earn our living'; 'we've always worked for what we have'; 'we help our own'. (Dick and Morgan, 1987: 235)

While Grieco (1987) quoted one worker as commenting:

> We've always had a good name as workers. None of us have ever shirked work. Oh, I'm not saying we've never given anybody any trouble, we have, but not as far as work's concerned. (Female tobacco worker, Basildon, Grieco, 1987: 31)

Grieco goes on to conclude that:

> Being known as good workers was seen as a form of insurance as well as a matter of morality. Because of their concern with their reputation as workers,

kin group(s) would only introduce 'good workers' to their employer. (Grieco, 1987:32)

As table 4.9 illustrates, three of the respondents from Bristol Laminated who received employment assistance in turn offered such assistance to friends and relations.

Table 4.9
Bristol Laminated, reciprocal help

Respondent	Network connection	Nature of assistance
Bristol Laminated 5	Brother-in-law Wife's cousin's husband	Put a '*word in*' Put a '*word in*'
Bristol Laminated 9	Brother	Put a '*word in*'
Bristol Laminated 10	Friends	Allowed his *name to be used*

The importance of family name is evident in the comments of BL5, who had obtained assistance from his father in law and later provided assistance for two relations' on his wife's side - his brother in law and his wife's cousin's husband:

> Q: Have you helped anyone get a job in here yourself?
> Yes, *my brother in law*. No, sorry, my sister in law's husband and *my wife's cousin's husband*. (What did you do?) *I put a word in*, I asked if there was any vacancies, *I said they were good people*. If they weren't good people I wouldn't have said they were good people. (BL 5)

The sensitivity which surrounds the sponsors reputation as a 'good' worker is clear from this quotation, with this worker only sponsoring these kin relations because he felt they were 'good' people. Another respondent offered reciprocal assistance to his brother who had initially obtained a job for him, before leaving to work abroad:

> Yeah, he broke service, went to New Zealand (What did he do there?) Same thing, but she got homesick, came home, so *I had to put a word in for him* to get him back in here. (BL 9)

This respondent provided the same help to his brother as was earlier provided to him. It also offers a good example of casual sexism, simply 'she got homesick', his brother's wife is not named or even referred to by family connection but just 'she'. In addition, the choice of words provides an indication of the way this respondent conceptualises work, his brother is described as breaking 'service', a term which is perhaps indicative of the sense of 'duty', of strong connection, if not with the firm at least with the type of work, an attitude which may be more conducive to an informal recruitment procedure. The third respondent who provided assistance to network members was not so much returning specific 'favours', but simply supplying the level of assistance he thought appropriate to friends:

> When I come in here what basically happened was that when the Board Mills shut and a friend of mine seen me down the pub and he said about jobs and I said you ought to try up here and if you try up here *tell 'em you know me*. He came up here and said that he knew me and about 8 or 9 others did - we all know Pete Spence and fair enough they all got a job. (BL 10)

The actual extent of assistance here is difficult to gauge as when the Board Mills in Bristol closed a number of redundant workers found employment at Bristol Laminated. What is clear, however, is the recognition and use of informal an network to help friends obtain employment. This worker had found his own job partially through the reputation of his family name and in turn when he had the opportunity he provided assistance to friends.

In summary the main findings were that the most common recruitment channel used at Bristol Laminated were informal, with family and friendship networks being used both frequently and intensively. It was argued that the casual and familiar manner in which family and friendship networks were discussed illustrates that such practices were taken for granted, that such mechanisms resemble an integral part of workplace culture in Bristol Laminated. It was further argued that, compared to the use of informal channels in Bristol Insurance, the nature of employment assistance at Bristol Laminated was of a more powerful nature and was more likely to be provided by a strong (usually kinship) network connection. The next section goes on to investigate the underlying rationale behind using networks.

4.4 The rationale behind using networks

Previous studies (Hedges and Beynon, 1972; Hill, 1976; Manwaring, 1984; Dick and Morgan, 1987; Grieco, 1987; Dawes, 1993; Atkinson et al, 1994) have focused on a number of advantages, to both managers and workers, which arise from the use of networks. Turning firstly to management, there are four commonly perceived advantages. The first is the low cost of informal recruitment methods, both in terms of time and money. As Rees (1966) highlighted:

> The problem facing the employer is not to get in touch with the largest possible number of potential applicants; rather it is to find a few applicants promising enough to be worth the investment of thorough investigation... Many employer hiring standards can be viewed as devices to narrow the

intensive field of search by reducing the number of applicants to manageable proportions. (Rees, 1966: 561)

Hence employers wish to reach not necessarily the greatest quantity of candidates but the applicants of the highest potential quality. Wood (1986) in his study of the recruitment systems of large manufacturing and retail firms found that personnel managers rated the limiting of applications received as one of the major advantages of using informal recruitment methods. His study took place in the early eighties, a time of acute economic recession, and he found that firms which relied on word of mouth recruitment methods were *not* overwhelmed with applicants as unemployment grew but that firms with more formal recruitment policies had to adopt different strategies. He writes:

> For example, we came across a retail store which had a policy of interviewing everybody who came to their stores. However, the personnel managers found that the number had increased to such an extent that they had to abandon this practice. Another company which had previously had recruitment and retention problems found, in 1981, that it was so inundated with applicants that it had to bring the telephonists into the selection process and consequently train them to screen out candidates over the telephone. (Wood, 1986: 111)

Jenkins et al (1983), too, in their study of the way organisations manage labour recruitment, found that:

> ... it (informal recruitment) also helps to prevent the gatehouse or personnel office becoming besieged by the flood of applicants which a newspaper advertisement or a card in the local Job Centre might produce. (Jenkins et al, 1983: 264)

On the same topic Lee and Wrench (1981) reported one manager who relied on word of mouth recruitment methods as saying:

> We haven't advertised this year. The news gets round by word of mouth. So far this year we have had eighty applications for six jobs. Another two hundred would come in if I advertised. (Lee and Wrench, 1981: 9)

The low cost and administrative efficiency of informal methods is one attraction to management. Another, and possibly more important, feature of family and friendship networks is that they produce relatively 'reliable' candidates, in the sense that one is more likely to get applicants of the same quality as the existing workforce (Courtenay and Hedges, 1977; Jenkins, 1982; Jenkins et al, 1983; Manwaring, 1984; Bresnen et al, 1985; Lee, 1985; Dick and Morgan, 1987; Grieco, 1987). Grieco (1987) writes of this advantage:

> ... this channel provides an efficient screening mechanism which will produce

> new workers with characteristics similar to the existing work force. (Grieco, 1987: 38)

A point which was echoed in the work of Jenkins (1982):

> If we've got a reliable person, then his son or daughter is likely to be fairly reliable. They'll have more commitment than the average guy. (Manufacturing employee relations manager, Jenkins, 1982: 29)

A number of authors have expanded upon this to argue that familiarity with the present workgroup also serves as an indicator of certain knowledge, or an approach to work, which will make the learning of certain (tacit) skills easier (Lee and Wrench, 1981; Hedges and Beynon, 1982; Manwaring, 1984; Dick and Morgan, 1987; Grieco, 1987). The concept of skills and the different perceptions of 'skill' is dealt with in greater depth in the next chapter, but, given the relevance of tacit skills to informal recruitment methods, it is briefly introduced here. Manwaring (1984) defines tacit skills as:

> ... those specific skills that new recruits require even in formally unskilled and semi skilled jobs... (Manwaring, 1984: 161)

The argument is that membership of a 'known' family or friendship network is an indication of the likelihood of an applicant possessing, or quickly learning, certain firm specific skills.

A third reason for employers using this method is the potential it offers for increasing control over the workforce (Lee and Wrench, 1981; Hedges and Beynon, 1982; Jenkins, 1982; Jenkins et al, 1983; Manwaring, 1984; Dick and Morgan, 1987; Grieco, 1987). Grieco (1987) writes of this:

> ... recruitment through existing employees acts as a form of control since responsibilities and obligations hold between workers so recruited: for if the sponsored antagonizes the employer, the reputation of the sponsor himself will be damaged; thus, the new worker is constrained by the interests and reputation of his sponsor. (Grieco, 1987: 39)

On the same point, two of Jenkins respondents gave the following comments:

> ... if we do have problems, then often the management doesn't have to get involved, the existing employee will sort that out. Likewise, I don't think that anyone will recommend someone if they're not a good prospect. (Public sector deputy divisional staff officer, Jenkins, 1982: 30)

> ... if the father's a solid and respected employee. He can take over from us, if his son steps out of line the dad'll belt him round the ear. He can keep an eye on him, make sure he gets up in the morning. (Manufacturing personnel

manager, Jenkins, 1982: 30)

The fourth, and related, potential advantage to management of informal recruitment mechanisms is the potentially positive influence hiring friends and relatives has on industrial relations (Scott et al, 1956; Jenkins, 1982; Jenkins et al, 1983; Dick and Morgan, 1987). For example, Jenkins (1982) quotes one manager as saying:

> ... we have in the past enjoyed a positive industrial relations climate. It's not just been a quiescent labour force, it's one which has been quite difficult and militant at times. But they accept that the foundation of the business is to make things to sell them. You can't actually put a quantifiable profit on that. But subjectively one feels that we are more likely to retain the commitment to the business by bringing in people who have already got an interest than by taking other people. It's as simple as that. (Manufacturing employee relations manager (Staff), Jenkins, 1982: 31)

This argument is taken further in a later paper (Jenkins et al, 1983), where the authors write:

> ... that the paternalism of the 'family firm' is a euphemism for a particular kind of industrial relations strategy: allowing the labour force to participate in recruitment in return for a degree of co-operation and industrial peace and quiet. (Jenkins et al, 1983: 265)

Connected to this is the fifth and final advantage to management, namely that patronage of kin and friends can be used as a form of payment, of rewarding loyalty (Bakke, 1940; Hill, 1976; Wood, 1986; Dick and Morgan 1987; Grieco, 1987). For example, Wood (1986) found that:

> Many firms do give preference to friends and relatives, or at least reported that they looked favourably on them. Those giving preference often saw it as a kind of fringe benefit for their current employees... (Wood, 1986: 111)

Recruitment through family and friendship networks also holds advantages for employees. The most important is that such networks provide higher quality information on employment opportunities and, as was noted earlier, provide such information before it has reached the public domain (Marsden, 1982; Manwaring, 1984; Whipp, 1985; Dick and Morgan, 1987; Grieco, 1987). Hence even when employers' state they recruit from people turning up at the employment site often this is not a random selection of jobseekers but is made up of people who have heard that 'such and such are looking for people...' The better quality of information may allow prospective employees to learn certain facts or tacit skills before the interview. As Rees (1966) wrote:

> The informal sources also have important benefits to the applicant. He can obtain much more information from a friend who does the kind of work in which he is interested than from an ad in the paper or a counsellor at an employment agency, and he places more trust in it. He can ask the councillor about the fairness of supervision in a factory, but he cannot get an informed or reliable answer. (Rees, 1966: 562)

A second advantage to workers relates to the potential for gaining some control over recruitment (Reynolds, 1951; Rubery, 1978; Jenkins, 1982, Jenkins et al, 1983; Manwaring, 1984; Whipp, 1985; Grieco, 1987). For example, Reynolds (1951) gave the following conclusion:

> Certain nationality groups and kinship groups had become so firmly established in the plant that it was no use trying to add an outsider as he would be 'frozen out' in short order. (Reynolds, 1951: 50)

While Jenkins (1982), in his investigation of whether informal mechanisms discriminated against black workers, commented:

> ... in an organisation with an all white or predominately white workforce, network recruitment will tend to ensure that this remains the situation. Particularly in a time of economic crisis this will help ensure that black workers remain in those employment niches they entered in the boom years of the 'fifties' and 'sixties' and do not move out of them. (Jenkins, 1982: 32).

Thus if workers can successfully 'close' the jobs market they may well become a more cohesive and more powerful group, with the potential for influencing not only recruitment but, more broadly, the labour process. A further advantage for employees in utilising friendship networks is access to the social relations which exist in the workplace (Manwaring, 1984). He writes of this:

> ... monotony may not be felt as boredom, because workers can find satisfaction at the workplace, rather than in work, through the social relationships which exist in the workplace. Such relationships will be stronger if they have already been formed in the community and are then reproduced. (Manwaring, 1984: 169)

It is possible, therefore, for workers to use an improved social atmosphere, created by family and friendship networks, to overcome the monotony attached to repetitive work.

This section, drawing on studies which have mainly taken place in the blue collar sector, has highlighted the advantages of informal mechanisms to management as being the low cost; the reproduction of workers with familiar characteristics and the likelihood that the sponsored recruit will already possess some knowledge of the working environment (tacit skills); the potential for increasing control and the potential for using employment favours as part of a system of payment through patronage. The advantages to workers include the quality and speed of transfer of information on employment opportunities; the potentiality of increasing control over the recruitment process and the likelihood that recruiting through family and friends will create a more friendly working environment. The next two sections go on to analyse the primary case data on why informal networks are used.

4.5 Advantages of networks

Bristol Insurance

This section turns to an examination of the reasons for utilising family and friendship networks which emerge from Bristol Insurance primary data. Given the secondary role assigned to informal channels by Bristol Insurance respondents, the interviews with office respondents often moved on to other issues, with the result that there was little discussion of the advantages of informal methods. Instead, and as was noted earlier, respondents emphasised the more meritocratic nature of formal channels and relegated family and friendship networks to providing information of a general nature. Nevertheless, the limited data which emerged around the issue of advantages, supports the secondary evidence examined in the previous section. Table 4.10 shows that 4 of the 18 respondents made 7 direct references to advantages of informal channels.

Table 4.10
Bristol Insurance, advantages of family and friendship networks

	Recommendation of sponsor implies reliable/trustworthy	Control	Cheapness	Better quality info	Total
Manager grade	bi 10; bi 11	bi 10		bi 11	2
Supervisor grade					
Clerical grade	bi 18		bi 17	bi 18	2
Response Total	3	1	1	2	7\4

Note: response total (in italics) may be more than number of respondents due to multiple replies

Two of the three managers who had used networks to recruit went on to discuss advantages as did two of the clerks, one who had used a network connection to obtain employment and one who had denied the existence of networks in Bristol Insurance but had experienced network recruitment in a previous job.

Turning firstly to the perceived advantage of trust and reliability, one manager made reference to previous employment:

> My father used to work for DCL (United Distillers) and it's a small town and *I got my summer job through my father*. There were brother's and father's, yes it becomes a family affair because it's *part of the known quantity*. (BI 10)

While another manager gave the following comments when discussing the recent recruitment of a new member of staff:

> ... for example when Julie joined us she did a post graduate diploma in marketing at the University and I called John Smith who works on that course and said 'have you got any *good* students' and because *I know John Smith well I know* he would give me a list of *good* students ehm he circulated the job round and *he supplied the references* because I was able to talk to him *informally* and that worked extremely well. Ehm effectively what it's giving you is *more information* so you ought to be able to make a better decision. (BI 11)

The importance of being of a 'known quantity' emerges strongly from both these quotations, of using networks to obtain better and more reliable information on the character of a potential employee (Jenkins, 1982; Jenkins et al, 1983; Manwaring, 1984; Grieco, 1987). The relevance to the recruitment process of being a 'known quantity' was also commented upon by one of the clerks at Bristol Laminated, this time in discussion of how he got his previous job in the post office:

> The job in the post office it was again my brother had just gone into the post office, he'd been there about two years and they were recruiting a few people, they were doing training courses to get people in and I applied and luckily I got in there (How do you think your brother being there helped you?) Ehm, they asked me if I had relatives in there, obviously they knew he was a relative, we're both living at the same address at the time, ehm and *I feel he had a good name at the post office*, that may well have helped. Eh he couldn't pull any strings to get me in, you know it's a big organisation you couldn't do that, but *I think him having a good name, keeping his nose clean, doing his job well, possibly did help me to get in*. Or at least it helped me to get the interview anyway I think... and then *it's up to you to prove yourself*. (BI 18)

Again the point about having a 'good name', which was noted earlier in relation to Bristol Laminated, is seen to be important. The fact that this respondent's brother had '*a good name, keeping his nose clean, doing his job well*' is assumed to carry implications of the respondent's character and suitability, with the suggestion that this worker, like his brother, would be a good, conscientious, worker who would keep out of trouble by *'keeping his nose clean'*. Another potential (managerial) advantage noted by one of the respondents was the implications for control, here, again, the possession of a 'good name' and reputation is seen to play a role:

> ... *You know somebody* who's active in the job market and you suggest that they apply. Now that's not giving them a right to the job but if they've *come proven*, most people wouldn't put forward someone who they didn't think was actually able to do it *because it would reflect on them*. So therefore the calibre is probably quiet high. (BI 10)

The implied meaning behind this is that more control is shifted to management, people would be reluctant to recommend friends or relatives who were 'poor' or potentially 'disruptive' workers because *'it would reflect on them'*. By taking some responsibility for the conduct of these friends or relatives management control is internalised within the workforce.

The third (again managerial) advantage, which was cited by the respondents was the potentiality of filling the vacancy quickly. This advantage was noted by a respondent who did not know of any network connections inside Bristol Insurance but who had experienced informal mechanisms in previous employment:

> ... where I used to work (Securicor) *I did recommend somebody to work there* and they got the job. (What did you say to the boss?) Well there was actually a vacancy in the office and I said that I knew somebody that was interested to the lady that was in charge of us and she said well ask them to fill in their cv or whatever the procedure was and ask them to come along them. (Did you end up training that person?) No, cause it was in fact my sister-in-law so I think they thought it was probably best that we did separate jobs, we worked sort of separately. (Was it a big help you putting a word in?) Yeah maybe, the job was vacant and *we needed someone quite quickly to fill it*. (Bristol Insurance 17).

This quotation supports the work of many earlier studies, which argue that the speed with which family and friendship networks supply candidates of the appropriate quality makes such channels cheaper and more efficient (Rees, 1966; Lee and Wrench, 1981; Jenkins, 1982; Wood, 1986; Grieco, 1987). The final advantage which was cited by Bristol Insurance respondents was the provision of quality information. This was evident both in the comments of one of the managers (BI 11 referred to above) and one of the clerks (BI 18) who, as was noted earlier, received information from his sister on the nature of the company and of the job.

In discussions of networks, one of the managers (BI 11), also referred to potential disadvantages:

... the *disadvantages are if you don't handle it properly* that you get into the position where you've almost *got to offer them the job*... so you've actually got to be quite careful in doing it. (BI 11)

The implication is that by discussing employment opportunities with friends and relatives who then recommend a network connection one may get into a position where one has to offer this network connection a job for fear of offending a trusted friend or family member.

The most important point to note about the data in this section is the relative scarcity of comments, this reflects the secondary importance of networks to Bristol Insurance employees, and the fact that interviewees instead stressed the prevalence and importance of more formal recruitment channels. However, to the extent that advantages were articulated, these were seen to support earlier work (Jenkins 1982, Jenkins et al, 1983; Manwaring, 1984; Wood, 1986; Grieco, 1987).

Bristol Laminated

As was noted earlier the Bristol Laminated employees who were interviewed had more personal experience of (particularly kinship) networks than those working at Bristol Insurance and, in addition, were more open and frank in their discussions of such networks. This greater exposure to networks and greater willingness to talk about the assistance given by family and friends is reflected in the comments on the advantages and disadvantages of such recruitment methods, which are more frequent (with eight of the ten interviews covering potential advantages), extensive and detailed than those of Bristol Insurance respondents. One immediate difference

Table 4.11
Bristol Laminated, advantages of family and friendship networks

	Recommendation of sponsor implies reliable/ trustworthy	Control	Cheap ness	Know ledge of factory	More friendly environ	Total
Manager	bl 6	bl 1;	bl 1	bl 6	bl 6;	2
Worker	bl 5; bl 8; bl 9	bl 3; bl 8; bl 5; bl 10		bl 3;	bl 2; bl 5; bl 8	6
Response Total	4	5	1	2	4	*16\8*

Note: response total (in italics) may be more than number of respondents due to multiple replies

between the two case study firms, again reflecting the type of assistance offered by the respective networks, is the emphasis placed by Bristol Laminated respondents on the help offered by family as opposed to friends. This changed emphasis implies a stronger level of tie which may partially account for the greater willingness to discuss the pros and cons of networks. Table 4.11 illustrates the summary picture.

As this table illustrates, eight respondents made 16 references to one or a combination of five advantages: that the recommendations of sponsor carries implications of trustworthiness or reliability; that there are implications for control; that such channels are cheap; that they give applicants prior knowledge of the factory and that such networks are more conducive to a more friendly working environment. Turning firstly to the importance of recommendations, this was referred to by one of the managers and three of the workers, with the production manager giving the following reply to a question on the advantages of a family recruitment network:

> Ehm, well I suppose you shouldn't, but you tend *to judge the offspring by the parent*, ehm so if you've got a *good* bloke who you've had experience of for some years and you know his *attitude* to work then you expect the *approach* of the youngster to be much the same... and the same works if you've got somebody who you're not very *happy with* then you tend not to want to look at their offspring either. (BL 6)

This quotation offers an honest assessment of one of the most frequently cited advantages to management, namely that family and friendship connections have implications of the reliability and trustworthiness of a perspective employee. This is illustrated by reference to *'judge(ing) the offspring by the parent'*, with the logic being that if you have a '*good*' worker with the correct '*attitude*' you expect his relation to have a similar '*approach*'. The implied meaning behind this concept of a '*good*' worker, which was also noted by respondents from Bristol Insurance, is of an employee who shares managerial aims and objectives. The offspring of anyone who substantially deviates from such an approach, or who management is not '*happy with*', will not be considered for employment. This managerial advantage was also cited by a number of the workers:

> Q: What are the advantages of this method?
> Don't know really, I suppose they knew I was his brother like, so I suppose *he's a good worker I expect they think his brother'd be the same.* (BL 9)

> The father was a *good worker*, the boy he may turn round and *look up to his father* and turn round and try and do as *good a job as his father had done. He'd try and progress like his father*, if his father had a job that's responsible. (BL 5)

Again the potential advantage to management is quite clear, with membership of a network carrying implications of the quality of the worker, a perception which was shared by some at Bristol Insurance (BI 10; BI 11; BI 18) and which supports earlier work (Jenkins, 1982; Jenkins et al, 1983; Manwaring, 1984; Bresnen et al, 1985; Dick and Morgan, 1987; Grieco, 1987). The second response also sheds some light on what is meant by a *'good worker'*. It was argued earlier that the meaning behind this concept was of a worker who shared managerial aims and objectives and this is clearer from the above extract where it is assumed that a *'good worker'* would try to *'progress'*. The emphasis of meaning is clearly on promotion, ambition and careerism, a process of meritocratic upward mobility which is most successful when one follows the objectives of the company and its management. The comments of the third worker who discussed the advantage of network reputation also made reference to the potential for increased managerial control:

> They knew someone who was working well and then they had relatives they knew they had *a better chance of getting a good worker from the same family* because even if they weren't a good worker their relatives would get onto them. (BL 8)

The two advantages are seen to be interlinked, with family reputation carrying responsibility which may serve to internalise control. This was noted by a number of the other workers:

> I think I know that when a friend or relation recommends somebody to the company or goes to the company and says 'my boy needs a job' eh and the company gives that boy a job I think *that person is more likely to not let him get away with things*, he's more likely to say *'come on pull your finger out'* like you know. (BL 3)

> There's an advantage with management but there's also a disadvantage with you. I got a lot of brothers alright but I wouldn't like to work with any of my brothers in here because I would *feel responsible for them*, the time I've been here. Eh a friend of mine has got his brother here and it was a little bit like that to start with. What they did do, they separated them and put them on different shifts. But when you do get the families in here you do feel a little bit responsible for them and your always kind of ehm, how can I say, *it could give you a good name or a bad name*. (BL 10)

This illustrates quite clearly that some of the workforce at Bristol Laminated are aware of the implications for control of recommending a network connection. The first quotation shows an awareness of the potential for internalising control while the second relates responsibility for a network connection to the importance of one's 'name' as a worker. The likelihood of such a recruitment method internalising control was also mentioned by one of the respondents from Bristol Insurance (BI 10) and was widely found in other studies (Lee and Wrench, 1981; Hedges and Beynon, 1982; Jenkins, 1982; Jenkins et al, 1983; Manwaring, 1984;

Dick and Morgan, 1987; Grieco, 1987). The personnel manager at Bristol Laminated linked the potential for increasing control with the low cost:

> Q: What do you think are the advantages of using that friends and family type of network?
> Ehm the advantages of it? There's quite a lot of '*you're my friend and now you're in the company so don't you misbehave cause it'll get to me kind of thing*', obviously it's cheap because *you don't have to pay for advertising*, ehm and it probably keeps the numbers down a bit cause 80 odd applicants is a bit of a pain. (BL 1)

Another manager noted the possibility that using family and friendship networks to recruit implied possession of certain tacit skills:

> Q: Does it help if new recruits know other people?
> It helps them settle down and get to *know the way that we operate* and the various different parts of the factory as well if they *know other individuals and can feel comfortable* talking with them. (BL 6)

This quote illustrates the potential importance of recruiting through family and friendship networks, with the implication that network applicants have gone through a period of pre-work socialisation and that membership of such a network signifies the ease with which a new employee will learn the tacit skills specific to each workplace (Manwaring, 1984; Dick and Morgan, 1987; Grieco, 1987). The last advantage to emerge from the data was the perception that recruiting through friends and relatives led to a more friendly and secure environment (Manwaring, 1984). In the case study data from Bristol Laminated respondents this was most often expressed through emphasising the family nature of the factory. For example, two workers gave the following comments during discussions of the advantages of network based recruitment:

> It creates a *nicer atmosphere* if it's a *family run place*. (BL 8).

> Well this used to be a *family company*, the company *looked after* its employees, I don't think that's the case now. Ehm *everybody knew everybody*, I mean I don't even know my managing director, he's been here two years. (BL 2)

The first quote links a family based recruitment process with a '*nicer atmosphere*' while the second respondent (talking of the past) emphasises a relationship between such a recruitment process and a more secure working environment where '*everybody knew everybody*' and where employees would be '*looked after*'.

In addition to these advantages both of the managers at Bristol Laminated (who had greater experience of, and exposure to, network based recruitment than those from Bristol Insurance) cited a number of disadvantages, mainly in relation to loss of control:

> ... if the workers that are here now know the father or the brother or whatever they would probably be *quite considerate* towards them, but they can very easily and very quickly get into the *culture* of the factory, which we're trying to change. And to bring someone in who knows the *culture* because their father's in the *culture* isn't a good idea. (Do you think looking to job centre's will change that?) Yes, that should change the *culture* because the people in job centres are looking for jobs, are *keen* to get jobs and are *keen* to make their mark. (BL 1)

This clearly illustrates that while recruiting through family carries the advantage that other workers would 'probably be *quite considerate*' towards the new workers there is the danger that these workers will 'very easily and very quickly get into the *culture* of the factory', which this manager wishes to change to one of '*keenness*'. This manager, therefore would like to change what are seen as deeply held customs and values to attributes which management find attractive, such as eagerness, enthusiasm and devotion.

Another potential disadvantage which was articulated by management, is the possibility that family members may combine in the face of certain managerial pressures or practices, with the consequent 'problem' for managerial '*discipline*':

> ... it's the 'it's my son you shouldn't be *disciplining* him' kind of thing. I know at the Bedminster factory they've got a lot of family influences and they do have problems there if they do *discipline* one person in the family the whole family tend to get involved. That's not quite so bad here, I mean it's a bit like that. Ehm when you turn someone's son down from them having applied, I have had one or two quite abusive conversations from father's whose sons are the bees knees. And 'you haven't given them a job, instead you've given this outsider a job and he's absolutely useless.' (BL 1)

> Well, I suppose it can cause problems from a *disciplinary* point of view it can be very difficult to *discipline* people and they can I suppose be protected if they've done something wrong the others tend to *close ranks* and look after them if they're a member of the family. It tends to get *a bit like the mafia*. And also it's very difficult to keep any secrets, everything goes through the place like wildfire. People can be out on holiday and still know because *there's connections all over the place*. (BL 6)

The first point to note is the belief that the pressure involved in recruiting through family and friendship networks may, when a friend or relation is refused employment, cause antagonistic relations. This potential disadvantage was shared by a marketing manager at Bristol Insurance (BI 11), who cited the possibility of awkwardness as one of the disadvantages of relying on network recruitment and then turning down a family member. The second point to note is the essentially confrontational attitude and perceptions held by these two managers, where the potential problem is one of '*discipline*', with the emphasis of meaning on a institutionalised hierarchy where subordinates may occasionally require punishment or incur a penalty. These managers, while being fully aware of the potential advantages vis-a-vis control, are also aware that family and friendship networks represent a potential threat to their authority, with the possibility that family members will '*close ranks*' in the face of '*discipline*' (Hill, 1976; Grieco, 1987). Finally, the second quote illustrates the density of such kinship networks, with the production manager expressing her concern at the difficulty of keeping secrets, with the possibility that workers will know what's going on even if their on holiday because '*there's connections all over the place*'.

The most significant difference between the data presented and analysed in this section from that in the previous section was, again, the number and nature of comments relating to network recruitment. Bristol Laminated respondents made more frequent, frank and open comments about network advantages. It was argued that this is a reflection of the greater exposure of Bristol Laminated employees to networks (with the more marked role of kin especially noticeable). Although the data from Bristol Insurance was more limited it was still possible to isolate some common and some conflicting views. One additional marked difference which emerged from the data was the perceived importance to Bristol Laminated workers and managers of the tacit skills which may be signified (and possibly transmitted through) family and friendship networks. The shared perceptions related to the importance of family name and reputation as signifying similar characteristics to the existing workforce and the possibility that this would increase managerial control. The next section goes on to investigate some possible reasons why there may be a difference in the role of informal networks between manual blue collar and non-manual white collar workers.

4.6 Formal vs informal: a contrasting rationale

The evidence which has been described and analysed in previous sections has been used to argue that the manual blue collar interviewees of Bristol Laminated utilise informal recruitment channels both more frequently and more intensively than the non-manual white collar interviewees of Bristol Insurance and conversely that formal channels are more important to recruitment in Bristol Insurance. Why should this be the case? It is not that networks play no role in white collar working environments, indeed the primary data from Bristol Insurance has illustrated that such networks are active in passing on 'low level' information on the nature of Bristol Insurance as an employer, or that formal channels play no role in blue collar recruitment, rather it is to argue that each sector concentrates on their respective channel because of that channels effectiveness in satisfying the recruitment criteria of *suitability* and *acceptability*. This dichotomy of criteria emerged from work in the field of discrimination with Jenkins' (1983) work on religious discrimination in Belfast, Curran's (1985, 1988) work on gender and the recruitment process and Jenkins (1986) and Lee and Wrench's (1987) work on racism and recruitment. Jenkins (1988) writes of these criteria:

> Both types of criteria are related to the efficient functioning of the worker and the workplace, as perceived by management. Suitability is functionally specific, inasmuch as it is concerned with the individual's ability to perform tasks required by the job. Criteria of suitability might include physique, particular experience or formal education, trade or professional qualifications. Acceptability is functionally non-specific, concerned with the general control and management of the organisation: will the recruit 'fit in' to the context in question, is he or she 'dependable', 'reliable' and hard working, will the new worker leave after a short time? Criteria of acceptability, highly subjective and dependent upon managerial perceptions, include appearance, 'manner and attitude', 'maturity', gender, labour market history and status. (Jenkins, 1988: 319-320)

I would argue that it is the potentiality of family and friendship networks to signify the possession of tacit skills (or the ability to quickly learn such skills) which relate to both suitability and acceptability in formally unskilled jobs which makes such a channel particularly relevant to the blue collar sector, where many manual jobs are officially classed as 'unskilled'. It was argued earlier that recruitment through family and friends helps to produce workers with characteristics similar to the existing workforce and that these imply possession of certain tacit skills (Corcoran, 1980b; Lee and Wrench, 1981; Jenkins, 1982; Jenkins et al, 1983; Manwaring, 1984; Manwaring and Wood, 1985; Dick and Morgan, 1987; Grieco, 1987). Manwaring, writing on tacit skills, comments that:

> ... using the extended internal labour market (EILM) provides an indication of a person's ability to learn and exercise such skills. The EILM is effectively an *informal apprenticeship system*. It can serve this function because the candidate is already integrated into the social relationships which exist within the workgroup... (Manwaring, 1984: 168, emphasis in original)

Grieco (1987) also notes the importance of kinship networks in passing on such firm specific skills:

> ... family and friends in the workplace can transmit the *tacit skills* in anticipation of the interview. Even for jobs which are formally unskilled, an applicant familiar with the specifics of production in that particular plant is likely once again to be at an advantage over other candidates. (Grieco, 1987: 40, emphasis added)

This point is supported by the work of Dick and Morgan (1987):

> Family aid to employment went beyond just asking for a job. Sponsors provided information on how to address managers... They were provided with *knowledge* about the job before being brought to the firm. Jack Bottomley for instance said, 'Dad told me about the dyepans, steam and hanks before I came in.'... One manager pointed out that 'the family could set the individuals straight about how things were run'. He included in this all the details about mealbreaks, finishing times, etc. as well as what he termed *'the little knacks of the job'*. (Dick and Morgan, 1987: 234, 236, emphasis added)

The role of family and friendship networks emerges clearly from these quotations, the argument being that network members go through a process of pre-work socialisation to a certain type of work, receiving '*tacit skills*' and '*knowledge*' through an '*informal apprenticeship mechanism*'. The importance of family and friendship networks in providing such assistance was also apparent from Bristol Laminated case study data:

> ... the person who recommends him obviously *knows the background and the history to the factory* and can *give that person advice outside of the factory as well as inside of the factory*. (So they might come in with certain knowledge?) Yeah that's right, or at least *the procedures if not the actual processes* he'd be working on but *he'd know the history of the factory and the people in the factory* and what he should be doing and what he shouldn't be doing before he walks in through the door. (BL 3)

The process through which tacit skills are signified and transferred between network members emerges clearly from this quotation, where this worker sees network applicants as possessing general knowledge of the factory 'processes' and advice as to common custom and practice in the factory. I would argue, therefore, that family and friendship networks are effective in communicating information to management on the degree to which sponsored applicants possess tacit skills (or the ability to quickly learn such skills) which are important in many, formally unskilled, blue collar manual jobs. To an extent, therefore, the 'informal apprenticeship system' which is represented by family and friendship networks may be seen as satisfying the managerial criteria of suitability and acceptability. The criteria of suitability is met by the tendency of such networks to signify possession of (or the aptitude to quickly learn) functionally specific tacit skills which are vital 'to the feel and discretion in even formally non-skilled production processes' (Manwaring 1984: 167), while the functionally non-specific criteria of acceptability is met by the pre orientation of 'manner and attitude' to a specific industry or firm which is associated with membership of a kinship or friendship network. How does this compare with the situation in non-manual white collar work? As was argued previously networks are evident in Bristol Insurance and as is argued in the next chapter tacit skills are also evident, so it is not that family and friendship networks as signifiers of certain tacit skills have no role in office recruitment, but rather that their role in satisfying the recruitment criteria of acceptability and suitability is not as significant as in manual factory work. To take the example of qualifications, certain qualification backed skills such as 'O' or 'A' levels[17] are required in even the most routine type of non-manual white collar work and I would suggest that possession of such qualifications signifies certain functional abilities (read, write, spell) as well as certain personal characteristics. Gintis (1971) Bowles and Gintis (1975) suggest that qualifications illustrate possession of certain motivations (such as sociability and stability) and values which may be compatible with that of the enterprise and so it may be the case that office managers use qualifications as communicating certain information about an employee's outlook which may signify the degree to which the applicant would 'fit in' to the workplace. It may well be the case, therefore, that one reason why each sector concentrates on their respective channel is the efficiency of that channel in effectively satisfying the recruitment criteria of suitability and acceptability.

Another possible explanation focuses on the historical development of informal recruitment practices in the blue collar sector as part of the continual struggle for power and control over the labour process. Lazonick (1979), in his comprehensive study of the development of cotton spinning from the late eighteenth century, argues that informal recruitment was an integral part of the labour process and necessary to the continued profitability of the industry. He writes:

> The minder-piecer[18] system relieved managers and overlookers not only of the need to directly supervise the young workers, but also, as an internal subcontract system, of the task of recruiting them... Operative spinners brought relatives and children of neighbours into the mills (in the latter case, paying the wages of younger piecers directly to their parents). They had an economic interest in seeking out the most dependable assistants, while at the same time their location in the families or communities of these assistants gave them an advantage in assessing the likely qualities of new recruits. (Lazonick, 1979: 244)

This offers an early example of managers/owners devolving power to certain grades of workers (in this case the minder-piecer's) in an attempt to increase both productivity and profitability, with the workers in question also benefiting in terms

---

[17]Ashton and Maguire (1986), in their work into the structure of the youth labour market, found that 86% of males and 79% of females whose first job was in clerical work had "O" or "A" levels, compared to 32% and 21% respectively for semi-skilled and sales jobs.

[18]Minder-piecers were responsible for the maintenance and operation of the mechanised spinning production process and for recruiting and supervising workers employed in this process (Lazonick, 1979).

of increased earnings and prestige. Similar findings were made by Joyce (1980) who, in his study of a Lanarkshire cotton town, stressed the strong interrelationship between the firm as a 'family' and the firm as a family employer, with the aim of maintaining quiescent industrial relations and profitability through a mixture of threats and patronage. As was argued in an earlier section, the role of informal recruitment as an area of consensus as well as conflict between managers/owners and workers in the blue collar sector has been highlighted in a number of more contemporary (blue collar) studies (Hill, 1976; Lee and Wrench, 1981; Jenkins, 1982; Hedges and Beynon, 1982; Jenkins et al, 1983; Manwaring, 1984; Dick and Morgan, 1987; Grieco, 1987). The work of Dick and Morgan (1987) into family networks and employment in a Yorkshire textile mill illustrates the extent to which this is still the case:

> The informality within the firm was reflected in ways other than simply how recruitment was conducted. Managers, staff and manual workers are well-known to each other from the many years that most of them have worked on the site. No one calls anyone by their surname. Managers are all known by their first name, including the directors. The chairman of Blackburns' board is called Mr Eric and the executive director is called Mr Paul. Many of the managers, too, have long established family ties with Blackburns. The family of the Managing Director and the executive director have been represented in the firm since the turn of the century. The financial Director and the Woolshop Manager inherited their positions from their fathers, as their fathers had before them. (Dick and Morgan, 1987: 237)

This demonstrates the continuing prevalence of strong family relations within a firm, with benefits flowing both to management and the workforce.[19] Rubery (1978) has argued that workforce groups such as trade unions may develop and erect barriers to entry which effectively close access to employment. This is supported by the case study data from Bristol Laminated which illustrated that managers were aware not only of the advantages in recruiting through family but also of the potential for increasing the unity of the workforce and by so doing weaken managements ability to 'discipline' workers. There could be a case, therefore, for arguing that the emphasis of blue collar recruitment on informal methods is part of a historical process, whereby both workers and managers saw the potential to gain control, power, or to keep the status quo and that this process continues to have an influence on manual blue collar recruitment. This is not to argue that there is no conflict of objectives or confrontation between managers and workers in the white collar sector (Braverman, 1974; Gordon et al, 1982;

---

[19] Dick and Morgan (1987) also found that sponsorship maintained its relevance even when entry was restricted to Youth Training Scheme entrants. At the time of their research eight of the ten YTS trainees had been given their place after a relative spoke for them.

Crompton and Jones, 1984), rather it is to argue that office work in general and clerical work in particular are the products of a separate historical process where the area of conflict with respect to recruitment has shifted to large personnel departments overseeing 'meritocratic' recruitment practices.

A third possible explanation for the different orientation in recruitment channels may lie with the extent to which recruitment is influenced by either a 'professional' personnel department or by line managers. Atkinson et al (1994), has argued that the greater the role of line managers then the greater the use of informal methods as 'line managers are less influenced by formal considerations of abstract good practice' (Atkinson et al, 1994: 31). So if it is the case (as it was in Bristol Laminated) that the line managers have more say in recruitment in manual blue collar work, this could account for the greater reliance on informal methods. The potential for personnel departments in blue collar firms to hold a secondary position compared to family and friendship networks is illustrated in the work of Dick and Morgan (1987), who found that:

> At the time of research the firm had a personnel department which was theoretically responsible for recruitment... In practice, however, this procedure was rarely followed. Workers within particular departments would often know well in advance that a vacancy was going to occur. They would then approach the departmental manager directly and ask on behalf of a relative about the job. The manager would then interview the potential newcomer and the person might then be promised the job before the personnel department knew there was a vacancy. In fact the first they might know about it might be when the family member concerned showed up at the personnel department asking to fill in an application form after they had already been offered the job! (Dick and Morgan, 1987: 236, emphasis in original)

Thus, it could be argued that the potential of line managers in blue collar firms to circumvent formal recruitment methods is not shared by line managers in white collar workplaces, where (as was the case in Bristol Insurance) the recruitment process is more influenced by 'professional' personnel departments following a set recruitment procedure.

I would suggest, therefore, that there are a number of reasons for the differing emphasis on formal and informal recruitment channels between manual blue collar and non-manual white collar work. Firstly, that the degree of use of recruitment channel is influenced by the degree to which management recruitment criteria of suitability and acceptability are satisfied. Secondly, that the historical development of the recruitment process for manual blue collar jobs has tended towards informal methods and that this has strongly influenced contemporary recruitment practices. Thirdly and finally that large offices may be more influenced by 'professional' personnel departments who are more keen to follow, and be seen to follow more 'meritocratic' recruitment policies which tend towards a greater use of formal channels.

4.7 Conclusion

The aim of this chapter was to investigate the recruitment channels of Bristol Insurance and Bristol Laminated, with particular emphasis to be given to an examination of informal channels, which other (larger) scale studies had shown to be a discriminator between manual blue collar and non-manual white collar work. The opening section presented and analysed secondary material from both America and Britain which demonstrated the importance of informal methods of recruitment. It was noted, however, that most of these studies were into primary industries (Hill, 1976; Wedderburn, 1965), blue collar firms (Dunnell and Head, 1973; Courtenay and Hedges, 1977; Manwaring, 1984; Dick and Morgan, 1987; Grieco, 1987) or single issue areas (Jenkins, 1982, 1986, 1988; Campbell, 1988; Morris and Irwin, 1992), with little detailed comparative inter industry case study work. Most of the comparative work has taken place through large scale surveys (Hedges, 1983; LMQ, 1984; IFF 1988, SCELI, 1992), which showed that one of the most important discriminators between manual blue collar and non-manual white collar work was the use of informal recruitment channels. This secondary material was followed by a detailed analysis of my case study work from Bristol Insurance and Bristol Laminated. It was found that although the main recruitment channel used by Bristol Insurance respondents was formal there was still a role for family and friends in providing low level information (on such things as remuneration and working conditions) which, it was argued, had an incremental influence on employment decisions and outcomes and may be under-represented in large scale (especially management based) surveys. This role of networks, both in the extent and nature to which family and friends were used, was found to contrast strongly with respondents at Bristol Laminated, where all of the workers interviewed had obtained their jobs through family or friends. It was argued that family and friendship networks may be seen, therefore, as common to both case study firms and as an important discriminator between them. Common to the extent that both case study firms use kinship and friendship connections, but discriminating in the sense that respondents from Bristol Laminated have different perceptions of such connections and use them more often and more intensively than those in Bristol Insurance. Having established the importance of family and friendship networks the next major section moved on to investigate secondary material which explained why such networks are used. It was found that management saw such networks as providing workers with similar characteristics to the present workforce, including (most importantly in the manual blue collar sector) tacit skills or the potential to learn tacit skills. In addition management saw the opportunity of using patronage to increase control of the labour process and pacify the workers. Such networks were also seen to offer some advantages to the workforce, firstly and most importantly, they were seen to provide accurate information on employment opportunities before vacancies reached the public domain and secondly were seen as a method of increasing workforce unity. The findings relating to reproducing present workforce characteristics and control were noted by Bristol Insurance and, with the addition of tacit skills, also noted by respondents from Bristol Laminated.

The last major section examined possible explanations for the greater extent and use of family and friendship networks in the manual blue collar sector and for more formal methods in the white collar sector and argued this was done because of the differing needs and the different historical processes in the two sectors.

The question then arises as to what this means for the underlying problematic of the research - the extent to which labour markets are characterised by flexibility, occupational mobility and the consequences this might have for the competitive structure of the labour market. Three points emerge from my analysis of the case study data. Firstly, at some level, informal word of mouth networks are used in both Bristol Insurance and Bristol Laminated and that their existence must not be seen as a dysfunctional labour market rigidity but rather as fundamental elements in the construction of workplaces. Such informal exchanges of information, such institutionally specific practices, therefore, must, therefore, be seen as endogenous not exogenous to the functioning of the labour market. Secondly, while informal networks are used in both firms, the nature and extent of their use differs to such an extent as to serve as a component in creating distinct workplace communities. In Bristol Insurance they are used to provide 'low level' information on such things as the 'nature' of the company as an employer while in Bristol Laminated they are used much more frequently and intensively. Thirdly, both these factors influence the potential for industrial mobility, in the sense that any unemployed workers from firms such as Bristol Laminated would be searching through the wrong channel (informal as opposed to formal) and that, even to the extent that office vacancies were 'publicised' throughout a family and friendship network, it would very probably be a network to which factory workers would not have access and, even if they had, would function in an unfamiliar manner. This difficulty is compounded by the fact that factory workers tend to be more reliant on such networks, so as strong employment orientated networks shrink in tandem with the decline in manufacturing employment, there are few such networks to replace them and one of the areas with more positive employment opportunities (offices) not only relies on separate recruitment channels and networks but perceives and uses these networks in different ways. The theme of difference, of non-competitive work groups, then, emerges strongly from the data on recruitment. This theme was also apparent in data on skills and it is to this we now turn.

5 Labour and skill

5.1 Introduction

> The demands on the skills of the labour force are likely to continue increasing. Higher levels of training and education will be needed for the increase in higher level jobs. New skills will be needed to take advantage of developments in new technologies and new materials. And as organisations strive to become more *flexible* and responsive so as to compete effectively, individuals will need a wider range of skills to increase their own *flexibility*. (Skills and Enterprise Network, 1993: i, emphasis added)

This quote emphasises the importance the government, often through Training and Enterprise Councils (TEC's) and independent training organisations, gives to increasing flexibility through encouraging workers to learn and be ready to learn new skills (Benn and Fairley, 1986; Finn, 1987; Skills and Enterprise Network, 1993). Given the central importance of "skills" to government thinking and policy making the second line of inquiry was into how case study respondents perceive skill. How do respondents from Bristol Insurance and Bristol Laminated conceive and conceptualise skill? And if respondents do articulate different perceptions to what extent does this imply non-competitive work groups which may act as barriers to flexibility and occupational mobility? This chapter seeks to answer these questions by identifying and investigating common or conflicting skill perceptions amongst case study respondents.

In order to set the later analysis of primary data in a theoretical context, this chapter opens with an analysis of the literature on skill. It will be seen that the debate surrounding skill is both complex and contentious, being influenced by historical precedents, gender perceptions and institutional norms. The discussion of the skills debate is opened by reference to Braverman's (1974) "deskilling" hypothesis, which stimulated much of the consequent discussions and served to bring skill conceptualisation back to the centre of research into the labour process. This initial discussion of Braverman's position is followed by an analysis of criticisms and alternative skill conceptualisations from which three broad, but by no means mutually exclusive, theoretical positions are seen to emerge. The first, most common among labour economists, links skills with the properties of an individual and consequently focuses on the need to build up "human capital" through training and education. The second, common amongst industrial sociologists, sees skill as an aspect of the job itself and investigates the organisation and requirements of changing systems of industrial production. The third (often articulated by social historians) links skill with political and social forces.

The complexity of the debate concerning skill which is evident in the literature also emerges from the analysis of the primary data which follows the overview of previous work into the conceptualisation of skill. The analysis of this data is split into three separate sections dealing with skill construction, skill perception and skill acquisition. The last section brings together the results of the analysis of the primary data and examines how these reflect upon both skill theory and the potential for industrial mobility.

5.2 The conceptualisation of skill

> ... within the capitalist system all methods for raising the social productivity of labour are put into effect at the cost of the individual worker; that all means for the development of production undergo a dialectical inversion so that they become means of domination and exploitation of the producers; they distort the worker into a fragment of a man, they degrade him to the level of an appendage of a machine, they destroy the actual content of his labour by turning it into a torment; they alienate from him the intellectual potentialities of the labour process in the same proportion as science is incorporated in it as an independent power; they deform the conditions under which he works, subject him during the labour process to a despotism the more hateful for its meanness; they transform his life-time into working-time, and drag his wife and child beneath the wheels of the juggernaut of capital. (Marx, [1867], 1976: 799)

This extract from Marx, describing what Braverman (1974) was later to label the deskilling of work, captures the power, passion and political nature of the skill debate. The nature of the changes which Marx saw accompanying increasing mechanisation under a capitalist system has ensured a lively and contentious debate around what is classed as skilled work and who are classed as skilled workers. This overview of skill theory begins with the work of Braverman, who, at least in Britain, stimulated the contemporary debate surrounding skill. The task centred definition of skill developed by Braverman is used as a starting point from which other skill conceptualisations (often linked to criticisms of Braverman's work) are introduced and discussed.

Braverman, with the publication of *Labour and Monopoly Capital* in 1974 sought to bring discussions of the labour process to the heart of the neo-Marxist debate.

Building on the work of Marx, he linked the labour process to class analysis and argued that work, both in the factory and in the office, had become increasingly routinised and deskilled, leading to an increasing homogeneity amongst the working class. In order to reach this conclusion two important assumptions were made, firstly that the working class existed as a class in itself and not of itself (in other words the working class is seen as relatively passive[20]) and secondly that skill is linked to technical, craft based, tasks carried out by that individual. Braverman writes of skill:

> For the worker the concept of skill is traditionally bound up with craft mastery - that is to say, the combination of knowledge of materials and processes with the practised manual dexterities required to carry on a specific branch of production. The breakup of craftskills and the reconstruction of production as a collective or social process have destroyed the traditional concept of skill and opened up only one way for mastery over labour processes to develop: in and through scientific, technical, and engineering knowledge. (Braverman, 1974: 443)

Braverman argued that the objective of capitalist management was to gain more control over the variability and uncertainty connected with the transformation of a worker's potential to work (labour power) into actual work (labour). Deskilling was simply one method of increasing this control. As the opening reference shows, Marx predicted that as capitalism developed the traditional skills associated with craftwork would disappear and machines would take over the heart of the production process. The result of this is that workers would lose the ability to perform all the tasks required in a particular trade and consequently becoming mere machine minders. This deskilling would widen the labour supply available for any particular task and consequently lower labour costs as workers were forced to accept a lower wage as labour supply grew. Braverman believed that the trend towards deskilling had not changed, but that modern scientific principles were now being applied to the task of deskilling. A skilled worker was defined by reference to work which combined control over both the conception and execution of production and was epitomised by the stereotype of the nineteenth century artisan. Management theory and practice was assumed to place emphasis on gaining complete control over the labour process which demanded a "scientific" attitude to production which would lead to improved productivity (Taylor, [1895], 1947). In this mass production, or what later became to be known as the "Fordist" system of production, tasks were split between the "mental" aspects such as planning and design which were controlled by management and the simple manual operations which were left to the workers. This process, Braverman argued, serves to systematically deskill the worker as elements of knowledge, responsibility and day to day judgement are progressively removed and replaced by routine, pre-planned

---

[20]For more on this see Wood (1982: 14).

tasks, until:

> What is left to workers is a reinterpreted and woefully inadequate concept of skill: a specific dexterity, a limited and repetitious operation, "speed as skill" etc. (Braverman, 1974: 443, 444)

For Braverman, then, skill was linked to the complexity of the task and was seen as epitomised by the artisan, who had undergone a prolonged period of training in the form of an apprenticeship. Other writers, adopting a task centred notion of skill and writing mainly in the field of industrial sociology, have supported the work of Braverman (Kumar, 1978; Crompton and Jones, 1984). Crompton and Jones (1984) applied Braverman's knowledge to clerical work and concluded that such work has been deskilled by technological change:

> The greater the level of mechanisation within both departments and organisations, the more likely was the work of the lower clerical grades to be rated as unskilled or semi-skilled... excluding programmers and systems analysts, over 90 per cent of those on clerical grades were in jobs that were entirely rule-bounded - although the complexity of the rules varied - and required no discretion or autonomy in carrying out the various job tasks. (Crompton and Jones, 1984: 73)

These authors, using a task centred notion of skill where control over the one's labour power is crucial to the degree of skill possessed, produced results which were used to support Braverman's theory of deskilling. Other contemporary work done in the field on manual work has also supported Braverman's thesis (Cockburn, 1983; Noble, 1984; Armstrong, 1988; Thompson, 1988; Wilson and Buchanan, 1988).

Turning to criticisms of and alternative's to Braverman's work, these fall into two broad camps: firstly (most common amongst labour market economists) the emphasis is shifted from skill being linked to the job itself to skill being defined by reference to the worker's capabilities which are built up through investment in human capital (education, training) and secondly (common amongst social historians) viewing skill not as a series of specific technical tasks or abilities but as being socially defined and created. Some writers, building on the work of the American labour economist Becker (1964) into the field of human capital have argued that increased mechanisation (particularly increased use of electronics) has led to increased skilling (Fuchs, 1968; Bell, 1974). This "skilling" hypothesis interprets skill as being linked to a worker's capabilities and as being created by education and training. Penn (1985) gives the following summary of the work of these theorists:

> The general argument... is that advanced industrial society requires an increasingly educated workforce. Arguments are put forward about the growth of "knowledge" as a new factor of production and the concomitant growth of

knowledge producing (universities, research institutes) and knowledge-consuming (electronics) industries. (Penn, 1985: 37)

The belief here is that "value" is increasingly being added in the production process through the nurturing and capturing of cognitive skills, which are increasing in line with the numbers of people gaining educational qualifications.[21] Between the poles of deskilling and skilling there has been the development of the compensatory theory of skill which argues that changing technology has resulted in both upskilling and deskilling. Researchers in this area have placed particular emphasis on the upskilling of machine maintenance workers which has occurred as a result of developments in the field of micro-electronics (Penn and Scattergood, 1985; Penn, 1990) and the upskilling of office administrative workers as a result of the computerisation of office functions (Penn et al, 1992). These authors conclude that:

> There is little evidence to support the deskilling thesis associated with Braverman. There were very few examples of computerisation being associated with a lowering of skills amongst workers in the establishments that had been interviewed. There was greater support for the skilling thesis associated with human capital theory. (Penn et al, 1992: 678)

There is, then, a considerable body of work, which emphasises the potential for new technology (particularly microcomputers) to upgrade workers' skill through increased education and training. Associated with the importance of new technology is the work of those arguing for the creation of the flexible firm (Atkinson, 1984, 1985a) and flexible specialisation (Piore and Sabel, 1984; Sabel and Zeitlin, 1985, Murray 1987). Although, as was argued earlier, this literature touches on much more than the technical it could be used, I would suggest, as part of the criticism of Braverman in the sense that he tends to dismiss the potential for the demands of new technology to encourage and introduce *new* skills.

Another criticism, still associated with the capabilities of workers, has focused on Braverman's tendency to place too much emphasis on a narrow, task-centred definition of skill and has argued for the inclusion of less well recognised, but nevertheless important, tacit skills:

> The narrowness of the definition of skill also, it is argued, leads to an overestimate of deskilling by downgrading certain job elements. In this respect, attention has been drawn to the importance of social skills in group working; the degree of discretion retained by workers because of unpredictability in raw materials and production processes; the idiosyncrasies of machines and work situations requiring specific skills; and the degree of

---

[21]For more detail on the increase in student numbers see Dennis (1994: 65-70).

unrecognised abilities - what has been called tacit skills -required for a broad range of tasks. (Burchell et al, 1994: 165)

The concept of tacit skill was introduced in the last chapter, where it was argued that the greater importance of "unofficial" skills in factories may partially account for the greater reliance on informal networks. Turning to a deeper analysis of this concept the emphasis is on what Beechey (1982) has described as "complex objective competencies" required for individual tasks and social, subjective skills vital for efficient production. The concept was popularised by Manwaring (1984) and Manwaring and Wood (1985), who built on Polanyi's theory of tacit knowing (Polanyi and Prosch, 1975) and Kusterer's concept of working knowledge (Kusterer, 1978), to develop the concept of tacit skills to describe and explain such abilities.[22] They describe tacit skills as:

> ... refer(ing) to the feel and discretion which form the basis for subjectivity in even non-skilled work and are vital to efficient performance in all work situations. (Manwaring and Wood, 1985: 177)

These authors identify three dimensions to tacit skills. Firstly, the undertaking of routine tasks involves a process of learning by which skills are gained by experience and may become so well known that they are practised unconsciously. Secondly, different degrees of awareness are required to perform certain activities. Thirdly, that because of the collective nature of the productive process workers must develop co-operative skills. Reference to abilities which are similar to such tacit skills has also been found by other authors in Britain (Cockburn, 1983; Penn and Scattergood, 1985) and America (Steiger, 1993).

The existence of subjective or tacit skills has two important implications. Firstly, as Cressey and MacInnes (1980) and Manwaring and Wood (1985) note, because some working knowledge remains *inside* each worker, there is a limit to direct management control of the labour process.[23] If it is the case, for example, that the

---

[22]Gramsci's [1948-51] (1991) comments on labour hoarding hint at an early recognition of tacit skills: "Since there has never functioned and does not function any law of perfect parity of systems and production and work methods valid for all firms in a specific branch of industry, it follows that every firm is, to a greater or less degree, "unique" and will form a labour force with qualifications proper to its own particular requirements. Little manufacturing and working secrets, or "fiddles", practised by this labour force, which in themselves seen insignificant, can, when repeated an infinite number of times, assume immense economic importance." (Gramsci, [1948-51], 1991: 313)

[23]Ainley (1993) writes of how tacit knowledge may still be relevant in production processes dominated by new technology: "Tacit knowledge may yet be directly retained by the use of keyboardless computers, in which mice and gloves

workers themselves are not aware they possess such skills there is some knowledge that management simply cannot gain access to and therefore cannot control. Secondly, if workers are presently rewarded on a formula which links, even approximately, pay and "official" skill then the abilities of those workers whose main skills are tacit may go unrecognised and hence unrewarded. This has special importance in areas of employment which require non-technical and social skills, such as office or retail jobs which demand good communication skills or nursing and teaching which demand listening and caring skills. These jobs are particularly likely to be filled by women (Employment Department Group, 1994) and there has been considerable work in this area, much of which has argued for the recognition and reward of such skills (Phillips and Taylor, 1980; Armstrong, 1982; Coyle, 1982, Crompton and Jones, 1984; Craig et al, 1980, 1985 and Horrell et al 1990). Tacit skills, therefore, reflect on the skill debate in two ways. Firstly, the existence of tacit skills would imply that even if one is to conceptualise skill in the Bravermanian sense of a series of task centred objective capabilities, that the series of *tasks* must be expanded to include functions beyond what is "officially" classed as technical, such as intense familiarity with particular machines, and expanded also to include social, non-technical job tasks such as caring and communication. Secondly that skill conceptualisation should take account of the subjective *capabilities* of workers as well as the complexity of *tasks*, thus allowing the inclusion of non-technical and social skills which are possessed by many individuals who are officially classed as unskilled.

Consideration of which set of tasks and which knowledge is considered as skilled leads on to the possibility that skill is socially created, that work and workers are classed as skilled or unskilled not because of any "objective" skill criterion but because social forces have shaped the occupational skill profile. There is an important distinction to be made here between "social" skills in the sense of good communication or interpersonal skills, and the "social" definition of skills. Henceforth "social" skills will refer to the possession of non-technical abilities and "political/social" skills will refer to the series of tasks and competencies which have managed to obtain skilled status. The interaction of such political and social forces in the process of creating skill leads to another criticism of Braverman, namely that he underplayed the power of workers and assumed that management dictated the principles and priorities of the labour process without significant worker resistance (Zeitlin, 1979; Stark, 1980; Wood, 1982; Cockburn, 1983). Stark (1980) comments:

> Not only does he ignore the conflicts between capitalists and the "scientific managers," but he also fails to integrate into his analysis the shopfloor and political struggles of workers against rationalisation. It is not unfair to argue

---

may be used to 'pull down' information and perform operations upon it inside an artificial 'cyberspace'." (Ainley, 1993: 23).

that Braverman portrays the capitalist class as veritably omniscient and the working class as infinitely malleable. (Stark, 1980: 92)

The first point which Stark makes is the possibility that management will adopt a strategy different from Taylorist "scientific" management or that such a strategy could be modified. Such modified managerial strategies to overcome worker resistance were developed by Friedman (1977, 1978) and Edwards (1979). Friedman (1977, 1978) developed a theory of responsible autonomy which has been described as:

> ... consisting of worker discretion and commitment to capitalist objectives (a job-redesign type of practice); as counselling, improvements in social relations, the stimulation of intergroup competition, suggestion schemes and participation; and as the concession of improved material benefits - high wages and incentives, job security, good fringe benefits and working conditions. (Wood and Kelly, 1982: 82-83)

Here the aim is to humanise work, to offer workers increased pecuniary and non pecuniary benefits in order to change their allegiance and follow managements' objectives of productivity maximisation. Manwaring and Wood (1985) use "quality circles" is an example of such strategies:

> Quality circles attempt to achieve more than just the enlargement of workers' knowledge for managerial gain. They attempt to draw on and develop the co-operative nature of the labour process. (Manwaring and Wood, 1985: 191)

Friedman also associated deskilling with a management strategy of direct control, where the discretion individual workers can exercise is reduced. According to Friedman (1978) there is continual tension between these two strategies. When there is excess labour supply and rigorous price competition the direct control strategy is suitable but when faced with a tight labour market or strong worker resistance job enrichment schemes are appropriate.

Another model of modified managerial strategy was developed by Edwards (1979), who shifted the emphasis from strategies of responsible autonomy to:

> ... the use of industrial relations procedures, through bureaucratic rules which channel conflict into manageable and acceptable ways and especially through the use of internal labour markets and dual labour markets which divide and segment the working class. (Wood, 1982: 16)

The logic of such an argument could be applied to the work of Atkinson (1984; 1985a) who recommends that management construct a flexible firm split into a number of different segments, with employment security varying from segment to segment. This could be interpreted as change which would serve to divide potential opposition to managerial control (Bowles and Gintis, 1975; Gordon et al, 1982;

Nichols, 1986; Potter, 1987, Pollert, 1988b, 1991; Curry, 1993). This point was emphasised by Pollert (1988b) who, as was noted earlier, argued that this debate contained little that was new and, furthermore, that it was strongly influenced by ideology:

> New, flexible technology thus becomes the saviour and economic transformer of what had been the subordinate sector. In each approach, all labour flexibility is celebrated as work enhancing, while decentralising and fragmentation are embraced. As such, the informal and secondary economies are legitimised, and the significance of the disjuncture between organised, collective and directly employed labour, and isolated, atomised production is masked. (Pollert, 1988b: 71)

Here Pollert argues that the "problems" of increasing production and greater efficiency are seen essentially as labour's and that the solution is to do away with *collective* trade union influenced skilled areas and replace them with *individual* contracts and bargaining. In short, management changes to the production process are seen as part of a strategy and struggle over workplace control. This theme of control has been used by other authors to argue that management measure skill less by reference to objective technical competencies than by assessments of the passivity, malleability and stability of potential employees (Collins, 1971; Gintis, 1971; Beynon, 1973; Bowles and Gintis, 1975; Hill, 1976; Blackburn and Mann, 1979; Lee and Wrench, 1981; Grieco, 1987; Steiger, 1993). Steiger (1993), for example, in his recent research into the perceptions of skill in the U.S. construction industry, listed the following in the characteristics of the "good craftsman":

> "Getting to work on time", "ability to get along with others and the public", "keeping busy", "doing what one is told", "keeps safety at the forefront", "positive attitude" and "low absenteeism".[24] (Steiger, 1993: 549)

The emphasis here is on the importance of possessing certain social characteristics which include respect for authority and a "positive" attitude to productivity. The debate around control, therefore, embraces discussions both of social skills and the political/social forces which decide what tasks and capabilities are classed as skilled. Continuing with the importance of the interaction of social and political processes in shaping skill perceptions More (1980) distinguished between "genuine skill" which arises from a given technology and "socially constructed skill" which may result from the influence of the workforce acting through unions, or by management as part of a strategy to increase control or

---

[24]The remaining characteristics listed in Steiger's notes were (in alphabetical order) "ability to 'see structurally'; ability to work without proper tools (all from plumbers); basic skills; honesty; physical strength; reputation; speed (all from non-union respondents); training; willing to learn/teach." (Steiger, 1993: 558)

appease the workforce. More (1980), by way of example, uses the work of Turner (1962) into the work of nineteenth century spinners:

> Turner's description of the spinners' tactics is a classic example of social construction of the straightforward kind... In late-nineteenth-century England the male cotton-spinners had for various reasons such as their early organisation in strong trade unions secured for themselves a level of wages usually associated with workers who had served a long apprenticeship, even though the actual work of the spinners did not take long to learn. (More, 1980: 20)

As this quote makes clear, by combining together through a trade union these workers succeeded in gaining the wages normally associated with a long period of formal training. This extract also highlights that it was *male* trade unionists who acted collectively to protect and/or enhance their working conditions and skill status. The potential for political/social skill construction to discriminate in favour of men has been noted by a number of authors (Lazonick, 1979; Phillips and Taylor, 1980; Pollert, 1981; Armstrong, 1982; Beechey, 1982; Cockburn, 1981, 1983, 1986; Crompton and Jones, 1984; Manwaring and Wood, 1985; Jenson, 1989; Bradley, 1989; Horrell et al, 1990). The historical nature of such closure is evident from the work of Lazonick (1979) and Cockburn (1983). Lazonick (1979), in his work into developments in the cotton industry during the industrial revolution, found that:

> While female mule spinners represented a small proportion of the Manchester Spinners' Society in 1795, opposition to their employment was an issue in virtually all the major spinners' strikes of the first four decades of the 19th century. In 1829 they were excluded from membership of the Grand General Union of Cotton Spinners. While the men agreed in principle to support attempts by the women to get wage-rates comparable to men, they were not prepared to aid their entry into the occupation. Rather they told the female mule spinners to form their own association. (Lazonick, 1979: 236)

There is, therefore, historical evidence of the protection of skilled status by men, a practice which, as Phillips and Taylor (1980) argue, still has contemporary relevance. Phillips and Taylor (1980), use as an example the relationship between skill and gender which was found by Craig et al (1980):

> In a recent study... it is suggested that the skill distinctions between the work of producing paper boxes and that of producing cartons can only be understood as historical associations between typically "male" work and skill. Paper boxes are produced by women working on hand-fed machines; the work is considered - and paid - as unskilled labour. Cartons are produced under a more automated process, and the work hence requires less individual concentration but it is treated as semi-skilled work. It is hard to escape the

conclusion that it is because of the similarities between the work of men and women in the carton industry that women in carton production are considered more skilled than box workers. Men and women work in a similar process; men are recognised as semi-skilled rather than unskilled workers; therefore carton production must be semi-skilled. The women producing paper boxes are simply women producing paper boxes, and however much the work itself might seem to qualify for upgrading, it remains unskilled because it is done by typically unskilled workers - women. (Phillips and Taylor, 1980: 84)

It is clear, then, that political/social construction of skill has consequences not only for the relations between capital and labour but also between men and women in the labour force. The importance of an approach to skill construction (described by Penn and Scattergood [1985] as the social determination approach) which recognises the power of both organised capital and organised labour to influence skill has also been stressed by other authors: (Mackenzie, 1977; Coombs, 1978; Rubery, 1978; Lazonick, 1979;[25] More, 1980, 1982; Stark, 1980; Littler, 1982; Penn, 1983, 1985; Penn and Scattergood, 1985; Thompson, 1988; Steiger, 1993).

In summary, the preceding review and analysis has illustrated the complications and complexity surrounding the issue of skill and supports the conclusion of Thompson (1988) that "Skill, in short, is a contested concept." The reasons for the antagonistic ambiguity which surround the concept of skill are related, I would argue, to its role in deciding which jobs and workers receive the higher wages and status associated with skilled work. Despite this complexity, however, it is possible to split skill into three (occasionally overlapping) conceptual categories (Cockburn, 1983; Martin, 1988; Penn and Francis, 1994): skill related to the capabilities of the worker, skill related to the complexities of the tasks done by the worker skill as being socially created. We now move on to an analysis of the primary data which, in addition to reflecting the conflict and complexity evident in the work on skill conceptualisation, also contains some common themes and perceptions.

---

[25]In his discussion of the introduction of new machinery into the cotton industry Lazonick describes how workers developed skills which were unique to a particular machine and by so doing protected their job: "Over the long run the effect of such delegation of tasks was that minders, by tuning and adjusting their mules... created a situation where no two pairs of mules worked in precisely the same way, thus to some extent making each minder less dispensable for the successful operation of his particular pair." (Lazonick, 1979: 240)

5.3 Construction of a skilled job

Bristol Insurance

Table 5.1 summarises the categories which emerged from discussions on what makes a job skilled:

Table 5.1
Bristol Insurance, classifications of a skilled job

	Training	Technical knowledge	Responsibility	Misc	Total
Managers	bi 10; bi 11	bi 6; bi 10	bi 9; bi 10		4
Supervisors	bi 7; bi 13; bi 15	bi 7; bi 13; bi 15	bi 7	bi 12	4
Clerks	bi 16; bi 17; bi 18	bi 14; bi 17		bi 18	4
Response total	8	7	3	2	*20*\12

Note: response total (in italics) may be more than number of respondents due to multiple replies

As shown 12 of the 18 interviewees gave replies relevant to skill construction. Despite the mixture of responses the majority of those interviewed made some reference to a relationship between a skilled job and a substantial period of training, a finding which supports the results of Penn and Francis (1994) who found in their study into skill (as part of the SCELI project) that:

> ... over three-quarters of the respondents in Rochdale characterised a skilled job in terms of training in some form. (Penn and Francis, 1994: 224)

The majority of the 12 responses from Bristol Insurance linked skill to either the length of training undergone by a particular *individual* (which links skill more with labour economists notion of human capital); the length of time taken to build up technical knowledge of the *task* (linking skill more with the industrial sociologists) or a mixture of these two. In addition there were two quotes which recognised the importance of social forces shaping what is considered a skilled job. Turning to training and the primary data, one clerk commented:

> Q: What do you think it is about certain jobs that class them as skilled as opposed to unskilled?

> Ehm, I don't know. You generally tend to think of skilled people using their brains and unskilled using their hands. But then there are skilled manual jobs aren't there? I suppose a lot of that comes out of training [What, the manual work?] No, being skilled, whether you're skilled or not. I mean, *to get a skilled job you have to be trained*. I think. (BI 16)

This response illustrates the difficulty some of those interviewed had in conceptualising skill, with this respondent first explaining skill by reference to a mental/manual split (which, as the next chapter shows, is a common differentiator between office and factory work), before concluding that this is too simple and that a skilled job is one which requires training. One manager went further, defining a skilled job as one which not simply required training but training of a specific type and length:

> Q: What is it about certain jobs that define them as skilled?
> (long pause) I suppose *jobs that have got a certain level of skill require eh require training* which could obviously be anything from a few weeks on the job training at one end of the scale through to the need to have a couple of degrees in the Institute of Marketing maybe at the other end of the scale. Whereas with an unskilled job theoretically you ought to be able to go in, do it from day one with a relatively small amount of training. (BI 11)

What is apparent here is that skill is defined with reference to human capital (through length of training), but this is not training which is done in isolation, rather it is training which is relevant to a particular (and technical) task. Thus the conceptualisation of a skilled job combines elements of both the labour economist (Becker, 1964) which is evident by reference to length of training *and* the industrial sociologist (Braverman, 1974) which is evident through training for a particular task. The association found in the previous set of comments between a skilled job and a lengthy, specialised, training was evident in another response:

> For me, *a skilled job is something where you have to have training*, either external training or on the job training, which if you came in on day one and you were asked to do that job, without having met that situation before you actually wouldn't know where to begin. I mean if you go into the manufacturing side you've got you're assembly line, *it's also the period of time that it would take to learn the job as well*, because certain jobs take longer to learn than others and if you're just adding a widget, then I think that's going to be a reasonably quick thing to learn... However if your trying to, if you don't just look after the widget, but you look after the wombat and the widget, that requires a degree of skill because you would actually have to work out the best way of putting all those bits together to make the thing work in the right fashion, whereas if you've only got the one bit to do, that's as far as I'm concerned unskilled whereas *if you've actually got a combination of things to do then you have to work out which is the best way of doing those*

things it may be that it's set down for you but you also have to know if you don't do it in that order it will have a dramatic effect. That's a skill. (BI 10)

Again, the complexity surrounding skill is immediately evident from this quotation with this respondent working through a definition of a skilled job which is seen to include references to building up human capital, exercising technical knowledge and carrying some responsibility. There is also a hint at a more Bravermanian task centred definition of skill, where a skilled worker has control over the conception and execution of the task. This is evident from the section where the respondent comments: "*if you've actually got a combination of things to do then you have to work out which is the best way of doing those things*". In other words a skilled job would be where one had to have knowledge of a series of productive activities, personally carry out such activities and carry responsibility for such activities. The shift in emphasis away from length of training per se to technical knowledge of the task at hand was evident in a number of other comments:

> Q: What do you think it is about specific jobs that define them as skilled?
> I don't honestly know.. . Maybe as I go on, I've only been here a year. *Maybe as I go on I'll learn more technically*, maybe I would be classified more as skilled. (BI 14)

> Q: What do you think it is about certain jobs that defines them as skilled?
> (long pause) There are certain jobs in our section which require more skill than others, which are *more technical,* more complicated. [What do you mean by technical?] You have to have a *greater knowledge of the computer system*, ehm, some jobs are very repetitive, some people do very repetitive jobs, really mundane jobs which will take them a few weeks to learn and then they can do the job, ehm other jobs you're learning all the time, sometimes you don't even ever come across the same thing twice. So they are quite involved. (BI 13)

> Q: What do you think it is about certain jobs that classes them as skilled?"
> Well, I couldn't be a marketing manager. That's a skilled job, I couldn't be a marketing manager. *I wouldn't know what to do.* I think you've got skilled areas. I don't know if all the jobs in the area are skilled. [So what is it exactly that makes certain jobs skilled?]. In accounting I suppose if you have done accounting *exams* you know the rules of taxation and that's important when you get to managers. (BI 15)

Here, again, there is reference to the length of time required to learn the job, although there is a shift in emphasis from external training to learning on the job, the common theme of time required to be proficient in a job is still evident. What is more interesting is the greater concentration on the relationship between skill and the task, articulated through the requirement for more technical knowledge. The meaning behind the term technical is important because it can be used in a general sense to refer to complexity of tasks per se or in a more particular sense to refer to the complexity of a *mechanical* task. This distinction is significant because while both senses are evident in the responses from Bristol Insurance only the mechanical is used by those from Bristol Laminated. Further analysis of the keyword "technical" illustrates that it has two main uses:

technical a. of or in a particular art, science, handicraft, etc., (*technical terms, skill, difficulty*). (OED 1989)
technical a. **1.** complex, complicated, detailed, intricate, specialised: *This is a technical matter, not easily understood by the layman.* **2.** mechanical, applied, industrial, polytechnic, technologic(al): *We thought he would be happier attending a technical school.* (Oxford Thesaurus 1991)

It is clear that of the two meanings BI 13 and BI 15 (quoted above) are using the primary meaning implying that any complex task (such as running a computer system or tax accountancy) may be described as "technical". However, other respondents from Bristol Insurance use technical knowledge more in the sense of applied mechanical knowledge. For example BI 10, whose comments were analysed earlier, was seen to use a mechanical example (technical knowledge of an assembly line production process) to differentiate skilled from unskilled jobs. This association of applied technical knowledge to skill was also evident in comments from other Bristol Insurance respondents:

> Q: What do you think it is about jobs that defines them as skilled?
> Well, to me *it's like somebody whose got a trade*, like a carpenter or somebody that's actually got *a trade so they've got a skill behind them*. Anything from carpet fitting to carpentry. (BI 17)

> Q: What do you think it is about certain jobs that define them as skilled?
> That's interesting, *when I think of skilled labour I think of manual work* and that could be anything from a senior mechanic to a brain surgeon I suppose. It's *something that involves using your hands*, taking it broader, I suppose it's to do with specialising... I think you tend to call people specialists in the financial service sector, you wouldn't say he's a skilled worker or something because that automatically to me anyway, and I think to most people would conjure up sort of *manual type job*. (BI 6)

Here the emphasis is seen to focus on a Bravermanian task centred definition of skill, with the idea that a skilled job is a trade or a manual job which requires conception and execution of learned technical knowledge. It could also be argued that the respondents have been influenced by political/social definitions of skill, with the stress not only on possessing learned knowledge but, crucially, executing such knowledge with one's hands, an idea which appears to have been strongly influenced by notions of the dexterity of skilled craftsmen.

The other skill association which received more than one reply linked a skilled job to the degree of responsibility. This was alluded to in the earlier comments of BI 10, where a skilled job was seen to be one which not only required relatively lengthy training and technical knowledge, but also carried some responsibility. Such an association was also noted by two other respondents:

> Q: What do you think it is about jobs that defines them as skilled?
> Well, the *level of initiative* that someone's required to take and the *level of problem solving* involved and the *level of communicating*. (BI 9)

> Q: What do you think it is about jobs that defines them as skilled?
> I think *being able to apply work in practice that you've learned* (Does your boss's job require more skill than yours?) not really, although I suppose there must be to a varying degree, *there's more responsibility* that goes with it... (BI 7)

This association of responsibility with a skilled job supports the results of Penn and Francis (1994) who found "responsibility" to be twelfth out of sixteen classified replies as to what constituted a skilled job. In my data the skill aspect of responsibility was seen to be linked to an occupational hierarchy and (perhaps reflecting their place in such a hierarchy) was recognised by three higher graded employees.

There were, finally, two responses from discussions on what constituted a skilled job which were not shared by any other respondents:

> Q: What do you think it is about certain jobs that decides this job's skilled, that job isn't?
> *Convention* I think, I think everyone's got skills to work no matter where they work and I think it's just through... *academic snobbery* is one of them... I don't know I think *it's historical*. (BI 12)

> Q: What is about certain jobs that define them as skilled?
> Ehm, it's difficult to say, I mean, as I say, I don't think I do a skilled job, I don't know what a skilled job is as such. To me, *skill is acquired through experience*, skill, as I say like an artist or a footballer or even an actor, something like that, is a specialised job in some way. *You've got the gift you can't necessarily get the gift, you've just got it*. Its difficult to say skill and experience, I mean anybody with *experience* can possibly do any job that they're *trained* to do. I don't think I've got any gift in any way that I can do this job better than anyone else. I just think I've been brought up the right way to do this job, through the previous jobs and obviously schooling, and it's just the experience I've gained along the way. (BI 18)

The first of these comments, from BI 12, shows a recognition that skills may be determined through a social process (what I have called the political/social)

(Rubery, 1978; More, 1980, 1982; Penn, 1983, 1985; Thompson, 1988; Steiger, 1993) and the second response, from BI 18, shows the complexity surrounding skill by referring to a number of factors which combine to create a skilled job. The data from Bristol Insurance, therefore, produced a number of descriptions and explanations of what constitutes a skilled job and was characterised by a complexity which was evident from the fact that some interviewees worked through their ideas on skill in even quite short replies. This data also illustrates the difficulty in applying any clear cut theoretical skill dichotomy to actual data. Respondents are seen to hold views which contain elements of all three theories of skill conceptualisation discussed earlier, with reference being made to the importance of training (human capital), the importance of possessing technical knowledge (task centred) and the importance of possessing a recognised craft (political/social).

Bristol Laminated

Respondents from Bristol Laminated were seen to share some skill conceptualisations with respondents from Bristol Insurance, but with an important difference, while both linked length of training and technical knowledge to a skilled job respondents from Bristol Laminated mentioned the latter more frequently, with particular emphasis on a Bravermanian task centred mechanistic conceptualisation of skill. The summary position is illustrated in table 5.2, which shows that 7 respondents linked a skilled job with the possession of technical knowledge (often linked with a trade); 4 with the requirement for training or experience and 2 with responsibility.

Table 5.2
Bristol Laminated, classifications of a skilled job

	Technical knowledge/trade	Experience/ training	Responsibility	Total
Managers	bl 1; bl 6	bl 6		2
Workers	bl 2; bl 5; bl 7; bl 9; bl 10	bl 2; bl 8; bl 10	bl 3; bl 4	8
Response total	7	4	2	*13*\10

Note: response total (in italics) may be more than number of respondents due to multiple replies

This emphasis on the importance of an apprenticeship backed trade in defining a skilled job also supports the work of Penn and Francis (1994) who, while finding that the most common association across all occupational groups was between skill and training, also found that:

> Manual workers, both the skilled and the nonskilled, were also significantly likelier to mention apprenticeships. (Penn and Francis, 1994: 226)

Turning to the primary data from Bristol Laminated and to the comments which associated skill with technical knowledge and/or a trade, references included the following:

> I see electrician as a skilled job, now engineer I don't think is skilled, no that's wrong, its semi-skilled isn't it because *the machinery's doing the work*. Once you've got your template made the machine does the work. But with an electrician, something like that *you're using your hands all the time*, aren't you. I think to me that's more of a skill. [What about unskilled?] *I'm unskilled because I haven't got a trade.* But then I wouldn't say I was unskilled but I am classed as unskilled. *There is no trade for what we're doing*. (BL 9)

There are a number of important points to emerge from this response. Firstly, the complexity surrounding skill conceptualisation is strongly evident, with this respondent recognising an official skill classification system *and* providing his own definitions of what makes a job skilled. Secondly, the central importance of technical knowledge of machinery to his definition of skill is evident, with this respondent using a definition of skill similar to that of Braverman (1974) where skill is seen to be not just knowledge of a machine but a job which allows the *application* of such knowledge, hence an electrician is seen as skilled because one is continually exercising one's knowledge through one's hands. Thirdly, there is an awareness of the importance of occupational closure in deciding what is classed as a skilled job (Rubery, 1978; More, 1980, 1982; Penn, 1983, 1985; Thompson, 1988). This is evident from his denial that he (and his job) are unskilled but recognition that they may be classed as such because "*There is no trade for what we're doing*". This association of skill with applied technical knowledge but recognition that such an association has to work within the confines of a labour market shaped by occupational closure was apparent in another set of comments:

> I'm semi-skilled, I'm semi-skilled in my field, outside of here I'm nothing. *Outside of this trade I'm nothing...* Unskilled work is building site work, labouring, not plasterers and that and not plumbers and electricians. [What about skilled jobs?] I would classify skilled jobs as electricians, eh printers. (BL 10)

Again, a Bravermanian conceptualisation of skill is utilised, with skilled work seen as work which requires detailed technical knowledge associated with jobs which (traditionally) require an apprenticeship. His own work is classed as semi-skilled, being between skilled occupations which require an official technical training such as electricians and printers and unskilled jobs such as labouring. He does, however, class his work as a "trade", but, I would argue, uses this word more in the general sense of an occupation than in the specific sense of a craft trade:

trade n. **1.** business, esp. mechanical or mercantile employment opp to profession, carried on as means of livelihood or profit (*a carpenter, a butcher, by trade*); skilled handicraft (*learn a trade*). (OED 1989)
trade n. **1.** commerce, business, traffic, exchange, barter, dealing(s), buying and selling, merchandising, marketing, mercantilism, truck: *We are establishing trade with Eastern Europe*. **2.** calling, occupation, pursuit, work, business, employment, line (of work), metier, job, vocation, craft, career, profession,: *Just what trade are you engaged in?* (Oxford Thesaurus 1991)

Of these two meanings I would argue that BL 10 sees his job as a trade in the sense of his "work" as opposed to a skilled handicraft. The discussions on the association between skill and possession of a trade led some of the respondents to compare their own job with that of printers employed at Bristol Laminated. These comparisons continued to demonstrate a perceived association between a skilled job and the necessity of possessing and applying task based technical knowledge but at the same time demonstrated an awareness of the strength of the political/social process which classifies certain jobs as skilled. For example, the worker who is quoted immediately above (BL 10) gave the following comments when comparing his job to that done by the printers:

> The type of work what they the (lacquers) do is the same as what the printers do... (goes on to talk of printers attitude) *we're the skillsmen, you're crap like*, it's always been that way. You've got the same difference between office staff and us as you have between tradesmen and us. (BL 10)

This provides an example of the recognition that while both jobs require a similar amount of "skill" (in the sense of applied technical knowledge) the printers possess a "trade" and, through articulating opinions such as "*we're the skillsmen, you're crap like*", the animosity which is created within the workplace is clearly apparent. This belief that the work done by operatives in the "semi-skilled" part of the production process was as technically complex as that of the printers was shared by another respondent:

> Q: What do you think it is about a job that defines it as skilled?
> A very good question, I don't, I can't honestly see the answer. There's some of the machines here, *I suppose they're classed as semi skilled* but eh, in my opinion they demand quite *a lot of skill to run them, in fact more skill than the printers*. Perhaps I shouldn't be talking like that, but that's the way it feels to me, that there's something not quite right somewhere. [Skill in the sense of technical knowledge?] There's a lot of *technical knowledge* that they require on these machines and what a lot of people here have thought in the past with

> some of these *so called skilled jobs* it's only the fact that they've had an *apprenticeship on them.* I mean the people on the (laminating) machines do the same thing really but they haven't gone to college and whatever. (BL 7)

The first point to note here is the degree to which skills are associated with the task carried out on the machinery - it is the *machine* which is seen as being skilled - "There's some of the machines here, *I suppose they're classed as semi skilled*". The second point to note is the strong association between a skilled job and technical knowledge. He argues that if skill was simply based on the degree of technical knowledge then the laminating jobs (which are classed as semi skilled) are as, if not more, skilled, than printing. Thirdly, he recognises the importance of political/social forces which act (through apprenticeship) to close off segments of the labour market and ensure that printers retain their skilled status. The animosity surrounding this issue of the degree of skill in terms of technical knowledge required and what is officially classed and rewarded as skill was also evident in further comments from this, and another, respondent:

> ... Ehm that's been one of the things we've thought here in the past. It's strange you should say this really because you get like *printers, as you know are tradesmen, and they get paid as such for being tradesmen.* But we've got *people here and their machines are more complex than what the printing machines are*, and it's been a sort of bone of contention for years. It's just sort of not recognised as such. We used to feel years ago, I mean when I started here some of the printers, they were tradesmen and they deserved to be treated as such because *they used to do everything from start to finish on their machines*. Although the machines now look much more complex than they were then in effect I should think, really and truly, they're easier to run now than they ever were for the older people, because they used to do *all the preparation of the stuff and setting their own print* but all that's done for them now. I mean we feel that they're only more or less *machine minders* now rather than running the machines. I mean the machines more or less run themselves a lot nowadays. (BL 7)

> Q: When you look at the printers is it clear to you that their jobs require more skill?
> Some of those machines what we, some of the converting machines are far, far superior and sophisticated to them... My opinion is it's (printing) not the trade it was 10 years ago, simply because *they don't mix their inks*, all they are, *they just watch their machines same as what I do*. (BL 9)

Again, the Bravermanian conceptualisation of skill is immediately evident, with skill being linked to conception and execution of task orientated technical knowledge. Indeed, under this definition of skill these workers can understand and respect the previous standing of printers as skilled craftsmen: *"they used to do everything from start to finish on their machines"*. The animosity comes from an awareness that despite the fact these jobs have (in a Bravermanian sense) become deskilled to such an extent that "*they* (the printers) *just watch their machines* ", they (because of the collusion or conflict between unions and management) retain the status of skilled jobs. This provides a good example of the distinction, noted in the previous section on, which was drawn by More (1980) between "genuine skill" and "socially constructed skill". More (1980) writes:

> ... there are two different routes to skill... (one route) to genuine skill, required because of the complexity of the machines or tasks in question. The other path leads, via perhaps a strong trade union which upholds high wages among certain groups of workers, to a differentiation of workers into grades, some of which are better paid and are regarded as more skilled; management may, or may not, play a collusive part in this process - for instance it might accept the situation if it thought that it would gain through giving workers a channel to promotion, however artificial. (More, 1980: 16)

The workers at Bristol Laminated, therefore, recognise that deskilling in a Bravermanian sense has taken place but also recognise (and to an extent resent) the political and social forces which ensure these jobs remain classified as skilled. An example of this process from the world of printing is available from Cockburn (1983) who, in her study of printworkers, found that the introduction of computers had deskilled the workforce. She quoted one compositor as saying:

> There was a hell of a lot of pride in the old work. With the new system, it's taken the soul out of the job. I don't buck against it. It's secured my livelihood. But if there is one thing I absolutely dislike about it, that's it, the soullessness of it. (Compositor, Cockburn, 1983: 116)

This illustrates a recognition of deskilling but, as Cockburn goes on to point out, the union had managed to retain the status and pay of a skilled job:

> *Skill in the man* was now out of kilter with *skill in the job*, and the union was only with great difficulty ensuring that *skill as a class political concept* held line in the turmoil of this employer inspired revolution. (Cockburn, 1983: 116, emphasis in original)

The printers, then, offer a good example of worker's combining to defend their skill status (Rubery, 1978; More, 1980, 1982; Penn, 1983, 1985; Thompson, 1988). As the comments from Bristol Laminated show, however, such a defence may well create antagonisms within the workforce. It could be the case, therefore, that management deliberately collude in this process to pacify one group of workers and, by so doing, divide and sow discontent amongst the workforce as a whole (Edwards, 1979; More, 1980; Nichols, 1986).

Turning to the association between skill and training (also found in the data from Bristol Insurance) the production manager at Bristol Laminated gave the following comments:

> I guess I tend to classify *the unskilled jobs as the ones which can be taught in a matter of a couple of weeks*, whereas the skilled ones, in relation to my department I would say an operator was skilled because it would take say 8 weeks to train him and then he needs to have a certain amount of time on different machines and then *it probably takes him several years to gain enough experience to become a successful operator*. But if you were comparing him with say a printer who has to go through an *apprenticeship* then he would be classified as unskilled. [So it takes 5 years to fully learn the machine?] Not so much the machine as the materials going through it and the different problems you might encounter. So you could operate the machine within 8 weeks but to actually gain the experience of *what to do when you encounter this particular problem with this particular material can take years*. (BL 6)

Here, then, training and experience are linked to skill, with the discriminator being both the length and type of training which is involved, with an "official" apprenticeship leading to a higher skill classification. There is also recognition of the existence of an official skill classification system which, despite the fact that it takes "several years" experience on a laminating machine to become an efficient operator, places laminating work and knowledge as semi-skilled and printing work as skilled. This belief in a relationship between skill and length of training was shared by three of the workers. The comments of BL 10 have been analysed above (where this respondent was seen to associate skill with training for a trade) two other workers gave the following comments:

> Q: What decided which job is classed as skilled, which as semi skilled?
> I suppose it's *degree of learning*, that comes with the job, the *amount of time it takes to learn that job*. (BL 8)

> Q: What sort of jobs would you call skilled in the factory, you know, is an operator clearly more skilled than an assistant?"
> Oh yes, *he's come through the system*, yeah and usually *an operator would be of quite a few years standing with that machine*. I mean I started about sixteen years ago and up till recently it was the same three guys, I was the assistant and the guy that was the second op, he got made redundant so I've moved up so hopefully when the operator, when his day comes, for whatever reason, retirement, wants to leave, redundancy, then I hope to move up to that slot. (BL 10)

The first quotation links skill with the "*degree of learning*" and the "*amount of time it takes to learn*" a job. This association between skill and length of time on the job also emerges from the second quotation where the respondent distinguishes between a skilled operator and an unskilled assistant by the fact that "*an operator would be of quite a few years standing with that machine*". This supports the findings from Bristol Insurance, where respondents were seen to associate skill with length of training/time it took to learn the job. Another theme, common to both Bristol Insurance and Bristol Laminated respondents, was the association between skill and degree of responsibility:

> Q: Does skill increase from an assistant to operator?
> Oh yeah, yeah definitely, obviously *when you're an operator you carry a lot more responsibility* than you do as an assistant, as an operator you have one maybe two men working under you so you've got to look after their interests as well as your own and *you're also responsible for what comes off that machine* as an operator and your differential in pay reflects that. (BL 3)

> Q: Is an operator clearly more skilled than an assistant?
> Oh yeah, *they obviously got responsibility of the machine*. There's all different settings, they've got to set the tensions different, heat settings, there's a lot to it, *it's a lot more technical.* (BL 4)

Similar to respondents from Bristol Insurance there is a perceived association between degree of responsibility and degree to which a job is seen as skilled. Also, like Bristol Insurance, this increased responsibility and skill is linked to hierarchy, with one of the reasons for an operator to be considered more skilled than an assistant being because their job carries more responsibility.

The first point to note from the Bristol Laminated data was the continual association between skill and technical knowledge of machinery and, given the nature of the work done by respondents this is, perhaps, not too surprising. The second point to note is the consistency of comments which described a Bravermanian conceptualisation of a skilled job, with a skilled job being a job which required the conception and execution of task based technical knowledge. The third, and given the experience of these laminating workers with the printers, again perhaps not surprising, point to note is the recognition of the depth and strength of political/social skill construction.

Turning to a comparison of Bristol Laminated with Bristol Insurance data the point which emerges most strongly is the essential similarity of opinion amongst Bristol Laminated respondents compared to the fragmentation of responses from those at Bristol Insurance. While the responses from the office workers of Bristol Insurance contained elements linking a skilled job to all three schools of skill conceptualisation: training (human capital), technical knowledge required for the task (Bravermanian) and importance of possessing a trade (Bravermanian; political/social), the comments of Bristol Laminated respondents (while recognising the importance of a trade and the strength of political/social forces) continually concentrated on a Bravermanian task centred conceptualisation of skill. Why should this be the case? I would argue that one reason why the comments from the factory workers of Bristol Laminated fit more easily into a Bravermanian technical task centred theory of skill is because of the essential similarity between the nature of their work and the nature and focus of Braverman's research. Much of the empirical work done in the field of skills has concentrated on technical work in general and the work of factories in particular and even, as is the case with Braverman, when clerical work is included, it is often conceptualised within a framework which has been heavily influenced by technical images of the craftsman and artisan. Given this, it is perhaps not too surprising that respondents who have worked and continue to work in an environment which recognises and rewards technical abilities and knowledge (and where new machinery and working practices are seen to threaten the nature of work and previous skill demarcation lines) tend to perceive skills in a similar way to Braverman. This can be contrasted with the case of Bristol Insurance, where the comments on skill are more ambiguous, containing elements of the three skill theory schools. I would argue, and am supported by data in the next section, that this reflects the greater confusion felt about skills by such non-technical workers. People who work in offices draw up their skill map by reference to their own skills (which are often social) and, crucially, the official versions of skilled work have been created by a series of political and social processes which have usually concentrated on the conflict (or co-operation) of management and unions in (usually male) technical environments. When these respondents, then, come to examine what is a skilled job, they are influenced by a number of (at times conflicting) considerations: what skills do they have and how are these recognised and rewarded (hence, perhaps, the importance given to qualifications, with overtones of recognition of human capital theory); what skills do they see recognised and rewarded outside their working environment (with the potential influence of the continual political/social processes which decide pay in different industrial sectors) and what skills do they perceive as having been recognised in the past (with the potential for the debate around the loss of skills in certain "traditional" industries to be influential). The next section moves on from perceptions of what constitutes a skilled job to perceptions of what skills are held by the respondents themselves.

5.4 Perceptions of skills

Bristol Insurance

The data which emerged from discussions of the skills held and skills which are perceived as being necessary for work in Bristol Insurance fell into two (broad) categories - social skills and technical skills. Table 5.3 (and the later table 5.4) detail the breakdown of this data.

Table 5.3
Bristol Insurance, breakdown of social skills

	Communication		Comm'n skills as "common sense"	"Female" skills	Total
	People skills	Good on the phone			
Managers	bi 1; bi 5; bi 6; bi 7; bi 11	bi 2; bi 3		bi 11	7
Supervisors	bi 4; bi 13; bi 15	bi 7; bi 13;		bi 7; bi 15	4
Clerks	bi 14; bi 16; bi 17; bi 18	bi 17; bi 18	bi 14; bi 17; bi 18	bi 14	4
Response total	18		3	4	25\15

Note: response total (in italics) may be more than number of respondents due to multiple replies

Table 5.3 shows that 15 of the 18 interviewees, in discussing on skill, highlighted the importance of social skills and that the most common skill personally held or perceived as necessary for office work was the social skill of "communication". The responses fell into three sections: communication (15 respondents); communication skills as "common sense" (3 respondents) and "female" skills (4 respondents). Turning firstly to the importance of communication skills, these fell into two categories, those who made reference to "people skills" and those who made reference to being "good on the phone".

Typical comments from discussions included:

> I've always worked in the service industries so a lot of my skills are *people skills*, I've learned a lot more about computers because we use them all the time... there's lots of different systems which are new but mostly I'm a *people person*. [Meaning what?] I would rather sit down and talk to somebody than write a memo to them, I would rather phone them up and get the information, I'm quite good at finding out things. (BI 4)

> It's particularly important to be able to *express yourself* and be able to handle yourself. (BI 2)

I would say it helps if they've done supervising and perhaps studied, I would say that helps. (pause) You need to be self motivated because you're left to do your own work really... You need, I was going to say numerate but I'm hopeless at maths, but you need to be able work to some degree with figures.. *be good on the phone*, be able to write letters, be able to *deal with people really*. (BI 13)

Ehm, you have to be good with figures, you have to be able to concentrate. Ehm, you have to have *good communication skills to deal with the people around the department*. Ehm, calm, not to get yourself into a flap. That sort of thing basically. (BI 16)

The clear emphasis here is on the social skills related to communication, which are seen as being a vital part of the skills portfolio of office workers and important for office work. The frequency with which such "people skills" were mentioned highlights one of the weakness's of Braverman's craft based definition of skill noted earlier. As Burchell et al (1994) note:

... perhaps the most telling criticism of the deskilling thesis is the one-sided nature of skill which is deployed. The vision of skill adopted by Braverman is that of the individualistic mechanic/artisan... (Burchell et al, 1994: 164)

The skills which the office respondents of Bristol Insurance saw themselves as possessing and the skills which are seen as necessary for office work are, to an extent, beyond the scope of Braverman's mechanical task based definition of skill and provide evidence for the need for skill definition to be expanded to include social as well as technical skills. The prevailing strength, however, of the influence of both the Bravermanian association of skill with technical craft skills and of the political/social association of skill with apprenticed trades, is evident from other comments where respondents recognised they possessed certain abilities but were uncertain about what they counted as *specific* "skills":

Q: What sort of skills do you think someone needs to do your job?
Eh, you do come in contact with the clients and often they get a bit irate, you have to be a bit *patient*. Ehm, try not to get too irritable... so *patience, tact, common sense, just common sense really*. (BI 14)

Ehm, I don't think you need any skill as such. I just think you need the *basic common sense* and eh, basically what I've had, I've always worked in an office, its just experience. Being able to *get on with people* obviously helps but the two main things are common sense and experience. [What about knowing how to answer the phone?] Again, I think that's *common sense*. I mean being at *home*, using the telephone to make a complaint... *it's all common sense... there's no actual skill involved as such, it's just being patient*. (BI 18)

Really only to be accurate and conscientious (prompted about phone) yeah, I suppose so. [Did you learn anything from the telephone course]. I think so, a lot of it's *common sense*. I mean you don't shout and be rude to a broker. [What about common sense?] I should think if you've never worked in an office or never had much to do with phone work you could treat them (the customers) completely wrong, not meaning to but you could go wrong on the phone. (BI 17)

The first point to note is the grade of the respondents who gave these replies: they were all lower graded clerks. Thus it tended to be the lower graded staff who, while recognising that being patient, getting on well with people and communicating effectively are important to office work were unsure whether these were "real" skills and so tended to describe such abilities as "common sense". The fact that two of these respondents classified a skilled job in terms of technical/trade requirements could be interpreted as demonstrating the strength of Bravermanian and political/ social skill construction working in concert. The second, and connected, point concerns gender. Two of these three respondents were women and, as the majority of clerks are women (Davies, 1979; Department of Employment 1992[26]), this reluctance to recognise such abilities as skilled could be influenced by the fact that women and their work are more likely to be classed as unskilled (Lazonick, 1979; Phillips and Taylor, 1980; Pollert, 1981; Armstrong, 1982; Cockburn, 1981, 1983, 1986; Manwaring and Wood, 1985; Curran, 1988; Jenson, 1989; Horrell et al, 1990). In discussions on skill some of the interviews explored the issue of gender:

Q: Have women got any skills in common?
Yeah, cause women like to *tidy up and keep tidy*. They are *tidy people* and accounting, office work requires you to be *tidy*. You've got to see beyond the surface, you've got to go in deeper, till you find out what the problem is. I think women are more interested in that sort of thing. Men just tend to, eh, don't want to try. (BI 15)

Q: Do you think there are any skills which you as a woman possess?
(long pause) I don't know, it's easy enough to say that if you're a woman you have the ability to *listen more and be a bit more sensitive* to what's going on around you but I think that really depends on the person, you can have a really hard headed woman and a really sort of sensitive man... you might get people's attention but not necessarily for the right reasons. (BI 7)

Q: How do you go about recruitment in your department (of 3-5 people)
... I've got an in built bias toward employing women, it's simply because of

[26]The Department of Employment's labour force survey (1992) showed that from 1984 - 1990 the proportion of workers in the occupational classification "clerical and related" was between 76% and 78% female.

> my experience at the University and you know as I said earlier women on courses worked harder, more conscientiously, turned in better work and eh for these sort of jobs where there's quite a lot of *attention to detail* you also want initiative and you want to know that when I'm not here it all keeps rolling. (BI 11)

> Q: Do you think women have special skills and that's why this type of job has more women?
> To be honest I don't think so. I think perhaps women can be a bit *more sympathetic*, in a way. I think they can be *a little more patient*. (BI 14)

The abilities which are seen to be "female" are seen to relate to "tidiness", "sensitivity", "sympathy", "attention to detail" and "patience". A common characteristic of these abilities is that they are "social" skills which are not formally recognised (Phillips and Taylor, 1980; Curran, 1988; Jenson, 1989; Horrell et al, 1990) by official classifications systems and official qualifications. This lack of formal recognition is compounded by the fact that (as some of the above data has shown) some women themselves do not recognise such abilities as skilled. This is supported by the work of Horrell et al (1990), who found that while women were more likely to stress social abilities as being necessary for their job there was:

> ... a tendency by women and part-timers to downgrade the skill level of their jobs... for example women or part-timers may be less likely to recognise that they have responsibilities in a job or to stress the importance of various factors and qualities. (Horrell et al, 1990: 211)

I would argue that these abilities and the fact that they are not recognised as "skilled" (both by those who hold such skills and those who decide what is classed as skilled) leads to the possibility that they are examples of office based tacit social skills. While most of the work done on tacit skills has involved research in either blue collar manufacturing firms and work (Manwaring, 1984; Manwaring and Wood, 1985; Dick and Morgan, 1987; Grieco, 1987; Steiger, 1993) these data illustrate that the concept is equally applicable in offices. Manwaring and Wood (1985) write of tacit skills:

> Tacit skills refer to the feel and discretion which form the basis for subjectivity in even non-skilled work and are vital to efficient performance in all work situations... An important implication of this conception of tacit skills is that the exercise of skill should not necessarily be seen as a conscious activity. (Manwaring and Wood, 1985: 177, 179)

I would suggest that when office workers describe learned abilities such as patience, sympathy and effective communication (which are "vital to efficient performance") as "common sense" they are not aware skill is being exercised. Skill is so linked up with historically influenced technical task based definitions that these abilities are seen as "natural" and therefore "unskilled" (Cockburn, 1981; Milkman, 1983; Jenson, 1989). There could be a case, as has been argued earlier, for shifting (or at least expanding) the definition of skill to include such non-technical abilities. Perhaps such an expansion of what is classed as a "skill" would also provoke a rethinking of the degree to which clerical work has been "deskilled" (Braverman, 1974; Crompton and Reid, 1982; Crompton and Jones, 1984). For example, in their study (introduced earlier in this chapter) on deskilling in clerical work Crompton and Jones (1984) used a task centred Bravermanian definition of skill, which concentrated on the degree of control each worker has over the conception and execution of their part in the production process. They write that:

> Our initial analysis will retain the task-centred approach... We regard "control" as essential to the definition of skill. (Crompton and Jones, 1984: 59)

And they go on to conclude that:

> In summary, therefore, the vast majority of the clerical and administrative employees we interviewed were in jobs that required them to exercise little in the way of skill; work tasks were on the whole governed by explicit rules and few could exercise discretion or self-control in their work. (Crompton and Jones, 1984: 64)

I would suggest, while not disputing that automation has had a (perhaps debilitating) effect on lower graded non-manual work, and agreeing with Lane (1988b) that the issue of proletarianisation is complex, that one of the reasons deskilling is so marked in this study is the narrowness of the definition of skill (Burchell et al, 1994). By concentrating on the mainly objective *technical* aspects of tasks, such as coding, batching and the updating of information these authors effectively play down the subjective *social* aspects of clerical and office work and the consequent *social* abilities of office workers, such as patience and good, effective, oral communication. Such tasks and competencies emerged strongly from Bristol Insurance respondents and, if included in the definition of "skill", may well lead to a rethinking of the extent to which office work has been "deskilled". There is another way in which non-technical skills influence the (particularly Bravermanian) debate which surrounds skill. Braverman argued that management were taking control over the mental aspects of work and leaving the workers as merely "machine minders". Yet if office skills include (indeed primary emphasis is placed upon) communication skills then this increased subjectivity may represent a barrier to managerial control. This point was made by Cressey and MacInnes (1980) and Manwaring and Wood (1985) with especial reference to blue collar tacit skills, but is equally true of office communication skills, whether they are consciously recognised by individuals (if not by "official" skill categories) or unconscious abilities. For if the task of the modern office is to facilitate effective communication between individuals then the skill, by lying *within* each individual, increases the subjectivity of that individual and will, therefore, be especially difficult for management to control.

Turning to the second main theme which emerged from the responses on skills held and skills necessary for work in Bristol Insurance, 13 respondents made 23 references to what I have described as technical skills, including, as table 5.4 shows, keyboard skills (8 respondents); qualifications (7 respondents); literacy (5 respondents) and education (3 respondents). I am using the term "technical" here not in the sense of applied mechanical knowledge (an interpretation evident in many of the comments from Bristol Laminated respondents) but as both a contrast to the more social skills described by respondents and in recognition of the more tangible nature of these abilities.

Table 5.4
Bristol Insurance, breakdown of technical skills

	Qualifications	Education	Literacy	Keyboard skills	Total
Managers	bil; bi 2; bi 6	bi 1; bi2	bi 1; bi 8; bi 11	bi 1; bi 3; bi 8; bi 11	6
Supervisors	bi 4; bi 13; bi 15		bi 13	bi 4; bi 13; bi 15	3
Clerks	bi 16	bi 14	bi 18	bi 17	4
Response total	7	3	5	8	*23*\13

Note: response total (in italics) may be more than number of respondents due to multiple replies

Two key points are immediately apparent from this data. The first is the continuing significance which is attached to communication, with the emergent emphasis being on technical skills which facilitate effective communication. So while office workers placed stress on their social skills such as being "good with people" they also saw as significant the ability to master the range of more technical tools which facilitated such communication and thus placed emphasis on practical skills such as literacy (signified by possession of qualifications) and working with computers (primarily written communication through use of a keyboard). The second point is the apparent higher grade/lower grade split, with supervisory and managerial respondents making more frequent reference to education and qualifications. Such employees may well emphasise the importance of qualifications because they themselves possess such certificates and by citing them as important "skills" they are reassuring themselves that they have built up human capital and are therefore "skilled". They may also, however, use such technical abilities as signifiers of certain social characteristics (Gintis, 1971; Bowles and Gintis, 1975). Bowles and Gintis (1975) write of education and qualifications:

> ... schooling may increase the ease with which the employer can extract labour from a worker with given labour power by generating or selecting individual motivational patterns more compatible with the class-based power structure and incentive mechanisms of the enterprise. (Bowles and Gintis, 1975: 80)

These authors see the possession of such skills not as simply transferring information about the ability of a worker but also about the likely productivity of a worker, with possession of qualifications implying possession of a set of values similar to that of the (capitalist) organisation. This point may be linked back to the previous chapter on recruitment where it was argued that one reason why formal networks were more common in offices was that such channels offered a quick guide to qualifications which carried significance both of a candidates acceptability and suitability (Jenkins, 1988). It could be the case, therefore, that higher graded employees in Bristol Insurance were using qualifications and education as signifying both possession of certain objective "tangible" technical competencies (such as being able to write) and as signifying possession of certain social characteristics (such as sharing managerial values). This enables the production and reproduction of both a "stable" and an "able" workforce (Blackburn and Mann, 1979; Morgan and Sayer, 1988).

Turning to the primary data, two managers expressed their belief in the existence and importance of qualifications to office work by reference to the lack of such qualities amongst factory workers:

> Q: How would you describe your average financial sector worker?
> Ehm, taken in the right spirit, I'm sure it will be, I think they have *a higher academic level*, yes? I think they are invariably either more *numerate*, more *literate* or a combination of both... (BI 1)
>
> Q: What sort of skills would you see your average manufacturing worker as possessing?
> If you really take it to the extreme I suppose one has the impression that *they will be less well qualified...* (BI 2)

These responses, given in reply to questions on differences between office and factory workers, are relevant here because of their skill inferences, with office workers seen as possessing more qualifications which are seen to imply greater knowledge of (and aptitude in) channels of communication. Two of the other higher graded staff discussed their own qualifications:

> Q: What skills do you have?
> Well I've got a *diploma in marketing* and I've obviously got a good seven

years experience, so I do understand marketing theory and the practicalities. (BI 2)

Q: Did you have to have qualifications for your job?
Well, I did an *HND in Hotel Management* (laugh) believe it or not, nothing to do with this. And because it was a supervisory position they took that into account. I think usually when you come in here you come in at a lower level. (BI 13)

The first of these responses illustrates a clear link between skill and holding a qualification, with this respondent giving a qualification as his first skill. The second response provides an example of where qualifications are taken as a proxy for skill with this respondent (to her own surprise) finding that a qualification in Hotel Management was recognised as important for a job as unit leader in customer accounts. Other respondents stressed the importance of more general educational skills:

Q: Any skills for general office work?
Literacy, numeracy and a certain sort of methodical approach. (BI 9)

In the job I've got you've got to be able to *read and write*. (BI 18)

Q: What skills are required for anyone coming into this office or any office?
Yeah, *a certain amount of education, a certain standard of education*. Like I said you've got to have *the basics*, be able to read and write, maths and whatever. (BI 14)

Here the emphasis is on having what was described as "basic" skills such as literacy and numeracy, abilities which enable the transferral of information between colleagues and customers and as such form part of a *communication* skills "package" which emerges as the most important capacity necessary for office work. The focus of these employees on qualifications and education could also be interpreted as carrying overtones of a more "human capital" skill association (Becker, 1964).[27]

The last technical ability which was stressed by Bristol Insurance respondents was familiarity with computers in general and keyboard skills in particular. Comments included:

Q: Any basic skills required by all workers here?
Eh, nowadays I'd say *computer skills*... that's a skill that people need, *common sense* and learning to get along with other people. (BI 17)

---

[27]For more on the particular role of education in increasing skills see Penn and Scattergood (1985), Penn (1990) and Penn et al (1992).

Q: What about more office based skills, do you think there are general skills you think you need to work in your little bit?
(pause) *Keyboard skills* would be useful, because we're all computerised, we've all got our own terminals, so being able to use a keyboard [What about phone skills?] Yeah that helps. But most people in the section when they start they go on a telephone techniques course so they learn, you know, they learn the correct skill for using the telephone, and also writing letters and writing memos, *just basic English* [They get taught that on the course?] Yeah there's a letter writing course and a telephone techniques course which many of them go on, to bring them up to the standard, the company standard. (BI 13)

Q: What skills do you think you had when you first came here?
Very little, very little indeed. I could use a calculator, I could use a telex, *I could use a computer* but I didn't have any particular skill because I hadn't actually concentrated on anything. (BI 15)

All three responses, with differing emphasis, note the importance of more technical, computer skills, with the underlying inference that such abilities were necessary for communication. The first set of comments offer an example of the technical/social split, with the technical skills on computers being followed by the social skills of "common sense" and working well with other people. The second respondent also links social and technical skills, with the technical emphasis on computer skills and literacy and the social emphasis on telephone techniques. Both these are seen as important for providing information within the company (over the phone and through computer networks) and with customers (again over the phone and through using computers to hold customer information and answer customer queries). In the third response BI 15 lists three technical skills, two of which involve communication (fax and computer), but denies that these are really skills. This reluctance to describe such "general" abilities as "skills" may be linked to an earlier assertion by this respondent that a skilled job was one which required qualification backed specialisation.

The skills which Bristol Insurance respondents see themselves as possessing and which are necessary for office work, therefore, fall into two main categories, social and technical, but with the common theme of communication and this data, as the next section shows, contrasts with that of Bristol Laminated.

Bristol Laminated

Table 5.5 shows the summary picture for Bristol Laminated and what is immediately apparent is the continuing emphasis on a Bravermanian mechanic/technicist conceptualisation of skill, with 9 of the 10 respondents making reference to their own skills as being connected with "working with machinery". Other skill comments related to: physical properties (4 respondents); intelligence required for factory work (2 respondents) and possessing the right "attitude" (3 respondents).

Table 5.5
Bristol Laminated,
breakdown of own skills and skills necessary for factory work

	Working with machinery	Physical properties	Intellig	"Attitude" of workers	Total
Managers	bl 1	bl 6	bl 6	bl 1; bl 6	2
Workers	bl 2; bl 3; bl 4; bl 5; bl 7; bl 8; bl 9; bl 10	bl 2; bl 3; bl 4; bl 5; bl 8; bl 9	bl 5	bl 4	8
Response total	9	7	2	3	*21*\10

Note: response total (in italics) may be more than number of respondents due to multiple replies

The common association by respondents from Bristol Laminated between skill and mechanical and technical knowledge which emerged from the last section in again evident in the data relating to skills held or seen as necessary for work in Bristol Laminated. All of the workers, when discussing their own skills or the skills necessary to work in Bristol Laminated, made reference to machinery. Typical comments included:

> *I've always felt easy working with tools and big machinery*, I mean eh and once you get on there, the skills that are required on our job, I mean obviously you must like physical work, you must be able to *work as a team*, knowing what the other man does and also to a point of getting on with other people, I mean you can't have one sour thumb, I mean the day is just a bad day if you've got one sour thumb. (BL 2)
>
> Q: Any more general skills people need to work in factories?
> Eh, obviously every sort of job is a skill in it's own, but the same thing applies it would only be in this industry. Every *single machine* here has got quite a high degree of skill to run them. (BL 7)
>
> I brought the skills from St Anne's Board Mills that I knew about paper, I knew how to make paper board and also I was trained up on *big machinery*. Because of the similarity between that it came in handy to get the job in here. Because it was roughly the same type of trade. So that came in handy. The trade I've learnt in here, right, if I have got to pass on. I have got training on

slitting machines, alright, which are all semi-skilled except the printers which are top dogs. (BL 10)

Here, the association of skill with machinery comes across strongly, with these respondents articulating a Bravermanian association between their skills and technical knowledge of machinery. This is evident from the comments of BL 7 who (again) is seen to attribute skill to the actual machine and BL 10 (who later described himself and the other laminating workers as "mechanically minded"). In addition to this Bravermanian association between skill and machinery, the deep descriptive detail of some of the work carried out on the laminating machines, illustrated the existence and recognition of tacit technical skills: For example, BL 7 gives the following description of working the was mixing machine:

> You had to make all the wax mixes up, all different type of mixes, different lacquers and things. Wax and rubber won't mix. To start off any basic rubber mix you had to start off with rubber and wax. Now the only way we could get that to mix was by crushing it in a machine, something like a mincer where you had two sets of solid blades. You would put the rubber in first and that would mash it up into tiny little granules and you had to very, very gradually put the wax in along with it until you finished up with what looked like dough. And it was hot, it was all done by friction, you had ice cold water going through the blades, solid great blades and those blades had ice cold water running through them but with the friction they would get quite hot and the skill was if you did it too quick it would never mix so you had to get it just right and it took quite a long time. You had to get the rubber to the right consistency first of all. The plan was to break that down and then you had to very, very slowly add wax until eventually it got to a nice creamy mixture. [How did you know when the rubber was of the right consistency?] Well that was it, it was *only just skill that told you that, there was nothing to tell you that it was right you had to know when it was right*. You were trained in that, obviously, initially, but eh I could tell at a glance, looking at it when it was just right. (BL 7)

This detailed description demonstrates the level of knowledge required in jobs which are officially classed as unskilled or semi-skilled and points to the importance of what Kusterer (1978) described as "working knowledge" and was later to be described by Manwaring (1984) and Manwaring and Wood (1985) as tacit skills. Such abilities are evident from the latter part of the above quote where this respondent's experience of the machine and the production process would allow him to "know at a glance" that the mixture was of the required consistency. This skill is similar to that identified by Penn and Scattergood (1985) who, in their work on skill, investigated three paper factories and concluded that the skills of the "beaterman" in knowing the correct colour of the pulp mixture was an *intuitive* based (or tacit) skill.[28] It was argued in the last section that respondents from Bristol Insurance possessed tacit social skills such as patience and good communication, abilities which had become such a common part of working knowledge as not to be recognised as "skilled", instead being described as "common sense". It was also noted that although the *concept* of tacit skills is clearly applicable to a multiplicity of occupational environments the majority of the empirical work had taken place in blue collar or manual sectors (Cockburn, 1983; Manwaring, 1984; Manwaring and Wood, 1985; Penn and Scattergood, 1985; Dick and Morgan, 1987; Grieco, 1987; Steiger, 1993). The data from Bristol Laminated supports some of the key findings from these studies. For example, Manwaring and Wood (1985), found that workers and managers were often not aware of the importance of tacit skills until something went wrong on the production process. They cite one respondent as commenting:

> I have lost count of the number of times we have a quality or productivity problem which the engineers discuss in their offices and the fellow on the shop floor solves. Once there was a water leak on the bulkhead. One welder knew all along what was wrong. The welding gun had to be used in an awkward position which often meant knocking the weld. These kind of problems can't be identified from drawings. (Senior car production manager, Manwaring and Wood, 1985: 178)

Here, it is the experience of working on a particular machine over a number of years which gives the shop floor worker the in-depth knowledge of the machine - knowledge which tends only to be recognised when there is a problem. This finding was supported by data from Bristol Laminated:

> Q: How long did it take you to learn the jobs?
> Well, you had laid down times. You get the basics in that time but for an operator it's years really because you're learning all the time, anything goes wrong, anybody can press a button, *it's when things go wrong that's where your knowledge comes in* and that takes years. (BL 9)
>
> Q: How well do people get to know their machines?
> Oh very well, you can teach anybody to run anything, but *it's when something*

---

[28]This recognition of what have been described as tacit skills has also been noted by Cockburn (1983) and Steiger (1993). Cockburn, in her work on the printing industry, argued that printers possessed an "aesthetic understanding of how a newspaper should look" (Cockburn, 1983: 114) while Steiger (1993), in his work in skill in the construction industry, found the least skilled of construction workers still possessed "unrecognised complexities and skills" (Steiger, 1993: 551). I would argue that these authors are also describing tacit skills - an in-depth, perhaps unconscious, knowledge of part of a production process.

> *goes wrong, it's that knowledge*, and it might not go wrong very often and you can tell by the sound, you're not exactly sure what it is but you know machines are like that... (BL 8)

These respondents from Bristol Laminated are describing an experience which closely mirrors that found by Manwaring and Wood's (1985) and Penn and Scattergood (1985), with tacit skills being particularly evident when "things go wrong". Another common recognition was the use of an analogy with one's car to describe tacit skills. This was found both by Manwaring and Wood (1985) and Kusterer (1978). Manwaring and Wood (1985) cited Kusterer (1978):

> Cars are basically the same, but every car is different... At first when you're learning you just learn the rules about driving. But as you get to know how to drive, you get a feel for the car your driving - you know, things like how it feels at different speeds, how well the brakes work, when it's going to overheat, how to start it when it's cold... Then if you think about old cars like these machines, been running three shifts for twenty years, some of them, like maybe you've got a car with no horn, that wants to turn right when you hit the brake, that don't start right unless you pump the gas a special way - then maybe you can start to see what it's like trying to run those junky old machines they've got down there... Now a good operator is like when you put her on a new machine she knows these machines so well she's got a feel for it, she picks up right away what she's got to do different on this new machine than she was doing on the other one. (Manwaring and Wood, 1985: 176, from Kusterer, 1978: 50)

The point here is that driving skill is not simply knowing how to drive, in the sense of learned mechanical movements, but rather consists of the increased knowledge and heightened awareness one achieves from driving the same car for a period of time. This, again, was supported by data from Bristol Laminated workers discussing how familiar they became with their machines:

> ... *it's like your car you know*, you know when it's not running right, you get that particular sound when it's running ok, it's just the same with machines, you get so used to them, and *that skill can't be taught, it's knowledge gained through years of experience.*" (BL 8)

> When they see a problem coming up on a roll they know what to do to put it right whereas a young one, or a new face, let me put it that way, he wouldn't know what to do for years. *Each machine has it's own little quirks like a car*, you don't drive two cars the same do you. Your car might be identical model to mine but it drives entirely different. So until you've actually been used to driving that car then eh, you'll be grating the gears and kangaroo juice etc. (BL 3)

As with other research findings these workers compare their own knowledge of machines with the familiarity which is built up between a driver and their car. There is, then, seen to be a strong tendency to associate skills with machinery and in this sense Bristol Laminated respondents are seen to utilise a Bravermanian conceptualisation of skill. In addition, the depth of descriptive detail which was offered demonstrates an awareness of machinery which goes beyond Braverman's relatively inflexible mechanic/artisan (Burchell et al, 1994) definition of skill to include tacit skills which have been learned over a period of time but are not formally recognised by a craft or guild.

Another, and linked, set of skills which emerged from discussions with Bristol Laminated respondents centred around the perceived requirements of physical strength or fitness, aptitudes which carried undertones of political/social closure, with certain requirements, such as physical strength, being seen as "male" and serving to close off parts of the labour market to women (Lazonick, 1979; Phillips and Taylor, 1980; Pollert, 1981; Armstrong, 1982; Beechey, 1982; Cockburn, 1981, 1983, 1986; Crompton and Jones, 1984; Manwaring and Wood, 1985; Curran, 1988; Horrell et al, 1990). The association between gender and strength is to found not only in contemporary work. For example, Lazonick (1979), in his work on the cotton industry during the industrial revolution, cites a civil engineer who argued for the use of fewer spindles (192 as opposed to 300) on cotton "mules", as this would require less strength and therefore increase the potential pool of labour to include women and children:

> It must be admitted, that wheels (i.e. mules) containing 300 spindles are unfit for any but men to work them; and the spinner will be more fatigued with working them fourteen hours; moreover, the small wheels may be worked by girls from sixteen to seventeen years of age, or by boys of fifteen, an advantage of no small importance to the master spinner. (Sutcliffe, 1816: 36, from Lazonick, 1979: 235)

There is a clear historical association between heavy factory work which requires physical strength and the required gender (male) of the workers who possess such abilities. The contemporary relevance of such traits for heavy factory work is shown by comments from a number of Bristol Laminated respondents:

> Q: What attributes are you looking for?
> Well basically we're looking for people *who've got the strength* to do the job but also who've got a *certain degree of intelligence*, there's quite a lot of detail involved in reading complex instructions and writing down information that's got to be accurate. (BL 6)

> Q: Can you name any skills folk would need for an operating job?
> I've always felt easy working with tools and *big machinery*, I mean eh and once you get on there, the skills that's required on our job, I mean obviously eh *you must like physical work...* (BL 2)

Q: Speaking more generally, can you think of any skills that everyone in the factory needs?
Ehm, obviously you need the aptitude to work by yourself, your own *initiative*, ehm obviously there are supervisors but obviously there are times when you need to make decisions yourself on what to do. What do you mean sort of skills, do you mean *actual physical skills* or (physical, mental) ehm I don't know really, it's awkward to say. Obviously *it's better if you're fit but actual skills*, awkward to say really. *Actually working in there it's sort of obvious but trying to explain it you got to stop and think.* Obviously you need a reasonable aptitude for figures and that. To start off basically *it's common sense* and as you get more experienced and more confident the job sort of comes. (BL 4)

Q: Other than experience are there any other skills people would need to come and work in a factory?
Well, *health and strength* obviously but that's all you need. (BL 3)

These comments, while noting the importance of intelligence (BL 6), teamwork (BL 2) and initiative (BL 4) share the common perception that certain physical qualities are important to factory work, with both workers and managers associating working on the shopfloor of Bristol Laminated with being "strong", "physical" or "fit". I would argue there is an underlying association here between these "physical" skills which are perceived as necessary to work with factory machinery and the gender of the workers who operate such machinery. This is not, of course, to argue that women are less likely to work with machinery, rather the emphasis is on the *nature* of the work, in particular the emphasis on heavy work with "heavy" machinery requiring specifically male attributes, with women often left to tend the "lighter" tasks and machines (Pollert, 1981; Purcell, 1982; Milkman, 1983; Cockburn, 1981, 1983, 1986; Humphries, 1987; Bradley, 1989; Thompson, 1989; Jenson, 1989). This distinction between working with machinery per se and working with "big and heavy" machinery was noted by Thompson (1989):

> In both the electrical and clothing industries, technological change towards *lighter* machinery and standardised, fragmented operations have led to the replacement of men by less trained women. (Thompson, 1989: 203, emphasis added)

Here, modern industrial work is seen to be suitable for women because its nature has changed in two important ways: it is simpler and, crucially, it is *lighter*. In the past at Bristol Laminated there had been a number of jobs which were done by women, but again these were of a "lighter" nature, including such things as counting pouches, counting sheets or packing sheets:

Q: Why do you think they're aren't any women working on the factory floor?
Well *all the womens' jobs went.* [Could women do the jobs that are here

> now?] Well a women could do any job, couldn't she really, but I wouldn't say it's a woman's environment. I don't think the treble shift factory job, doing a lot of *manual* work is really a woman's environment. I don't think women were made, were put on this earth to do *hard manual graft*. You've got some jobs, on my job, you've got to get off and you've got to use a bit of *muscle*. I mean a woman couldn't do that. I mean a woman could do any job if she put her mind to it but I don't think it's a women's job. (BL 5)

> Q: Anything about the jobs that would stop women doing them?
> No, they got hoists for heavy objects now, there's not so much of a *physical aspect* to a lot of the jobs as there used to be. It's just eh, the way things have been done over the years. (BL 8)

> Q: Anything to stop women doing these jobs?
> Oh they couldn't do them [Why not?] It's too heavy, you're talking about *big*, no they couldn't that. Well personally I don't think so, I know there's some *strong* women about, but no. Might be jobs upstairs, slitters, but then again that's lifting. But down here on a *big machine*, no. There's too much pushing and shoving, you're talking about *big heavy bars*, they couldn't lift that.(BL 9)

> Q: Why are there no women on the factory floor?
> Ehm, in my area it is quite a *physical job* and although we have lifting equipment its not sophisticated enough yet, although I think in the next two years we'll get to a point where the lifting equipment would enable a woman to do the job. Then it's a matter of getting over historical prejudice, of women being able to do that sort of thing. [But there used to be women?] Oh yes, we had a sheeting department and packaging dept and it was *fairly light work* which women were able to do fairly easily. As we sort of condensed our business about being a bit more specific about what we were producing it's tended more towards heavy rolls and more strength involved. (BL 6)

This feeling that certain jobs are gendered was found by Pollert (1981) who, in her study into female factory workers at a tobacco firm in Bristol, cited male factory workers who argued that they were not suitable for "weighing" (tobacco) because they were physically unsuitable for this type of "light" work. She quotes one employee:

> Steven: Take weighing, for instance, which you've seen these girls doing. I don't think I could do that all day. Take my hand, for instance - my hands too big. I couldn't do it, my hands aren't nimble enough. (Chargehand, Pollert, 1981: 80)

The comments from male Bristol Laminated respondents reflect a similar belief in the gendering of jobs, with males more suitable for "heavy" work and females for "light" work. In the first quote (from BL5), the worker believes that "women could do any job" yet concludes that manual work is simply not right for women. This gendering of jobs is also apparent in the quote from BL 9 where these jobs are seen as essentially male jobs and are consequently associated with strength. Women who have this attribute are noted as being somewhat unusual and "unfeminine", this respondent comments that "I know there's some *strong* women about" and another respondent noted that "*outward girls* could do the job quite easily" [BL 2]). This representation of women working in what is perceived of as a male environment as being "unfeminine" was also highlighted by Cockburn (1986) who found that certain jobs connected with applying new technology were:

> Consistently represented to me as masculine jobs, since men alone (and indeed by no means all men) could offer (the required) range of abilities. A woman who could do a job of this kind would be, as they put it more than once, "an Amazon", "a butch type", "a freak of nature". She would be so unfeminine as to be a subject of mirth. (Cockburn, 1986: 182)

Thus the perception is not so much that women are unable to perform the work tasks, rather that such tasks and such an environment are, a priori, "unfeminine". The ambiguity surrounding this issue is evident in the above quotes, where there was disagreement over the extent to which modern lifting equipment negates the need for strength, but consensus that women are either unable or unsuitable for work which involves heavy lifting.[29] Thus it could be the case that, as Braverman (1974) argued much of the physicality of factory work has been reduced by the introduction of new technology, but it does not necessarily follow that the attitudes which associate themselves to such physicality are superseded by new technology. A number of respondents (three) went further in their comments on other attitudes and opinions which were seen as masculine and typical of a masculine environment:

> There was talk of employing women on the factory floor, there was a few, they had a few pregnant ladies sort of thing, sort of put them off a bit, you know what I mean. People were more interested in *doing the women* than they were doing their jobs. (BL 3)

> Well, no but we haven't got the toilets and how you going to get on with the blokes and are you going to be upset by some *swearing* or you know blokes are *different* working than the girls up in the offices. (BL 2)

> We have a woman manager right now and I'd be a liar to say I didn't find it difficult. Because when I talk to a woman right... Sometimes if I disagree, not

---

[29]For a discussion on the extent to which women took over "skilled" manual jobs during the "dilution" of skills which occurred during World War I see More (1980) and Phillips and Taylor (1980).

being nasty, if I disagree with you then I would tell you so but if you disagree with a woman or a woman disagrees with you you've got a different set up. You've got a set up where if I started effing and blinding at you alright you would want to deal with me the same back, you can't do that with a woman. My morals won't let me do that... we are a *different breed*. (BL 10)

The attitudes and opinions of these male factory workers are seen to move beyond simple biological determinism to include certain social attitudes which are assumed to exclude women. This belief that the social environment might be harmful to women also has historical precedent. For example, Humphries (1987), writing of the sexual division of labour and women's work in nineteenth century England found that:

> Subcommissioner Symons reported that a meeting of 350 working colliers from the Barnsley area passed with only five votes the motion that the "employment of girls in pits is highly injurious to their morals, that it is not proper work for females and that it is a scandalous practice." [30](Humphries, 1987: 939)

Also, Cockburn, in her study into the printing industry, found that historically

> Girls were not considered suitable for apprenticeship. Physical and moral factors (girls were not strong enough, lead was harmful to pregnancy, the social environment might be corrupting) were deployed ideologically in such a way that few girls would see themselves as suitable candidates for apprenticeship. (Cockburn, 1981: 46)

These two quotes demonstrate that reasons for keeping men and women in separate occupations have traditionally included opinions on the social as well as the physical environment. This interaction between social and physical biases which Cockburn believes excludes women from certain jobs are supported by my contemporary data from Bristol Laminated, where male workers stress that women are not suitable for their work because they do not have the requisite physical properties and/or would feel uncomfortable in such a social environment. This combination of linking male work with heavy machinery and certain social attitudes and modes of behaviour was summed up by two of the respondents as "macho":

> Q: What do you think are the main barriers (between office and factory work)?
> I think it's probably the confidence on one side, factory workers haven't got enough confidence to feel that they could make that swap, they tend to regard the office workers as a breed apart. And there's also this perception that we

[30]For further information see original document - Parliamentary Papers (1842).

> do all the work cause we're on the machines and they don't do anything, just shuffle bits of paper around. *Bit of a macho thing*. And I think on the other side there is a certain amount of prejudice because factory workers are regarded as being thick, stupid and awkward. Which is not true. (BL 6)
>
> Q: What other things might put the lads off leaving here and going to work in an insurance company or something?
> Ehm, well I suppose the obvious one would be wondering if they had the sort of education to do it I suppose, perhaps they could well do the job but they may think or may wonder whether they've got that sort of qualification, that's pretty obvious. Ehm, I don't know, perhaps it's a sort of funny feeling about some, perhaps they feel they're more sort of *macho on the factory floor*, sounds daft I know but I suppose it's the sort of thing some of them might feel." (BL 7)

The first of these quotes, from BL 6, shows a clear association between machinery and machismo while the second links the "factory floor", with a feeling of machismo. The sensitivity surrounding such an association is also evident from the second quotation, where the respondent distances himself from such a view ("they" possess such an opinion) and attaches the disclaimer that it "sounds daft". The inference is that some men shape their concepts of masculinity by their work (and the abilities and skills which are perceived as going with such work). Cockburn (1986) wrote of this:

> A man takes on a manly persona by grappling with machinery - and with the social "machinery" of the firm. A woman takes on a feminine one precisely by being technically incompetent. (Cockburn, 1986: 185)

There is, therefore, an extent to which one's gender creates (and recreates) perceptions of the particular type of person who possesses particular types of skills and abilities and is therefore suitable for particular kinds of work. This process of creating areas of employment which are bounded by gender orientated perceptions of skill is reflected in some of the data from Bristol Laminated and supports the work of others in this field (Phillips and Taylor, 1980, More, 1980; Cockburn, 1981, 1983, 1986; Pollert, 1981; Manwaring and Wood, 1985; Penn and Scattergood, 1985; Jenson, 1989).

The preceding analysis has shown how certain technical capacities and technical tasks can be divided by political/social forces. There was also some evidence from Bristol Laminated that management were interested in social characteristics. It was argued in the last section that higher graded employees at Bristol Insurance may have placed more emphasis on qualifications because these are used as a proxy for certain social characteristics of workers, such as reliability and a certain "attitude" to work and implying, as Blackburn and Mann (1979) suggested, that management were as interested in "stability" as in "ability". There is seen to be a similar interest amongst the two managers interviewed at Bristol Laminated, with the emphasis on the "attitude" of the worker. For example, the senior personnel officer at Bristol Laminated commented that:

> ... one of the old personnel officers used to go for early 30s married man with two kids and a mortgage because that way they hung on in there. (BL 1)

This supports the work both of Blackburn and Mann (1979) and Mackay (1971) who, in his study of the British engineering industry, found management's ideal worker to be male, around 30, married with small children, related to other employees and with a stable educational and work history. The logic was that this worker would have so many financial commitments that he will be viewed as being more "responsible" and will consequently be easier to discipline. This personnel manager, in discussions on recruitment, went on to stress the importance of possessing the right "attitude":

> ... so for the fork lift truck driver's job it was somebody who probably had fork lift truck driving experience anyway, because that helps to get them up and running fairly quickly and also just a general *attitude* of being willing to do anything and that included picking up a brush and clearing away waste and all the rest of it and in answer to the question why are you leaving your job, because some people were leaving permanent jobs for temporary jobs which seemed really peculiar, some of them would say "well they put me on the brush" and we'd say "oh" and others would say "I'm really bored, I'm a fork lift truck driver and half the time I've got nothing to do, I've painted lines, I've swept up, I've done anything I could possibly do" and we'd say "Oh, I like that sort of *attitude*." He's one of the one's who started. (BL 1)

Here it is not so much the actual ability to do the job, which is looked upon as almost secondary, as *social* traits, such as the potential recruit's "attitude" (especially towards flexibility).

The data in this section have again highlighted the association of Bristol Laminated respondents with a Bravermanian task-centred conceptualisation of skill. There was also a sense in which the respondents from Bristol Laminated went beyond a Bravermanian skill conception which concentrates on objective competencies to include tacit skills specific to certain machines and certain production processes. In addition, there was seen to be a strong gender element in the data on skills held and skills perceived as necessary for factory work, with respondents making reference to the need for physical strength and fitness and allusions to the social environment of the factory which was particularly masculine. The final point which emerged from the data was the potential importance of certain social characteristics such as "attitude" which are seen as being as (if not more) important to management as the ability to technically carry out the required task.

Comparing the two sets of data, a number of important points arise. Firstly, while both sets of respondents perceived themselves as possessing different skills, with Bristol Insurance respondents concentrating on social skills and Bristol Laminated on technical skills, they both articulated skill conceptualisations which were linked to their respective job tasks. Consequently respondents from Bristol Insurance concentrated on the possession of social abilities (which some saw as "skills" and others as "common sense") which they perceived as being essential to effective communication - the central task of office work - while respondents from Bristol Laminated concentrated on the possession of mechanical skills and technical knowledge which they saw as being essential to working with machinery - the perceived central task of factory work. While there were, therefore, elements of labour economists' skill conceptualisation and industrial sociologists' task centred skill conceptualisations in the comments of both sets of respondents tended to see themselves as skilled in the context of their *jobs*.

5.5 The acquisition of skills

Bristol Insurance

The majority of the data in this section refers to how respondents believe they acquired their own skills and, in some cases, how they thought skills in general are acquired. The summary picture for Bristol Insurance is shown in table 5.6, with 11 respondents discussing this issue and making 17 references to how skills are obtained.

Table 5.6
Bristol Insurance, how skills are acquired

	Experience	Training	Natural	Society	Total
Managers	bi 2; bi 3; bi 6; bi 9	bi 5; bi 9	bi 5; bi 9	bi 5	5
Supervisors	bi 7; bi 13	bi 7	bi 4		3
Clerks	bi 14; bi 16; bi 18		bi 18		3
Response total	9	3	4	1	*17*\11

Note: response total (in italics) may be more than number of respondents due to multiple replies

The most common explanation of how skills are acquired was seen to be in terms of experience (9 respondents), followed by natural abilities (4 respondents), training

(3 respondents) and society (1 respondent). Turning to the primary data, examples of quotes which made reference to acquiring skills through experience included:

> Q: How did you acquire your skills?
> ... if I go back to my *experience* out on the road, ehm, whilst the job itself I probably wasn't particularly good at, I feel *the experience* of having done it meant that I can bring to the job I'm doing now *the knowledge* of knowing the people we're selling to... some of the problems that they've got. (BI 3)
>
> Ehm Partly *experience, as you go along you learn, you watch other people and you see people doing things in certain ways...* (BI 6)
>
> ... I think *you learn as you go along...* I would say the management side, the supervisory side I've learned as I've gone along, and the job as well. I've never done anything like this before. I think *you just learn as you go along*. (BI 13)
>
> In my case, all I know is that it's age. *You learn it just by going through life.* I mean I could have worried an awful lot about this when I was younger... I just think it's *learning from other jobs, learning through age, learning from your own experiences,* as you get older. *I don't think you can be taught it,* you can be helped a lot but I think *basically it comes through going through your own life, you know, your own experiences*. (BI 14)
>
> Eh well, *not from any particular course* I would say, just from *day to day life*, jobs that I've done before, people that I've had to deal with that sort of thing, *experience really. Rather than training*. (BI 16)

The most significant point to emerge from these responses is the perceived importance of experience to skill acquisition. There is seen to be a shift in emphasis from earlier comments relating to skill where the importance of training (both formal and informal) was stressed, with the focus shifting to personal experience (both inside and outside of the working environment). It would appear to be the case that when dealing with *general* concepts related to skill respondents made reference to what are formally recognised methods of classifying skill, namely training (linked with qualifications or a trade) or possession of technical knowledge (again represented through possession of qualifications or a trade), but when explaining the *particular* instance of how they gained their own skills respondents stressed the importance of personal experience. This experience is seen to fall into two broad categories, those who felt they had learned on the job, either through personal activity or watching others and those who believed they had learned from experiences outside work, a process which was described as learning from "*life*". Given the importance of social skills which emerged from discussions with Bristol Insurance respondents the second of these is particularly interesting. These respondents, who emphasised the possession of good communication skills as being important to office work, are seen to partially explain the acquisition of such abilities by reference to experiences *outside* work, a process which may, to some extent, explain why some regarded such abilities simply as "common sense". For if one's abilities are created through a learning process which includes activities outside paid employment, and one is operating within a system which is (broadly) seen to reward formally recognised specialised training (which has been shaped by a historical process which gives priority to applied technical knowledge), then it is possible to understand why some respondents did not recognise their own social abilities as skills per se, but instead saw such abilities as being commonly learned and commonly held and therefore relegated to a standing of tacit skill or "common sense". Returning to the dichotomy between general and personal skill acquisition, two respondents gave the following replies:

> Q: How do people acquire skills?
> I think, ehm, *you can go on courses* and things like that, I think it helps to *learn from experience* and from your own mistakes, I think. (BI 7)

> Q: How are skills created?
> They generally, I think you've got some *natural people* with natural flair with words and sort of visual abilities, but then they're fairly few and far between, so generally speaking people, we tend to give them *on the job training and show by example* what can happen. (BI 9)

Here, in questions relating to the *general* acquisition of skills respondents are seen to emphasise training. This provides further evidence for my earlier argument that there is a contrast in conceptualisations between the personal and the general. So when Bristol Insurance respondents are asked about *general* concepts there is a tendency to turn to formal, socially accepted (and some would argue created) criteria such as training and qualifications (vocational and non-vocational), but when discussing the *particular* respondents are more likely to emphasise the importance of learning by experience (which is seen to include activities inside and outside of the workplace). There is, obviously, some commonality here, with both the earlier comments relating a skilled job to training and the later comments relating skill acquisition to experience being linked to time, with the idea being that a skilled job or a skilled person is created over a period of time. Not all of the respondents, however, saw skills in this way. A number saw skills as being "natural":

> Q: So when you talk about skill what sort of things would you put into that category?
> Skill? Ehm, I honestly don't know. I mean, to me somebody whose skilful is someone like an artist or somebody like a footballer or something like that but in the job that we do I don't think you've got to be skilful at all I think you've just got to have *common sense*. (BI 18)

> Q: How do people acquire skills, like being good at people skills or being good at numbers?
> I don't think you can *I think that's something you're either good at or you aren't*, you might not discover that it's something that you're good at, you might only discover it by chance, I've tended to fall into different jobs... (BI 4)

The first set of comments, from BI 18, supports earlier responses from this interviewee which saw skill linked with natural abilities and classed the abilities necessary for office work (such as patience and good communication skills) as "common sense". The belief that certain skills are "natural" is also apparent in the second response, from BI 4, detailed above. But while BI 18 recognises skill as a particularly specialised talent, such as that of a footballer or artist, BI 4 applies this concept to broader skills such as numeracy and communication skills. This respondent described herself as possessing "people skills" and there may, I would argue, be some similarity between the manner in which BI 4 describes the acquisition of such skills and the way in which other respondents described the acquisition of "common sense" (skills such as being good on the phone and possessing patience). For it may be the case that while this respondent is aware such abilities are not randomly distributed amongst the population they are not conscious that such abilities are learned and, unlike other (older) respondents who recognised that such skills are acquired through "life", sees such abilities as "natural" phenomena. One final respondent related the acquisition of social skills to "society":

> Q: How do you think people acquire these social skills?
> Social skills are *created by the society in which you live* so if people come into an insurance or marketing environment from a totally *alien environment* they're not going to get on are they so I suppose the broad answer to that is insurance attracts and requires people from a middle class sort of average background very similar to the people that their selling to. (BI 5)

This comment illustrates a recognition of the power of political/social forces in shaping skill, with this respondent arguing that the workforce reflects the class position of the company's clients and is, consequently, middle class.

The main finding of this sub-section has been that respondents recognise a process whereby skills are acquired through experience, both inside and outside work. It was noted that this emphasis on a personal process of informal learning through experience contrasts with earlier data which stressed the importance of training in making a skilled job. This may suggest that when asked what makes a skilled job the emphasis is on relatively formal criteria such as training, technical knowledge or a trade but when asked how they themselves have learnt their (especially tacit) social skills, the emphasis shifts to personal and informal learning processes.

Bristol Laminated

The summary picture of comments relating to how skills are acquired is shown in table 5.7:

Table 5.7
Bristol Laminated, how skills are acquired

	Experience	Training	Total
Managers	bl 6	bl 1; bl 6	2
Workers	bl 2; bl 3; bl 4; bl 5; bl 7; bl 8; bl 9; bl 10	bl 7; bl 10	8
Response total	9	4	*13*\10

Note: response total (in italics) may be more than number of respondents due to multiple replies

Similar to respondents from Bristol Insurance the data from Bristol Laminated gives primary emphasis to the importance of personal experience in gaining skills (9 respondents) and secondary emphasis to training (4 respondents), but (perhaps reflecting the continued relevance of a Bravermanian technicist skill conceptualisation), unlike Bristol Insurance where some respondents noted the importance of experience outside work, the overwhelming emphasis was experience at work. Turning to the comments relating to experience, it was argued earlier that respondents from Bristol Laminated recognised the personal possession and importance of tacit skills and described the learning of such working knowledge (Kusterer, 1978) as being based upon experience. Comments (some of which were cited earlier in relation to tacit skills) on this process of acquisition included:

> ... *it's when things go wrong that's where your knowledge comes in* and that takes years. (BL 9)

> (tacit) *skill can't be taught it's knowledge gained through years of experience*. (BL 8)

> Q: What do they do when things go wrong?
> A lot of it is *down to experience*, something will happen and they'll think that happened before and I did so and so and that sorted it out. (BL 4)

> Q: How are these skills learned, through time?
> That (knowing your machine) has just been *picked up through time*, yeah. I

mean eh it all depends on who you group with, I mean some lads just want you to know - that. I think they feel threatened that somebody might be coming up through the ranks, ehm, and it gives some people self importance that they're number one and to be seen in that light. I mean that's not my cup of tea... (BL 2)

Q: How do you get those skills?
I don't know, *I've always done the jobs*. I think I'm a plodder, maybe that's what's makes me a good temperament to work on the trucks. I'm older, no offence to you, I don't think young people have any patience. (BL 5)

Here, similar to Bristol Insurance, when asked how they acquired their own skills, the importance of learning through experience comes through strongly, but, unlike Bristol Insurance there is no difference between general notions of what constitutes a skilled job and how one acquires one's own skills. While for Bristol Insurance respondents there was seen to be a contrast between the general level of skill involved in conceptualising what constitutes a skilled job (training) and the personal level of acquiring one's own skills there was seen to be continuity in the responses of Bristol Laminated respondents. I would suggest this is caused by Bristol Insurance respondents making reference to "traditional" skill signifiers (such as training for a trade and/or building up technical knowledge) when conceptualising what constitutes a skilled job yet turning to their own experiences when describing how they acquired their own (very often social) skills. In contrast, Bristol Laminated respondents were working *within* the sector whose mechanical jobs and technical knowledge were the "traditional" benchmarks used for deciding what is classed as skilled. Consequently, it is not surprising that such respondents should make reference to technical knowledge when conceptualising what it is that makes a job skilled and again make reference to their experience in building up such technical knowledge when explaining how they believe they acquired such skills.

Turning to training, where this was mentioned in relation to their own skills, it's importance was played down:

Q: What did the training involve?
You get *three months training*, then you get put on a machine on your own and *you get so many cock ups it's unbelievable*, you really suffer. But after about a year you got it and as soon as you got it that's it, you're laughing. Because the job becomes second nature and as soon as the job becomes second nature you get it so perfect, in your own mind that you can cut down times you can cut down this, *cause experience comes in*. That's where it (skill) comes in, when you can go off one machine and on to another and be as good. (BL 10)

Q: What did the training involve?
There wasn't any sort of set training programme as such. It was more or less

something you derived over a time. It came with *watching other people* do it to start with and then obviously doing it yourself. *You did it all by experience really*. (BL 7)

Q: Earlier on you were talking about the skills necessary for operating machinery, could you go into any more details about what those skills are? They're just operating skills really, ehm the print area that we've got is actually a skilled area. They used to do a five year apprenticeship, they don't now they do a two year city and guilds course, that's predominately college and then hands on here... but for *general factory workers* we would take them into our finishing department where they would learn the skills of that and then when the time came they would be trained up on other things as the vacancies occurred. (BL 1)

The first two responses which are detailed above demonstrate, again, the importance of experience over training. The first respondent quoted above states that the three months official training is insufficient - *"you get so many cock ups it's unbelievable"* and that to became efficient on a machine takes experience. This poor opinion of official training was shared by the second respondent, who maintained that one learned through one's workmates and "*experience*". The third response, from the production manager, illustrates the importance of socially controlled skill status. The skills of the majority of the laminating workers (who see themselves as possessing as much technical knowledge skill as printers) are described as "just" operating skills compared to the printers who have to go through an apprenticeship.

This subsection, then, has pointed to both a similarity and a difference between Bristol Insurance and Bristol Laminated. Common to respondents from both case study firms was a powerful association between personal experience and the acquisition of skills. However, while this supports earlier data from Bristol Laminated which linked a skilled job to detailed technical knowledge it contrasts with earlier data from Bristol Insurance which tended to link a skilled job more with training. This difference was explained by reference to the influence of socially and politically defined skill, with office workers making reference to "traditional" skill benchmarks (based on training and technical knowledge) in describing general concepts such as what makes a skilled job and making reference to their own experiences (both inside and outside the working environment) when explaining how they acquired the (mainly social) skills necessary for work in an office, while factory workers made reference to such "traditional" Bravermanian technical skill conceptualisations both to describe general concepts such as what constitutes a skilled job and particular beliefs such as how they obtained their own (technical) skills.

5.6 Conclusion

In summary, the data on skills has produced a number of interesting results which reflect both on skill theory and carry implications for labour market flexibility in general and the potential for occupational mobility in particular. Turning firstly to skill theory, what emerged most strongly was the tendency for the comments of Bristol Laminated respondents to fall (broadly) within the Bravermanian mechanic/artisan task centred conceptualisation of skill. In each section, describing a skilled job, describing their own skills and describing how these skills were acquired, the comments of Bristol Laminated respondents generally fell within the context of Braverman's conceptualisation of skill. I would argue that these findings reflect upon the potential to make the labour force within one firm more flexible, in the sense of a workforce where people could move easily and quickly between jobs (Atkinson, 1984, 1985a; McCormick, 1985; CBI, 1985, Keenan and Thom, 1988). For if it is the case that some factory workers possess a notion of skill which recognises and respects learned technical abilities within the context of a craft then efforts by management to create a flexible labour force by introducing new technology and "multi-tasking" may meet with considerable opposition as workers may either not see such work as "skilled" and/or may view it as a managerial attempt to increase control over the productive process (Bowles and Gintis, 1975; Gordon et al, 1982; Nichols, 1986; Potter, 1987, Pollert, 1988b, 1991; Curry, 1993). This tendency for Bristol Laminated data to fall within a Bravermanian task centred conceptualisation of skill was contrasted in the first section with Bristol Insurance data which was seen to contain elements of all three schools of skill conceptualisation. It was argued this was due to Bristol Insurance respondents being influenced by a number of skill conceptualisations which, while concentrating on the technical, drew ideas and beliefs from a number of sources. There was more commonality, however, between the two sets of respondents in how their own skills were perceived and acquired. Both described different skills (office respondents describing social skills and factory workers technical/mechanical skills) but both linked their own skills to the tasks required by their respective jobs and described a process whereby skills are acquired through experience (with some at Bristol Insurance noting the importance of experience gained outside the workplace). Hence Bristol Insurance respondents placed stress on what they saw as the most important aspect of their jobs - communication, and consequently placed most emphasis on social skills, such as "being good with people", while Bristol Laminated respondents conceptualised their skills in terms of their jobs and employment histories and consequently stressed the importance of possessing technical knowledge and being "familiar with machinery".

Turning to the second, and related, area of interest - how these data affect the potential for mobility between factories and offices. The analysis has produced results which provide further evidence for the essentially problematic nature of mobility between factories and offices. Perhaps the most important potential barrier emerges from the essential solidity of responses from those interviewed at Bristol Laminated, who are seen to continually associate skill with mechanical tasks which require applied technical knowledge. These workers perceive their own skills as linked to working with heavy machinery in a factory environment. Thus their skills are not only associated with the technical but are also influenced by political and social processes which "gender" certain jobs. Thus it could be the case that not only would the skills of such male factory workers be irrelevant in an office environment but that the workers themselves may be reluctant to see office work as "skilled" (in the sense of technical knowledge applied in a male environment). The data on skill acquisition, where the role of personal experience and not training is emphasised, adds a further complication. For if it is the case that skills (and the recognition of the possession of skills by one's colleagues) are acquired through a long process of experience (including, perhaps crucially, social skills gained outside work and influenced by gender perceptions) then any "reskilling" which has at its base formal training courses to overcome such technical differences as typing will not be effective. The implications for industrial mobility between factories and offices which emerge from this data on skill are not, therefore, particularly favourable. Although the skill conceptualisations of both sets of respondents are in many ways similar (in the sense that both link their own skills with their own jobs and see these skills as being acquired through personal experience) this similarity serves only to accentuate the differences and problems facing mobility, with the (male) factory workers reproducing their technicist definition of skill by reference to their own work and employment experience and office workers doing the same (with different results). This leads to a situation where respondents have built up different technical and social skills which are exercised in different working environments and where skill recognition and reward have been influenced by different social, institutional, historical and political processes. As in the last chapter on recruitment, therefore, the data from Bristol Insurance and Bristol Laminated is characterised by difference, differences which present further evidence for the existence of non-competitive work groups. The extent of the non-competitive nature of these two work groups emerges more clearly in the next chapter, on the perceptions respondents held of each other and each others work.

6 Work and workers

6.1 Introduction

> ... some (of those in employment) probably fewer than ever before, will be working in conventional, full-time jobs within conventional firms. Many more will be working for themselves or in vibrant small businesses. Most will vary their working pattern several times during their lives to suit their personal circumstance. (Guardian, 19th September, 1994)

This quote from Paddy Ashdown, the leader of the Liberal Democrats, in late 1994 neatly summarises the cross party belief that labour market flexibility is a natural feature of the labour market landscape and that a defining feature of this landscape is for employment patterns to be fragmented, both in terms of working time and type of work. This situation is contrasted with the past, characterised by "conventional" jobs with "conventional" firms. The aim of this chapter is to analyse data from Bristol Insurance and Bristol Laminated respondents to investigate how they see each other, both in terms of type of person and type of work. If it is the case, for example, that each pictures and perceives the other in radically different terms, terms so different that one must talk of non-competitive work groups, of different work cultures, then how likely is it that the flexible future described above will come about? To what extent do "conventional" attitudes which one may assume accompany Ashdown's old fashioned "conventional" jobs and "conventional" firms have contemporary relevance? This chapter, using data on the third major area of investigation - how respondents see each other, attempts to answer these questions.

The chapter is structured around the two major themes which are seen to emerge from the data: the common recognition of a mental/manual split between office and factory work/workers and the common perception that the labour market is structured hierarchically, with office work above factory work. The resulting data and analysis are used to present further evidence which acts against the prevailing paradigm of occupational flexibility set out above and present in recent government publications (Hakim, 1987; Skills and Enterprise Network, 1993; Employment

Department Group, 1994; Watson, 1994; Beatson, 1995). It is seen that the pictures and perceptions articulated by respondents add to the model of non-competitive work groups which were also present in views and values on skills and channels of recruitment. The chapter structure reflects the themes of a mental/manual split and a hierarchy of occupations, with an analysis of the comments of Bristol Insurance respondents being followed by an analysis of the comments of those from Bristol Laminated.

6.2 Perceptions of work and workers

Bristol Insurance

The data which emerged from questions on barriers and perceptions have been split into two broad (and overlapping) sections. The first deals with descriptions of factory work and workers (summarised in tables 6.1a and 6.1b) and the second with aspects of office work and workers (summarised in later table 6.2) which serve to differentiate the two industrial sectors. Tables 6.1a and 6.1b are put below and will be referred back to throughout the first sections of this chapter.

Table 6.1a
Bristol Insurance, perceptions of factory workers

	Factory workers					Total
	Workin g with hands	Physical/ strong	Dextrous	Clothing	Low intelli gence	
Managers	bi 2; bi 5; bi 6; bi 10	bi 1	bi 1	bi 2; bi 3; bi 11	bi 1 bi 3 bi 8	7
Supervisors	bi 7; bi 15	bi 4; bi 12; bi 15	bi 4	bi 7; bi 13; bi 15	bi 7; bi 12	5
Clerks	bi 14; bi 18					2
Response total	8	4	2	6	5	25\14

Note: response total (in italics) may be more than number of respondents due to multiple replies

Table 6.1b
Bristol Insurance, perceptions of factory work and working process

	Factory work					Working process		Total
	Manual	Rout ine	Mach inery	Poor pay	Dirty	Tangible product	Free dom	
Managers	bi 9		bi 3; bi 6			bi 2; bi 5; bi 6; bi 10	bi 1; bi 8; bi 9	7
Supervisors	bi 4; bi 12; bi 13	bi 4; bi 7; bi 13	bi 7	bi 15	bi 12	bi 7		5
Clerks	bi 14; bi 16		bi 18	bi 16	bi 14	bi 14		3
Response total	6	2	4	2	2	6	2	24\15

Note: response total (in italics) may be more than number of respondents due to multiple replies

Turning to table 6.1a, while there were a number of different descriptions certain common themes are seen to emerge, in particular factory factory workers are perceived as being characterised by manual capacities such as being physically strong and used to working with their hands. A good example of the interplay between descriptions of factory workers and images of factory work is offered by the data relating to the type of clothing worn. As table 6.1a shows, 6 respondents made remarks relating to clothing in their descriptions of factory workers. The common contrast was between the suit and tie of the office and the "overalls" which were perceived as being worn in the factory. This contrast is evident from the following three quotations:

> Q: What picture do you have of your average manufacturing worker?
> Expect to see them in *overalls*, some sort of *boilersuit* or whatever, some sort of outfit as opposed to a *suit*. (BI 2)

> Q: How important would you say things like dress are in acting as a barrier to mobility?
> I would say that (dressing up) would put people off. I know at Rolls Royce that's one of the things they, I think the shop workers call office workers the "*tie brigade*" because they wear *ties* so yeah, I suppose they wouldn't want to wear a *suit and tie*. To *dress up*. (BI 13)

> Q: How would you describe your average manufacturing worker?
> I just think of them as *overall* people. People who wear *overalls*, not *white collars*. People with protective shoes on their feet. (BI 15)

Common to these descriptions is the contrast between the office *"suit"*, or "*white collar*" and the "*overalls* or "*boilersuit*" of the factory, with the inference that clothing creates a certain identity. On this, Morgan (1992), writing of Dalton's (1959) study of managers has written:

> Dalton's study of managers deals with the familiar distinctions between "line" and "staff" management, noting that these were not simply differences in functions but also differences in education, age and style of dress, the last having all the connotations of "dirty" and "clean". The relatively clean and smart suits of staff management might seem offensive or provocative to line management, who may wear work clothes and, symbolically or actually, may have their sleeves rolled up. (Morgan, 1992: 86)

I would suggest that a similar distinction is being described by the office respondents quoted above with the contrast between the "overalls" of the factory worker and the "suit" of the office worker serving to identify each with a certain type of work, contrasting dirty manual work with clean office work. This "manual" image is further strengthened by reference to the descriptions of the work done in factories (table 6.1b), which is described as variously: dirty; manual; routine; linked to machinery and offering low pay and by the other characterisations of factory workers (table 6.1a), who are portrayed as: working with their hands; physically strong and fit; dextrous and of low intelligence. The general theme, which carries overtones relating to the gendering of jobs, is one of manual work and manual workers. Typical comments included:

> Q: How would you describe your average manufacturing worker?
> Somebody who had *manual dexterity*, who was fit, who was reasonably *strong* and who had the aptitude for doing very repetitive routines, or quite repetitive routines in some cases. I'm not decrying that they would have any sort of abysmal academic level, don't get me wrong... I think *physical* skills and the *dextrous* skills of being able to adjust machinery or press the right button at the right time and observe things that are going through. I think it's all about those sorts of things, *alertness* and *fitness* and if *lifting's* involved somebody that can cope with that, no back problems and things like that. (BI 1)

> Q: How would you describe your average manufacturing worker?
> Men, or women on a production line. *Men doing the really, sort of manual jobs* and women on a production line. [Do you see them as having any sort of skills?] Depends on what they're manufacturing really, I mean they could be doing the same sort of *repetitive jobs* or they could be doing something that's quite skilled. Something that they've learned, that you couldn't just walk in

and do. Which is the same as it is here really. Some things you can pick up in a few days and others it takes months or years to learn. (BI 13)

Q: What skills would you need to go into manufacturing?
I would have to rethink my whole life, I would have to start thinking about, ehm, I couldn't care less what people said to me for a kickoff, not worried what *language* they used (nervous laugh) not that that worries me, but I'm going to come against *different language*. I couldn't, I certainly wouldn't care if I got *dirty* or not, ehm, you know, if me nails broke or, I don't know, or *grind* and *dirt* and things. I would just have to have a completely different think of what I'm doing. (BI 14)

Q: Going back to working in a factory what sort of things would put you of going into work in a factory?"
I'm sure the *pay wouldn't be very good*... I mean I wouldn't leave this job to go and work in a factory. But if there was a factory job going I wouldn't not apply for it because it was a factory job. I mean a job's a job, really as far as I'm concerned. [Probed if anything else, then she said she'd worked in a factory before, temporarily before Christmas one year when she was out of a job. I probed on the difference in work environment] Well, I mean it's the same basic structure isn't it, your supervisor then your big bosses, other than it's a bit more *manual*, well sometimes it's a lot more *manual*. The, you know, the structure is basically the same. A lot of it's more sit down and concentrate and in a factory it'd be more *manual*. (BI 16)

These comments illustrate a number of important perceptions of factory work and workers, including notions of pay, dirt, strength, fitness and the language used in such a manual environment. There is seen to be a fairly strong correlation between these descriptions and the skills factory workers saw themselves as possessing, which, as was seen in the last chapter, include reference to machinery and the possession of physical strength. Flowing from these descriptions (and again mirroring the skills data from the previous chapter) are implications of the gendering of jobs, with (especially heavy) work being linked to men (Lazonick, 1979; Phillips and Taylor, 1980; Cockburn, 1981, 1983, 1986; Pollert, 1981; Game and Pringle 1983; Morgan, 1992) The perception articulated by BI 14 above that factory environments would be characterised by bad "language" was also found by Cockburn (1981), who, writing of the tactics of men to keep women out of printing, found that:

> The composing room was, and in most cases still is, an all-male preserve with a sense of camaraderie, pin-ups on the wall and a pleasure taken in the manly licence to use "bad" (i.e. woman-objectifying) language. (Cockburn, 1981: 48)

Pollert (1981), while also finding that female factory workers had to put up with "sexist patronisation" (Pollert, 1981: 142), found that they could (and did) turn such an environment to their advantage:

> I was once politely reprimanded for chewing gum on the factory premises... in front of the girls. It was a case of the supervisor demonstrating his authority to the girls. But up came one of the girls, and, loudly telling me not to take any notice, gave him a half-motherly, half-sexy hug. He was stunned - utterly undermined. (Pollert, 1981: 143)

It is the case, therefore, that although women may have to put up with sexually oppressive supervision at work, they can (at times) turn this to their advantage. Table 6.1b also illustrates that while some respondents saw factory work as "routine", a more common perception was of factory work involving the production of a tangible product, with implications of the recognition of craft skills. Factory workers were seen as using "their hands" to "create" physical products, a work process which was often contrasted with the relatively intangible product produced in insurance.

> Q: What do you think would put manufacturing people off coming to work in an office?
> Because I think they would think of an office environment as a soft option. There are people who like to *create* something which often in an office environment you're not doing and you're *making*, you're *building* things and you've got something at the end... something *physical*... whereas in an office environment it's very difficult to say what you've done at the end of it. (BI 10)

> ... And again it's easy to get into a rut. I mean if I had my life again I wouldn't do this job. I'd certainly steer clear of it. All my life I've done a job where I've done something in accounts, something in the accounts side of it. Whereas really I'd love a job where I could be a bit more *creative*, I could *make* things, I could *use my hands*. Not particularly my brain, I could *use my hands* more, I'd just *make* things rather than write letters and ehm work out how much people owe and, no matter what job I've had I've always done something like that in the accounts side of it. And because I started off doing that kind of job, the next job you go to its "what experience have you had" "oh I've done this" "Oh yes, well we have got a job for you in the accounts section you see." and it goes on and before you realise you're stuck in a rut. (BI 14)

The emphasis which emerges from these quotes is of an association between factory work and a creative process, with the potential to express one's creativity seen as being a positive aspect of factory work. This perception of the work done in factories and the implied reference associating factory work with applied technical knowledge is similar to the way factory workers themselves classified a skilled job (see last chapter), with a strong (Bravermanian) association between skill and craft. The importance of these positive perceptions of factory work as involving "creativity" and "working with one's hands" is enhanced by the descriptions of office work and workers articulated by Bristol Insurance respondents, which are summarised in table 6.2:

Table 6.2
Bristol Insurance, perceptions of office work and workers

	Office work		Office workers	
	Mental	Office work as to sedentary	Qualifications	Total
Managers	bi 6; bi 8	bi 2; bi 5 bi 6; bi 8; bi 9	bi 1; bi 2; bi 6; bi 11	6
Supervisors	bi 4; bi 12; bi 15	bi 12	bi 15	3
Clerks	bi 16	bi 16; bi 18	bi 14; bi 16	3
Response total	6	8	7	*21*\12

Note: response total (in italics) may be more than number of respondents due to multiple replies

As table 6.2 shows discussions on perceptions of work and workers moved on to office work and workers in 12 of the 18 interviews. Of these 12, 8 respondents reported office work as being sedentary and this was often seen as contrasting strongly with perceptions of factory work and seen as a barrier to mobility:

> Q: What are the potential barriers to workers moving from manufacturing to the service sector?
> I suspect that the difference is that they would be much more *tied down to sitting at a desk.* I suspect if you're talking of a blue collar worker you're talking about someone who's used to *doing something with their hands or something more creative.* (BI 2)
>
> I think there are loads of jobs in Bristol and a lot of them are in financial institutions. Ehm but not everybody wants to do that, *I could see people going spare sitting in front of a desk all day every day*, they'd much prefer to be *working with their hands* or *doing something a bit more sort of tangible...* (BI 5)

> Q: Would manufacturing workers be attracted to coming to work in an office? No, not really because if they've taken to work where they're *moving around a lot*, fairly *physical* they probably wouldn't want to be *stuck behind a desk all day*... (BI 6)

> Self belief in being able to do the job, maybe they think there's more in the job than there actually is. Thinking the jobs boring, a lot of the people that I talk to ehm, like me mates and people like that who do manufacturing jobs, they say "How can you work in an office? Its got to be boring". They think working in an office is *sitting down and doing paper work*, you know, a lot of it is, but its just, I would think, as enjoyable as what they're doing. Ehm I think that's got a lot to do with it, how people actually see the job that they're going for. (BI 18)

The perceived contrast which is seen as a significant barrier to mobility is between the sedentary nature of office work and the mobile and creative nature of factory work. What is interesting is not whether factory work does in reality offer the opportunity for more physical movement (certainly some assembly line work does not [Blauner, 1964; Beynon 1973]) but the *perception* that it does. Indeed these responses may tell us more of the dissatisfaction of these office workers with the sedentary nature of their work than the reality of factory life, but these perceptions add to the image of factory workers as being engaged in manual labour which is seen to separate the two working environments. As Morgan (1992) notes, this distinction (highlighted as a discriminator between the work of men and the work of women) is as much about types of work as types of worker:

> The "mobility/immobility" distinction similarly does not simply refer to distinctions between men and women but also distinctions between men. "Mobility" here has a variety of connotations. A common feature of a definition of a "good job" is the ability to move around at or outside the place of work. It is likely that men and women share this perception... (Morgan, 1992: 83)

As Morgan (1992) argues, this distinction (while carrying overtones of masculinity) goes beyond gender differences and emerges as a general difference between factory and office work. Some respondents took this concept of mobility further and implied that it meant not just more mobility in the sense of physical creativity, but also more personal freedom which offered the opportunity for more social interaction at work:

> Q: What picture in your mind do you have of the average manufacturing worker?
> ... I don't know if some people feel there's a greater degree of *personal freedom* on a production line than on a row of people entering statistics into a computer. I would imagine that it's quite possible that someone working in

a manufacturing plant could never *sit at a desk 8 hours a day, it would bore them rigid.* (BI 8)

Q: What are the negative aspects of office work?
I think somebody who is used to working on the factory floor where they can have the radio on and *have a laugh and a natter* while they do whatever it is they do *manually* might find it a bit of culture shock if they came into an office where you're expected to *sit there with your head down* and there's no sort of pipe music or radios on and not so much kind of banter and chatter... I guess it would seem a bit *claustrophobic* just sitting at a desk... a bit more *constricting* I would have thought as well. (BI 9)

Here, again, the theme of sedentary office work being contrasted with manual factory work is evident but the contrast goes beyond the purely physical to include the idea that there is more "social" freedom in factories. This notion that the factory environment lends itself to "larking around" was also found by others (Roy, 1960; Beynon and Blackburn, 1972; Pollert, 1981; Thompson, 1988). The perception that a factory environment leads to a more friendly social environment was taken further by a personnel manager from Bristol Insurance who had worked for a number of years in a manufacturing company and argued that close working relations inside the factory were replicated outside the factory:

Q: How does the social life of Bristol Insurance compare with that of Imperial Tobacco?
(laugh) Don't you ask me that. Smith's had the nicest sports club I've seen in the West of England... and I joined there at 18 and until I became too sort of decrepit to turn out I was up there nearly every night enjoying and playing my sport. *Wonderful meeting environment...* Perhaps it's not quite so important but I would certainly say that manufacturing has the edge on commercial ventures when it comes to that type of provision. But I think, in general terms, if a person came out of manufacturing from that type of environment, and I don't think age is material because you can enjoy places like the Smith's ground just playing skittles or playing darts or playing snooker, you don't have to be racing around the field. I think *ehm* potentially they would find a difference in some of the *ehm social rapport*. I don't think people in an office, necessarily are prepared to spend as much time with their colleagues in a social environment... I would say that if you're in a factory invariably, say there were ten of you working on a plant in a factory I would say invariably five of you would live close together and four of you would probably be at the pub together two or three times a week if not seven. Yeah. I would say that the number of occasions that would happen in an office environment, other than where there is a *formalised event* organised, I would say people invariably go their separate ways after work... but I think people in a factory environment might find that a bit, eh, *more impersonal*, in general terms, in an office, the larger the office the more *impersonal* it can become. (BI 1)

It is argued here that it is not simply the quality of sports facilities which creates a friendlier social environment but the closeness of relationships in the workplace. The word "*rapport*" is chosen to describe the type of social interaction and the nature of the difference between factory and office. The emphasis of meaning is on an understanding and communicative relationship, which is assumed to be created by the more "personal" nature of the factory working environment. This is supported by the work of Beynon and Blackburn (1972) who, in their study of workers in a food producing factory, found that 296 out of 297 workers felt either extremely or quite friendly with members of their work group. These findings can be contrasted with the research into office workers undertaken by other authors (Crozier, 1971; Prandy et al, 1982). Prandy et al (1982), for example, found that social interaction at work was relatively unimportant in deciding overall work satisfaction, instead their respondents concentrated on satisfaction with the intrinsic job and satisfaction with promotion while Crozier (1971) found, in his study of French white collar insurance workers, that:

> ... they (office workers) expect cordial relations with their colleagues, but prefer a certain distance to be maintained. Eighty-five percent of them never get together with their colleagues outside work, and the fifteen percent who do seem to apologize for it. (Crozier, 1971: 110, emphasis added)

The image of factory work and workers which emerges is of a distinctly manual culture which is seen as requiring strength (with the consequent overtones of masculinity), the necessity of physical movement and the opportunity of larking around. This image of "manual vs mental" is seen to be strengthened by comments from Bristol Insurance respondents which compared the level of intelligence required between the manual work of factories and the mental work of offices. This differential requirement of intelligence was taken further by some respondents who saw factory work not only as less intellectually demanding but factory workers as possessing less intelligence, a difference which is seen not simply to discriminate between the two sets of workers but which sets office work and workers above factory work and workers. Breaking such data down three common themes were identified: office work was associated with mental work (table 6.2); reference was made to the qualifications necessary for office work (table 6.2) and explicit reference was made to the relatively lower intellectual ability of factory workers (table 6.1a). Turning firstly to the commonly articulated association between office work with mental work, table 6.2 shows that 6 respondents made reference to this, and the following two extracts give a fuller understanding of the explicit contrast with the manual work of factories:

> Q: How would you picture your average manufacturing worker?
> *Manual* as opposed to *brain* level, much more *practical* skills. (BI 12)

> Q: What sort of barriers could you see to people coming from manufacturing to here?

> I think they might like it if they came to work in an office [Why?] it's a bit more, eh, you use a bit more of your *mind*. Whereas if you're sat there packing things in boxes you're not really *thinking* are you. You could be *thinking* of something completely different other than those boxes. (BI 15)

In the first quotation office work was associated with "*brain* level" work, while in the second quotation it was alleged that, compared to a factory, "you use a bit more of your *mind*" in an office. The "superiority" of office work was also hinted at in the second set of comments where it was assumed that the opportunity to utilise "higher order" mental skills would entice factory workers away from jobs that involved no "thinking" to offices where one could use one's "mind".

Another common method of stressing difference in terms of a mental/manual split was the perception that office work required the possession of qualifications: as table 6.2 shows 7 of the respondents made reference to the importance of qualifications to office work and the related belief that factory workers lacked these qualifications. For example, in response to a question asking what sort of things would put manufacturing workers off working in an office one clerk replied:

> (long pause) I don't know, ehm, a lot of office jobs they say you've got to have a minimum of so many "O" levels, that sort of thing. Not having the *correct qualifications* or experience I think would put someone off... (BI 16)

Another commented, when talking more generally about manufacturing:

> I often connect working in a factory when I was about... it was a quick option, it was an easy option. If you left school at 16 probably *didn't have much qualifications* to get anything else or *didn't want to prove themselves* and decided to do something, *not that I would say simple but like*, sort of heavy work, quite tiring work at the end of the day, long hours, not much money. (BI 15)

Both support the findings of Crompton and Jones (1984) and Marshall et al (1988) that offices are characterised by possession of qualifications gained through education. These extracts support comments which were analysed in the last chapter on skills where possession of qualifications and an education were seen as necessary for office work and they also support the argument made in chapter two (on different recruitment channels) that qualifications are more important in office recruitment partially because they can be used as signifiers both of a candidates acceptability and suitability and can be effectively screened for through formal channels. This is evident from the quote from BI 15 who is seen to associate the possession of qualifications with a positive attitude to ambition which is contrasted with factory workers who "didn't want to prove themselves". Connected to this is the potential for education/qualifications to create certain cultural standards which serve to give occupational status groups increased power in the job market. On this point Collins (1971), has argued that:

> Education may be regarded as a mark of membership in a particular group (possibly at times its defining characteristic), not a mark of technical skills and achievement. (Collins 1971: 1008)

It could be the case, therefore, that possession of a qualification backed education separates office and factory workers in a number of ways: actual practical abilities (literacy); signifying to management certain social characteristics (Gintis, 1971; Bowles and Gintis, 1975; Dawes, 1993) and (re)creating occupational status groups which differentiate offices and factories (Collins, 1971; Marshall et al, 1988).

Moving on to the more explicit comments on the perceived low intelligence of factory workers (table 6.1a), while this was hinted at by some of the clerical grades in Bristol Insurance (i.e. BI 15, quoted immediately above, who indirectly refers to factory work as "*simple*" which carries an inference as to the [lower] mental capacity of those who carry or are prepared to carry out factory work) the majority of explicit comments on the relatively low intellectual ability of factory workers came from higher graded respondents. For example, a marketing assistant gave the following reply in response to a question asking for a description of a typical manufacturing worker:

> Oh, God. Well the only ones I know are people who actually work in factories. Ehm, one of my nephews works building washing machines and he hated it, he did build cars then he went and built washing machines, and he absolutely hated it. You imagine it to be very physical, *very manual as opposed to, as it would sound, as opposed to mental work* ehm I don't think it's necessarily harder, it's just different... (BI 4)

This quotation reveals a (common) reluctance to state explicitly that manual workers were less intelligent or more stupid than office workers, with the above respondent commenting: "You imagine it to be very physical, very manual *as opposed to, as it would sound, as opposed to* mental work ehm I don't think it's necessarily harder it's just different." Here the repetition of "*as opposed*" and the injection of the pre-delicate hitch (Coxon and Davies, 1986) "*as it would sound*" illustrates the sensitivity surrounding this opinion.[31] This reluctance to discuss "intelligence" was also found by Crozier (1971) who, in his study of white collar insurance workers in France, noted that "The white-collar employee's work is called "intellectual", but immediately the phrase "so to speak" is tacked on" (Crozier 1971: 175). Another extract, this time from a recently recruited graduate worker, is more explicit about the differing levels of intellectual ability:

---

[31]There were also hints from respondent comments on recruitment that using family and friends to get a job was "sensitive". See chapter 4: BI 2; BI 18; BL 1.

> Q: Picture the average manufacturing worker?
> The impression that would conjure up in my mind is someone working on a shop floor doing a routine job. [Is there any particular age or gender that comes to mind?] Male, 40. [What kind of skills?] Knowledge of the job, the knowledge to be able to use the machines. I wouldn't, this sounds awful, I wouldn't consider them to be *intellectuals*. Although while saying that I'm sure there's a lot of people in here aren't... (admits this is a stereotype but then goes on) I would instantly think of somebody *working with their hands*, or actually *making something tangible*, which obviously we don't do. Very much more cut and dried. (BI 7)

The implied contrast here is between people who work with their hands and those who work with their heads. Added to this is the explicit reference to factory workers being less likely to be *"intellectuals"*. Again the sensitivity surrounding comments relating to intelligence and a mental/manual split is evident, this time from the pre-delicate hitch "this sounds awful". I would argue that part of the reluctance to be honest about opinions of varying degrees of mental ability in different industrial sectors is that respondents are aware of the potentially hierarchical implications of such beliefs and are hesitant about making explicit statements which have inference for status or rank (and, perhaps at the extreme, for class). Another two respondents from Bristol Insurance (both managers) were more explicit in their references to differing intellectual abilities:

> Q: What sort of skills would you see your average manufacturing worker as having?
> ... I've not been around factories but I would think that the routines are totally different, ehm it's usually shift work, which is different. If you really take it to the extreme I suppose one has the impression that they will be *less well qualified...* people would say are you *suggesting they're thick*, but I wouldn't say that, I would say they're bright in different ways... (BI 2)

> I do believe that there's probably a feeling that manufacturing skills are less (pause) sorry the *eh* shall we say the *demands* if you like of *ehm* of working on a shopfloor are somehow *less significant* than the demands of working in an office [What do you mean by significant?] I mean it's easier, *you can be dumber and work in a plant* than you can, I'm not actually sure that's true. If you look at what you tend to hear management saying about the levels of ability of the people they recruit from schools they're nearly always highly critical: "can't spell, can't write, can't do anything - you know can't add, can't spell, can't write and they're 16." Either the people who go into manufacturing industry are even less well educated, which is a pretty unlikely scenario, or in fact there isn't a difference it's just a perception of if you work in an office you must be brighter. (BI 8)

Here, again, the sensitivity surrounding explicit comments on intelligence is evident, with both responses showing signs of hesitation and uncertainty. However, interestingly, here these sensitive beliefs are "projected" onto others, for example, in the first quote, it is other "people" who believe factory workers are "thick", with this respondent saying he, personally, does not hold this belief. This is obviously a difficult area - to what extent do respondents mask opinions which may be ideologically/socially sensitive by articulating their thoughts through "others"? The interview with BI 2 sheds some light on this, for after the tape recorder was switched off we continued talking about how people tended to move into similar occupations to their parents, and he gave the following comments: "I didn't like to say that but I suspect that they either *think of you as academics* or that way inclined, or labour, that's the wrong word but you know what I mean, *manual.*"[32] Then we discussed how many people could not read and he said "I was careful with that but there are a lot of people who can't read properly."[33] I would argue that these comments illustrate the potentiality for some to conceal opinions which they believe, for whatever reason, to be sensitive. The strong response emerging from these comments, then, is of a belief that qualifications and intelligence are an important differentiator between both office and factory work and workers.

Not all the respondents, however, thought there would be difficulties in moving between the two sectors. BI 17, for example, gave the following comment:

> Q: Can you think of any barriers to movement?
> No as long as training provided. [Would someone who'd worked in a factory for years find it difficult?] Well, I should imagine the *different atmosphere*, the *different* set up... not that they couldn't learn what that job would involve but I should imagine it'd be totally different to what they'd been used to. (BI 17)

This quote shows that while the majority of Bristol Insurance respondents recognised important distinctions and barriers, this was not unanimous amongst interviewees and that one (BI 17), while recognising differences, could think of no barrier that training could not overcome.

The picture emerging from these comments is of a set of a quite separate work culture with Bristol Insurance respondents perceiving differences both in terms of the nature of work and the nature of workers. The next section moves on to Bristol Laminated data.

---

[32]These extracts are from comments made off-tape which were written into note form immediately after the interview. Although not, therefore, directly from tape, they closely approximate what was said by this respondent and have therefore been put in quotation marks.

[33]Ditto.

Bristol Laminated

This section moves on to an examination of the data from Bristol Laminated and, as the following analysis shows, many of the perceptions of office work and of barriers to mobility mirror responses from Bristol Insurance respondents and support comments which were made earlier in relation to skill. Turning firstly to the summary picture:

Table 6.3
Bristol Laminated, perceptions of office work and workers

	Office work			Office workers		Total
	Paperwork	Seden tary	Phones	Educ/ quals	Clothing	
Managers	bl 1		bl 1	bl 6	bl 1	2
Workers	bl 2; bl 4; bl 6; bl 10	bl 2; bl 4; bl 8; bl10	bl 7	bl 2; bl 4; bl 5; bl 7; bl 10	bl 10	7
Response total	5	4	2	6	2	*19*\9

Note: response total (in italics) may be more than number of respondents due to multiple replies

What is immediately clear is the shared conception of a manual/mental split. The "manual" aspect emerges from comments which see the factory work of Bristol Laminated as involving familiarity with machinery and certain (masculine) properties, such as physical strength. This both supports earlier comments made by Bristol Laminated respondents and illustrates the accuracy of the perceptions of Bristol Insurance respondents with regard to factory work and workers. The "mental" aspect is evident from comments which describe office work as involving "paperwork", being sedentary and office workers possessing "education" and qualifications.

Table 6.4
Bristol Laminated, perceptions of factory work and workers

	Factory work			Factory workers			Total
	Machines	Shift work	More friendly	Physical	Macho	Intell	
Managers			bl 1		bl 6	bl 1	2
Workers	bl 2; bl 3 bl 6	bl 3; bl 4; bl 5; bl 9	bl 3	bl 2; bl 3; bl 4	bl 7	bl 3; bl 4; bl 5; bl 10	8
Response total	3	4	2	3	2	2	*16*/10

Note: response total (in italics) may be more than number of respondents due to multiple replies

Adopting a similar structure to that used in the last section, comments relating more to the work and workers in the "other" (i.e office) sector will be followed by an analysis of data on factory work and workers. Turning firstly to perceptions of clothing, this would appear to less of a differentiator for Bristol Laminated respondents than for Bristol Insurance respondents, with only 2 of those interviewed (compared to 6 at Bristol Insurance) mentioning clothing in discussions. Where it was mentioned, however, similar conclusions were drawn. The personnel manager at Bristol Laminated (BL 1), linked working in an office with "dressing up", while another respondent gave the following comments during a discussion of the different type of clothing he would have to wear if he got promotion (to an office job) at Bristol Laminated:

> I wouldn't like to wear a *collar and tie* [Would you feel uneasy in that?] You always like to think of yourself as *being one of the boys*... (BL 10)

This supports earlier responses from Bristol Insurance which were used to argue that dress carries implications of status, with this respondent not wishing to join what a Bristol Insurance respondent (BI 13) described as the "*tie brigade*", because he liked to think of himself as "*one of the boys*". Here the difference is less "dirty/clean" than "formal/informal", with this respondent associating more formal dress with the more formal (and distancing) working environment of the office.

Another perception, common amongst both sets of respondents, was the notion that office work was sedentary and involved less movement than factory work:

> Q: Would you ever think of going to work in an office yourself?
> ... ehm the thought of being actually *stuck* in that office, I know you're not

sort of *tied down* but you're *stuck* there to a certain extent. When I was on the milkround I liked being in the *open air* but it's not too bad in here because we've got a fairly large factory so we're still, it's not sort of *too closed in*. (BL 4)

(This worker had worked in an office as a trainee draughtsman when he first left school and was asked why he left).
Lack of activity, I've got a low tolerance to *boredom* and just *sat in one place*, drawing, was not it, you know. I have to be *moving* about a bit. I mean this job I'm doing now is brilliant for that, you don't get enough chance to be bored. (BL 8)

It is clear from these quotes that these respondents share the image held by Bristol Insurance respondents of the essentially sedentary nature of office work, with it being seen as variously *"boring", "sitting in one place", "stuck"* and *closed in"*. This match of perceptions illustrates the strength of the positive perception of work which allows physical mobility (Morgan, 1992) and, through its identification with factory work, demonstrates its role as differentiator and as a barrier to mobility.

The factory workers of Bristol Laminated also identified office work with "paperwork" and stressed the perceived need for office workers to possess "education" and "qualifications". These provide further support for the perceived distinction between "manual" factory work and "mental" office work and mirror the perceptions of the skills necessary for office work which were articulated by Bristol Insurance respondents and were analysed both in the last chapter and the last section. Turning firstly to the comments of the personnel manager at Bristol Laminated:

Q: What do you think would put manufacturing workers off going into an office type of environment?
Ehm, from our men's point of view a lot of them just want what they call "a little part time job" (after redundancy) because a lot of them have done shift for so long they've had enough and they just want to potter a little bit. Most of them don't like *paper work* so an office would be a non-starter. (unprompted) It's not because they don't dress up or anything because although they're in overalls a percentage of them will still look tidy and when you see them out in the street they're as neat as pins. It isn't so much the atmosphere or the environment as the *paper work* and the *writing*, and *phones* wouldn't be, for the older ones phones wouldn't be acceptable either. The younger ones are a different kettle of fish. (BL 1)

The first point to note from this extract is the reference to a relationship between office work and "dressing up" which was highlighted earlier. The second point is that the emphasis of difference is seen to be of a very *practical* nature, concentrating on the importance of *"paper work"*, *"writing"* and *"phones"*. The lack of literacy skills, especially amongst the older members of staff at Bristol Laminated, was also apparent from later comments from this respondent relating to reading and writing:

> From the ones that we've employed in the last four years we've made sure of that (possessed reading and writing skills)... we did tests [Did any fail?] I was only on the edge of that but I think they did find some that probably couldn't cope. [Before that there were no tests?] They went by things like the application form but that's dangerous 'cause the wife usually does it and all they do is sign their name on it. So now I usually ask the question - "Did you fill in the application?" and some of them say "Oh no my wife did it for me" really pleased with it whereas it's no use to us at all. I had a suspicion yesterday, I was making someone redundant yesterday, he was delighted, he wanted to go anyway, I said to him if you can complete this form and let me have it back and he said "would you like to do it now for me, *I don't like paperwork*'"and he's sort of 55,56. (BL 1)

It is apparent that some of the workers at Bristol Laminated do have relatively poor reading and writing abilities and adopt various techniques to overcome this potential difficulty. It is also quite clear that when workers at Bristol Laminated talk of *"paperwork"* they are referring to literacy skills. That this anxiety is not simply held by older workers is shown by the comments of a lacquer mix operative, in his thirties, who gave the following response to a question on potential barriers to industrial mobility:

> I'm still ambitious, believe it or not, I still want to get on. But a lot of people on my level *worry*, and this is the only problem, when we set to *worry*, and I'll be honest with you, is, ehm, is our *education* from the past, we haven't took full benefit of it. If you asked me to *read* and *write* and all the rest I would *panic*, I would *panic* and a lot of people on the workfloor would do the same. I mean that, I would *panic filling out forms* and I would *panic* doing this and that... most of that side of things would make most of the manufacturing people, people on the floor, production workers, *panic* like hell. And that is wrong. This is where the *barrier* is, you got the *barrier* where you think that "oh he's *intelligent* 'cause he can *read* and *write* properly, I'm not, because I *can't spell*." I'll go home and read a book all day long but if you ask me to spell those words I couldn't. *That's the difference, we've all got this feeling*. We can camouflage it, we can hide it where we are but we still got the skills, we still got the sense. We know what to *write* 'cause we *write* that same type of stuff all the time. So we're not going to show that we're *thick*. But the problem of showing that we might be *thick* or someone saying (picks up bit of paper and theatrically pretends to read it, then throws if down) "can't spell," it drives you up the wall. Saying that, it's also my own fault, 'cause I could go back to school and I could learn more, but to go back to school takes a lot of guts and say look "I'm not as clever as I should be,

would you help me." They're on about retraining but if I'm in a class and everybody's young (expression here one of apprehensive fear). I'll get by, I'll sit down and *write* anything, but I wouldn't want to show you it after. But I'll go home and get it sorted out and I'll get it rectified and I'll get it sorted out on me own. It's the same as swimming, I can't swim, but I still go swimming but no one knows I can't swim. I can still camouflage that, and that's a lot what happens on the workfloor. That's why you've got this problem when you say "Can I go on that side of it?" (meaning move from factory to office) a lot of people in my situation wouldn't because of the *embarrassment* of maybe the way what we are. That is it honestly." (BL 10)

This powerful quote highlights not only the very practical nature of some of the differences between the sectors, but also offers an example of the social forces which may act as barriers to simple notions of retraining. For not only does this respondent perceive a practical barrier in the form of literacy but he also sees a substantial social barrier, where feelings of inferiority will mix with awkwardness and pride to form an attitude where he (and his colleagues) are unwilling to "go back to school". This recognition of a relationship between office work and paperwork and the associated need for literacy and qualifications was evident in a number of other comments:

Q: What sort of skills do you think they (office workers) need?
I really don't know, I mean obviously they must like *bookwork*, *working in the same place all the time*, in an office environment, keep yourself *clean*, if you know what I mean, I mean when you work *on a machine* your bound to get oil and eh that's not everybody's cup of tea. (BL 2)

Q: Would you ever think of going to work in an office yourself?
No, I don't think so, no. [What would put you off?] Well, obviously, the type of work, *paperwork*. I'm not daft obviously, but I know my limitations I don't think I'd be to good with too much *paperwork*. (BL 4)

Q: So what would put you off going to work in an office?
No... Maybe I look at it that I haven't got the *qualifications* anyway. I would imagine that to go into office work you've got to have a *qualification*. I got no *qualification*. I left school with no *qualification*, I've got no *qualification*. I look back and I think I did do a lot of things wrong when I was young, but it's alright saying 30 years on isn't it, you know what you should have done. My wife always says to me "well somebody's got to this job and somebody's got to do that job not everybody can be brainy and walk off and get all the jobs, somebody's got to do the *menial* jobs." I don't call it a *menial* job, it's an important job in the firm but they could always get somebody else to do my job. (BL 5)

What emerges from these comments is a recognition of educational inferiority and an associated feeling of insecurity. These workers believe that working in an office requires skills and abilities (reading, writing, familiarity with "paperwork") they do not possess and see themselves as unsuited for such work. This recognition of educational inferiority and inadequacy was not, however, accompanied by a belief that factory work required any less "intelligence". On the contrary, some respondents from Bristol Laminated were explicit about the knowledge and understanding required for work with machinery:

> Most jobs in Bristol Laminated are semi-skilled, unless you're a printer or an electrician or an electronics man, it's all semi-skilled work. You've got to be *intelligent*, you've really got to give yourself completely over to the machine, you can't muck about, you can't take your eyes of the job because you're doing such critical work. Medical packaging's what we're doing, you can't afford to make a mistake. (BL 5)

> I'll tell you now office work's a doddle compared to factory work. It's easier physically, *can't be any harder mentally* because if you're working on a machine you're always thinking what's going on and yet I see the average office person seeing themselves above a factory floor person. (BL 3)

These quotes support earlier data on the skills possessed by factory workers (analysed in the previous chapter on skills) which were seen to include in-depth (often tacit) knowledge of machinery with consequent implications for intelligence, in the sense that such work requires alertness, perceptiveness and understanding. In addition to this level of knowledge, factory workers also showed their "intelligence" through various ruses and tactics. For example, BL 10, whose quote is given above, is clearly aware of the common association between literacy skills and intelligence but describes the various techniques that he (and his colleagues) develop to overcome the potential literacy problem: "We can camouflage it, we can hide it where we are but we still got the skills, we still got the sense." Another example of the ingenuity which hints at the existence of alert and quick minds (i.e. intelligence) at work in factory environments is described by Thompson (1988) who, in his work into skills amongst Coventry car workers, relates how a bookie operated within the factory during working hours:

> He was rather a fat chap, he used to have big trousers, and he worked on the saw mill, and he worked on the circular saw - I've never seen a bloke like it - he's as quick as I'm talking to you - but he used to go down to the gentleman's toilet which was just outside the mill, about ten to two... right up to ten to two you could go and have a bet on the two o'clock race. He'd tell you what's run the first race - how he got to know I don't know. (Thompson, 1988: 64-65)

I would suggest, therefore, that intelligence can be interpreted as meaning possession of a certain amount of learned knowledge signified by educational qualifications (which has implications of social status) and/or of possession of a quick mind. It could be the case, therefore, that office respondents were using references to education and the intelligence required for "mental" office work not simply to describe real practical differences but also in order to identity certain social traits which may imply that office work and workers are above factory work and workers in an occupational hierarchy.

Turning to comments from Bristol Laminated respondents which made reference to factory work (table 6.4), there is, again, seen to be commonality between these descriptions (which emerged often in the form of contrasts with perceptions of office work) and the perceptions of factory work offered by Bristol Insurance respondents which linked factory work to working with machinery and requiring physical skills. The first two quotations which are examined are from a second operator on a polythene extruder who, for the six months previous to interview, had been involved in the introduction of a new computer system (called Capture) which involved some office (mainly paper) work. The first extract is in reply to a question on whether he would like to move to office work:

> No, no that wouldn't interest me. [What would put you off it?] Ehm the environment itself, you know I am a *physically*, I do like *physically* working hard. I mean I've been on Capture for six months and it hasn't to me been as rewarding as what I thought it was going to be. I mean whereas with a machine you get on with it, with Capture there's a lot of *politics* going on at the moment about how much money we spend on it, I'm not interested in that, I just want to get on and do a day's work... When I go back on the machine I won't be sorry to leave it, I shall get back to *humping* this and *humping* that. (BL 2)

The first point to note is that the aspects of factory work which this respondent finds attractive - "*physically* working hard" and "*humping* this and *humping* that" are the same as the perceptions of factory work articulated by respondents from Bristol Insurance, where both "*lifting*" and "*physical*" are used to describe manufacturing work and workers. This commonality reflects the accuracy of the perceptions of the aspects of work which differ between factory and office. The perceived contrast between factory and office work is clearer from an examination of a later response from BL 2, this time in reply to a question on the work of his family and friends:

> One's an accountant from the water board, he's different from me if that's what you're going to ask (this was not my intention) ehm whereas I'm more *robust*, I would say he's not, if there was anybody going to do something silly it would be me and not him, ehm he's a different type of person to what I am. John out Filton, now he's half office, half out on the road, *robust* like myself... my next door neighbour, he's an accountant, he's different from me.

> [Do they have different skills?] I could not see him working on a machine, it's not in his makeup to be like that. We both enjoy our gardens, whereas I would get on with it, *physically* get on with it, there's a lot of *thinking* done by the neighbour, no he doesn't seem as *robust* as me, *I'm not saying any I'm any more of a man*, no, I'm not saying that. (BL 2)

This provides some important and valuable insights into the meanings and values this worker attaches to aspects of his character and how these shape his attitude to work. This respondent immediately states, unprompted, that he is *different* from his accountant neighbour John and, using gardening as being analogous to attitudes to work, states that he differs from his friend to the extent that while his office working friend adopts a mental (thinking) approach to gardening he adopts a manual (physical) approach. These manual and physical properties of "robustness" which this respondent sees himself as possessing and which he believes are necessary for work with Bristol Laminated contrast quite dramatically with the more cautious, planned, thinking approach of his office worker friend and provide another example of the perceived mental/manual divide between office and factory workers.

There are also strong indications of the gendering of occupations here, with this respondent (completely unprompted) commenting that "... he doesn't seem as *robust* as me, I'm not saying any I'm any more of a man, no, I'm not saying that." It was noted earlier that respondents can adopt certain techniques to disguise opinions they see as contentious and that one of these is to push such perceptions onto "others". I would argue that this response offers an example of a different technique but with a shared aim, namely the outright denial of something *before* it is mentioned. It is always going to be difficult to separate out a "genuine" denial from one designed to disguise a sensitive opinion, but I would suggest that a common feature of the latter is that the denial takes place even though the topic denied is not being discussed. Hence, in the quotation above, BL2 seems to almost pre-empt a discussion of gender and masculinity.

One aspect of factory work which was not mentioned by office respondents but which was seen as attractive to some of the factory workers interviewed was shiftwork. As table 6.4 shows, 4 respondents made reference to shiftwork. Three of the four responses relating to shiftwork were positive in nature, with the general view being that shiftwork gave more freedom and flexibility, both in work patterns and leisure time. The first of the quotes below is from a respondent discussing the different cultures in a factory and office, while the second is in reply to a question as to what would put this worker off going to work in an office:

> ... more often than not you got to be a bit sort of *restricted* in the way you act. Plus another thing with that is sort of the *day work*, I'm not to keen on *9 to 5 hours*, I've got kids obviously. I quite like *shiftwork*, I get a fair bit of time with them. (BL 4)

Nine to five routine. I've worked shift work for so many years I couldn't go back on days. [Anything else?] No, I don't think so, just never wanted to work in an office. (BL 5)

Here the main attraction of shiftwork is seen to focus around the greater degree of personal flexibility which it allows, with BL 4 arguing that he can spend more time with his young family. I would suggest that the positive perceptions of shiftwork, or rather with the increased freedom which is associated with this working pattern, represents another practical barrier to industrial mobility.

This section has highlighted the similar nature of many of the perceptions respondents in the two industrial sectors hold of each other and has produced data which support many of the findings in the last chapter on skill. The most important distinction to emerge was of a mental/manual split. This was articulated in a number of ways: by reference to different types of dress (with implications of a dirty/ clean and or formal/informal divide); by reference to the "manual" skills necessary for office work (with, through the emphasis on physical strength, implications of the gendering of occupations); by reference to the sedentary nature of office work and the mobile nature of (manual) factory work, and by reference to the "mental" skills necessary for office work, such as literacy and qualifications (with it being argued that these may play a role in signifying membership of a social group as well as providing information of practical abilities). Running through this theme of a mental/manual split was the impression that mental work was "superior" to manual work. This was perhaps most obvious from the comments of some (higher grade) respondents from Bristol Insurance who (in terms parodied by a production manager at Bristol Laminated) portrayed factory workers as possessing low "intelligence". This is not to argue that the picture of manual factory work was universally negative (indeed there were positive images of movement which were associated with factory work), rather it is to argue that, on balance, and with a hesitancy which may hint at knowledge of the sensitivity surrounding issues of hierarchy (which carry implications for class), office workers saw themselves and their work not only as fundamentally different but also as "superior" to factory work and workers. These perceptions of difference are seen to emerge more strongly in comments which relate directly to an occupational hierarchy and to movement within such a hierarchy, and it is to this that we now turn.

6.3 Occupational hierarchy and ambition

This section turns to an examination of comments relating to occupational hierarchy and ambition. It opens with a brief discussion of official classification systems, before turning to an analysis of the primary data. The broad thrust of the responses points to a hierarchical conceptualisation of the labour market similar in structure to the Registrar-General's Social Class scheme (HMSO, 1966). This schemata was first developed in the early part of this century by a medical statistician (Stevenson,

1920) who collected and analysed data on infant mortality by occupation and developed a conceptualisation of society which had as its centre a recognition of a hierarchy.[34] As it developed the emphasis shifted from recognising a "natural" hierarchy based on ability and mortality to a hierarchy of *social* status:

> As stated in 1970, following a by then well-established formula, the aim was to provide categories that were "homogenous in relation to the basic criterion of the general standing within the community of the occupations concerned." (Prandy, 1991: 636 and OPCS, 1970)

The origins of this conceptualisation lie in the work of Weber (1968) and his work on status. This has been developed by Collins (1971) and Turner (1988) to include groups which share common cultures such as dress, mode of speech and outlook on life. The latest classification system, the Standard Occupational Classification (SOC), has been developed by combining the Department of Employment's classification of occupations (Classification of Occupations and Directory of Occupational Titles: CODOT) with data from the Office of Population and Census Statistics (OPCS) (Thomas and Elias, 1989). This system of classification is hierarchical, with each set of occupations further subdivided into major, minor and unit groups. The central importance of "ordering" occupations in the Registrar General's scale of occupations was also found by researchers in the United States (North and Hatt, 1947) and Reiss (1961); in the UK (Hall and Jones, 1950; Glass, 1954; Goldthorpe and Hope, 1974) and in international studies (Erickson et al, 1982). These studies produced graded hierarchies similar to those of the Registrar General, with, again, all manual work being placed below office work. The common approach of these researchers was to present pre-prepared categories to varying number of respondents who were then asked to rank these occupations.[35] This mass survey method may be contrasted with the approach

---

[34]Stevenson was attempting to refute the claim of nineteenth century hereditarian eugenists that interventionist public health schemes were diluting the physical stock of the country by encouraging the survival of the children of the "lower orders". To do this he collected data on fertility and mortality by occupation, hence the centrality of occupation to the official classification scheme. (Marshall et al, 1988)

[35]The exception here is Goldthorpe and Hope's research where respondents were given some choice, Coxon and Davies (1986) write of Goldthorpe and Hope's method "Five or ten representative titles were selected for each of the 124 occupational categories, which yielded a pool of 860 titles. Subjects were first invited to rank order a fixed set of 20 titles, and then to insert into their rankings a randomized subset of 20 from the 'pool'." (Coxon and Davies, 1986: 32). Respondents had, therefore, "choice" to the extent that they were offered a wide range of occupational titles which had been derived from a relatively wide range

adopted here in the sense that respondents were not presented with any pre-prepared list of graded occupations, rather concepts of hierarchy flowed, unprompted, from the data. As the following examination of the data goes on to argue, the broad perception is of a hierarchical conceptualisation of the labour market similar to that of the Registrar General's social class scheme, with office work and workers being placed above factory work and workers.

Bristol Insurance

The data from Bristol Insurance on a mental/manual split (particularly that referring to the differing degree of intelligence) was used earlier to argue for the existence of an occupational hierarchy. The potential for such occupational distinctions to carry overtones of hierarchy involving class were apparent in a study by Abbott (1987),[36] where it was found that in investigating what was meant by class labels the most popular occupational characteristic ascribed to the working class was "manual". This section builds on the earlier picture of a mental/manual divide through analysing references to class, status and hierarchy which emerged from discussions on perceptions of factory workers and potential barriers to mobility. The summary position is illustrated in table 6.5, which shows that in 8 of the 18 interviews discussions on difference and barriers moved into areas related to stratification.

Table 6.5 shows that 6 of the respondents made direct references to class, 3 made reference to the different status of factory and office work and 3 made reference to an occupational hierarchy. Turning to direct references to class, one of the most interesting comments came in reply to a discussion relating childcare and the promotion prospects for women in the two industrial sectors:

> I would imagine in manufacturing industry there would be more sort of *traditionalist* views about that sort of thing (women leaving when they have kids) simply because I would imagine you'd have a larger proportion *of working class people* and it tends to be *working class ethics* that the women are chained to the kitchen sink type of thing, even these days. [Is this only with the working class?] No, not entirely, not solely working class but I do think it's a big *working class* thing. I mean certainly in *middle class* or *upper middle class* a lot of women are pressurised by their husbands to stay at home and read articles about it. "Oh

---

of occupational categories.

[36]Abbott (1987) conducted research into the class position and class images of 342 working married women in social scale C1, where it was found that "routine non-manual women's perceptions of social class and of their place in the hierarchy are comparable to those found in research on middle-class men." (Abbott, 1987: 101)

darling it just wouldn't look good at the office, can't have wifey out working it'd look like I can't support them", so the wife ends up staying at home and doing charity work. So it does exist but I would have thought generally speaking it would have been a more *working class ideal* that the man goes to work and supports his wife and children. (BI 6)

Table 6.5
Bristol Insurance, references to stratification

	Ref to class	Ref to status	Ref to hierarchy	Total
Managers	bi 1; bi 5; bi 6; bi 8	bi 1	bi 1	4
Supervisors		bi 7	bi 13	2
Clerks	bi 14; bi 16	bi 14	bi 14	2
Response total	6	3	3	*12*/8

Note: response total (in italics) may be more than number of respondents due to multiple replies

The first point to note here is the clear articulation of difference between the two working communities. Although the terms "middle" and "working" class are used in a rather loose fashion, what is clear is that one is associated with offices and the attitudes one would expect to find in office while the other is associated with attitudes which are perceived as being typical of factories. The second point of importance is the implied belief in the superiority of the office attitude, which is compared positively to the more "*traditionalist* views" of manufacturing industry. The keyword here is "traditional" which, as Williams (1988) has argued, has overtones of backwardness:

> ... tradition and especially traditional are now often used dismissively... Indeed traditionalism seems to be becoming specialised to a description of habits or beliefs inconvenient to virtually any innovation, and traditionalist is almost always dismissive. (Williams, 1988: 320)

I would argue that it is in this sense that the above respondent uses "*traditionalist*" and that the emphasis of meaning is on a set of attitudes influenced not by independent individual thought but by the conventional customs of the community which are seen as relatively old fashioned and unsophisticated. I would suggest, therefore, that by applying the term to those who work in manufacturing industry (described as "working class") this respondent is expressing the superiority of office attitudes, with the consequent implication of a hierarchical conceptualisation of the working community.

Another respondent, in a discussion of possible barriers between the industrial sectors, was more explicit about the importance of "social class":

> Q: Can you think of any barriers (between factory and office work)?
> *Social*, possibly, ehm people who work in factories, people who work in offices different, really, *social class*. I don't mean necessarily better, but *different type of people* that you *socialise* with that sort of thing. So I think that would probably be a barrier, not knowing the *sort of people* you're going to end up working with. (BI 16)

The immediate emphasis is again on difference, with people who work in factories being perceived as belonging to a different "*social class*". The second point of interest is the inference of the superiority of the "*social class*" of people who work in offices. This is evident both from the fact that, unprompted, this respondent adds "I don't mean necessarily better, but *different*" and the choice of words to describe this difference. The keyphrases here "different *type* of people" and "*sort* of people". The emphasis of meaning is clearly on a different class or group of people and the implications of superiority come from the context in which these different classes are discussed. For example, this respondent notes that one would not choose to work with the "*type*" and "*sort*" of person who works in a factory, but would only "end up" in such a situation. The implication is that it would be distasteful to work beside factory people with the inference that office workers, at least at the personal level for this clerk, are superior to factory workers. This perception of superiority is clearer from the comments of another of the respondents from Bristol Insurance, who in a reply to a question on potential barriers between industrial sectors, gave the following response:

> Cause people like me, that sound's awful, but I mean people that work here, suddenly you shove them in a factory floor. And they'd say "well I'm not going to do that, *I'm worth something more than that*" because they automatically think they are *worth more, if they're here*. Which is fallacy, because people work hard wherever you are. (BI 14)

The sensitivity surrounding the process of hierarchical ranking is immediately apparent, with this respondent adding the caveat "that sound's awful" when it becomes apparent she is about to rank explicitly other workers (and implicitly herself). This respondent, as is done often in interviews when one is discussing a topic which is in any way controversial or sensitive, externalises this process of social ranking from herself to "people that work here" who would not wish to be "shoved" (i.e. not go voluntarily) on to the factory floor because, as they work in an office, they are "*worth something more*". The perception that office work is superior to factory work and that the people who do this work are above factory workers in an occupational hierarchy comes through strongly, with two references being made to office workers believing that, because of the type of work they do, they are "*worth more*" than factory workers. The complexity and confusion surrounding this process of ranking is also evident from this extract, where, in the last sentence, it is argued that this process of ranking is a "fallacy, because people work hard wherever you are." I would argue that this respondent is confusing a hierarchical ranking process which is in some way influenced by perceptions of social status with one which is decided by work effort alone. To the extent that a ranking process is decided by effort alone then a conclusion that office workers are "better" than factory workers may well be a "fallacy" because "people work hard wherever you are" but if, instead, this process of ranking is seen to be influenced by the *social* status of a particular occupation the perceived attitudes of this respondents colleagues are more understandable. Williams (1988) has written of this confusion:

> ... with the development of clerical and service occupations, there was a crucial ambiguity about the class position of those who worked for a *salary* or even a *wage* and yet did not do manual labour. (*Salary* as a fixed payment dates from C14; *wages and salaries* is still a normal C19 phrase; in 1868, however, "a manager of a bank or railway - even an overseer or a clerk in a manufactory - is said to draw a salary", and the attempted class distinction between salaries and wages is evident; by early C20 the *salariat* was being distinguished from the *proletariat.)* Here again, at a critical point, the effect of two models of class is evident. The middle class, with which the earners of salaries normally aligned themselves, is an expression of relative social position and thus of social distinction. The working class, specialized from the different notion of the *useful* or *productive classes*, is an expression of economic relationships. Thus the two common modern class terms rest on different models, and the position of those who are conscious of relative social position and thus of social distinction, and yet, within an economic relationship, sell and are dependent on their labour, is the point of critical overlap between the models and the terms. It is absurd to conclude that only the working classes work, but if those who work in other than "manual" labour describe themselves in terms of relative social position (middle class) the confusion is inevitable. (Williams 1988: 65-66)

I would argue that the confusion evident from the respondent cited above reflects the ambiguity surrounding issues of ranking and consequently of class highlighted by Williams. That is to say there is an awareness that in a purely economic sense both sets of workers are in a similar situation - both work hard, but that political, social and historical forces interact to influence the skill *status* of different occupations. In later comments this respondent expands on potential barriers to industrial mobility and gives some explanation of why factory workers would not fit in to an office environment and by so doing sheds light on why office workers believe they are "*worth something more*":

> Q: What sort of things do you think might put manufacturing workers off from coming in here?
> (really quick response) The fact that they'd think that they'd be *out of their class*. They would think that nobody would speak to them, the fact that they would think that people here, well perhaps they would think first of all that they couldn't do it and I'm sure a lot of them have got a lot more brains than people have here. But perhaps they'd think they wouldn't *come up to the standard* so they'd be frightened and then perhaps they would think that people would be a bit intolerant of them. Perhaps they would think that *their image* wouldn't fit. *The way they talk, the way they act, their manners, their dress and all the rest of it.* And so they'd feel uncomfortable. (BI 14)

In this quotation the respondent concentrates on the perceptions of factory workers and the emerging emphasis is on how feelings of inferiority may well make factory workers uncomfortable in an office environment. It is assumed that factory workers would "think that they'd be *out of their class*" and "wouldn't *come up to the standard* (required in office's) so they'd be frightened". This concept of a "*standard*", which it is assumed, factory workers would not meet, provides further evidence for the perceived superiority of office work and the concept of an occupational hierarchy which this implies. By placing office work and workers above factory work and workers the implied hierarchy is similar to the recently developed SOC (Thomas and Elias, 1989) and the social class index of the Registrar General on which this is based (HMSO, 1966). This extract also gives a clear indication that it is *social* differences which are seen as the main discriminators between factories and offices: "*their image* wouldn't fit. *The way they talk, the way they act, their manners, their dress and all the rest of it.*" The potential importance of dress as a status signifier and differentiating factor between factory and office has been discussed in an earlier section. However, the extract above expands on this and adds a number of other cultural traits which are close to the definition of status groups offered by Collins (1971):

> In general, they comprise all persons who share a sense of status equality based on participation in a different culture: styles of language, tastes in clothing and decor, manners and other ritual observations, conversational topics and styles... (Collins, 1971:1009)

The similarity between Collins's definition of a status group and the above respondent's description of why factory workers may feel "uncomfortable" in an office environment is quite striking. The respondent focuses in on what Collins believes to be the most important discriminators in shaping a status group - image, dress, pronunciation and manners and uses these to explain potential industrial immobility. These perceived discriminators are supported by the work of Crozier (1971) who, in a study of white collar insurance workers in France, found similar perceptions of blue collar workers, namely that they have poor manners, they do not speak the same language and their dress is more untidy.

Continuing the investigation and analysis of the "status" theme which was uncovered in the data, one of the personnel manager's at Bristol Insurance gave the following reply to a question on differences between the manufacturing and the office sector:

> I don't think that there is a *status differential* these days as there always was in the past. I mean, when an uncle of mine worked at Wills, he was there in the 30s and 40s, there was quite a *status difference* between staff and factory people. Staff were people that worked in the office and the factory people were *second class citizens* if you like, they dined in different dining rooms and they had different loos and all this crap... going back to the question, what can the TEC (Training and Enterprise Councils) do, I think it's a case of making people sell themselves and making people feel comfortable sitting amongst people who, they might have thought were, who would regard them as *inferior*. (BI 1)

Earlier it was argued that respondents adopt various techniques to avoid direct association with opinions which may be regarded as sensitive. This quotation offers another example of the "projection" technique, where status differences are initially assumed to be "in the past" (the 1930s and 1940s). That this respondent still believes these issues have contemporary relevance is apparent from the fact that he sees "make(ing) people feel comfortable" in amongst others who "would regard them as *inferior*" as the main barrier to industrial mobility which should be tackled by Training and Enterprise Councils. The references to the perceived superiority and consequent conceptualisation of a hierarchy of occupations are clear and powerful: in his uncle's time "the factory people were *second class citizens*" while today office workers may "regard them (factory workers) as *inferior*". The emphasis of meaning is quite clear - factory work and workers are perceived to belong to a *lower* level of occupation. This perception that manual factory work and workers are lower in status than office work is supported by the research of Prandy et al (1982) into white collar work, who concluded that: "One point emerging here is that our respondents see themselves standing well above manual workers in status." (Prandy et al, 1982: 65)[37]

---

[37]These authors conducted 1924 structured interviews with male non-manual workers (including managers and clerks) across a number of different employing establishments and one of the areas covered was the status of non-manual as opposed to manual work. The perception of occupational status was measured by asking each respondent to mark on a scale, with "manual worker" on one end and "top manager" at the other, where his job would be put by most people (a) in his company and (b) by the community at large. Possible scores ranged from 0 to 60 (with manual worker scoring 5 and top manager 55). The average scores for non-manual white collar work were 29.7 by the community at large and 28.7 by colleagues in his company, indicating recognition of an occupational hierarchy

A connected theme which emerged from discussions with Bristol Insurance respondents was that they saw themselves as possessing a positive attitude to career ambition, and contrasted this with factory work and workers, who were assumed not to share the same aspirations or be in a working environment which would allow such aspirations to be met. Thus office workers not only conceptualised an occupational hierarchy which saw them and their work "above" factory work and workers but also valued the possibility to be promoted within their company.

The findings from the data that office workers value the potential for promotion is supported by the work of other authors (Blau, 1963; Crozier, 1971; Prandy et al, 1982; Crompton and Jones, 1984; Lane, 1988b; Marshall et al, 1988). Crompton and Jones (1984), in their research on clerical work found that, while women were less successful in obtaining promotion, the majority of both male and female routine non-manual clerks were *interested* in promotion.[38] In addition, these authors, while arguing that clerical *work* has become increasing proletarianised, recognised that clerical *workers* appreciate and desire promotion, a value system symptomatic of a "middle class" attitude. They write:

> Emphasis on the non-manual career, particularly for men, reflects a long-established sociological contrast between the "middle class" and the "traditional working class"; while the former expects that "advance will occur - that careers will progress" and consequently possess a "marked orientation towards the future", the latter's major concern, it is suggested, is "with being able to *maintain* a certain standard and style of living" accompanied by an "emphasis on the present and... lack of concern for planning ahead"' (Goldthorpe 1969: 118-121). This "middle class" perspective has been described as highly "individualistic", in contrast to the "collectivist" perspectives of the working class. (Crompton and Jones, 1984: 80)

The importance of "personal advancement" to office workers was also emphasised by Prandy et al (1982) and Marshall et al (1988). Prandy et al (1982), in their study of male white collar workers, found that the positive implications for status implicit in a career structure was perceived as being a "reward" in itself, while Marshall et al (1988) established that one of the reasons why routine non-manual workers were more likely to view their work as "much more than just earning a living" was that they felt their job allowed them to use their initiative.

---

shaped by status perceptions.

[38]The research into clerical work in three firms found that interest in gaining promotion declined with age and, for women, with "life-cycle stage". For men it fell from 100% of those aged 25-34 to 58% for those 35 and over while for women the figures were 79% for young, unmarried women; 65% for young, married women; 64% for older women with no employment break and 29% for older women with a break in employment.

Turning to Bristol Insurance data on ambition, table 6.6 illustrates that in talking of their own work and that of factory workers reference was made to ambition by a total of 9 respondents, including managers, supervisors and clerks.

Table 6.6
Bristol Insurance, references to ambition

	Direct ref to ambition	Refs to seeking promotion/career	Employment seen as career not job	Total
Managers	bi 1; bi 9	bi 1; bi 9	bi 3; bi 11	4
Supervisors		bi 15	bi 7	2
Clerks	bi 18	bi 14; bi 16; bi 18		3
Response total	3	6	3	*12*/9

Note: response total (in italics) may be more than number of respondents due to multiple replies

The breakdown of this data illustrates that comments included direct reference to ambition, reference to seeking a career through promotion and the likelihood of seeing employment as a career and not as a job. Turning to more detailed comments, a personnel manager at Bristol Insurance who has worked in manufacturing gave the following reply to a question comparing office with factory workers:

> Ehm, taken in the right spirit, I'm sure it will be, I think they (the office workers) have a higher academic level, yes? I think they are invariably either more numerate, more literate or a combination of both. I think they have, possibly, more *ambition*, *career aspirations* and I would think they would put more time of their own into their future, i.e. by studying or something like that than the factory hand who would be waiting for a *promotion* hopefully but if not they tick over from day to day. I think there's a bit more *ambition*. Now that's not decrying, that's not being snobbish or decrying the factory worker. I think the office worker typically would have *goals* or *objectives* much clearer in their minds than people who went into a factory. And again I'm not decrying the comparison in academic levels but I think that would be understood. (BI 1)

The description of factory workers offered by this respondent is mostly negative and closely resembles, both in tone and content, earlier comments on the perceived low level of intelligence of factory workers. The negative description of these workers is similar to that found by Coxon and Davies (1986) who, in their research into images of social stratification, found that "... the incumbents (of unskilled jobs) have few qualifications, and there is more than a suspicion that they are neither bright, dedicated, nor ambitious." (Coxon and Davies 1986: 130). The perceived negative characteristics of factory workers are even more marked when contrasted with BI 1's positive description of office workers who are described as having "*career aspirations*", "*ambition*", and as seeking "*promotion*", "*goals*" and "*objectives*". The emphasis is on movement, of advancing oneself through employment. It is through this idea of upwards progress that the hierarchical conceptualisation of the labour market becomes clearer. This concept of hierarchy, and particularly its relevance as a signifier of class or rank, was noted by Williams (1988):

> Career is still used in the abstract spectacular sense of politicians and entertainers, but more generally it is applied, with some conscious and unconscious class distinction, to work or a job which contains some implicit promise of progress. (Williams 1988: 53)

The positive emphasis on movement implicit in the use of this keyword is contrasted with the absence of a similar attitude amongst factory workers and represents an important differentiator between these two sets of workers. In addition, the assumed "superiority" of office work and workers is hinted at by the fact that this manager states three times that he is "not decrying" the factory worker (this may, again, be indicative of the sensitivity, apparent in earlier comments relating to intelligence, surrounding the issue or ranking).

The relevance of ambition to office work and workers and its perceived absence from factory workers is evident in another quotation. Part of this extract was used earlier with reference to the recognition of the sedentary nature of office work, but here the response is used for its reference to ambition:

> Q: What barriers do you think stop manufacturing workers from moving to the service sector?
> *Self belief* in being able to do the job, maybe they think there's more in the job than there actually is. Thinking the job's boring, a lot of the people that I talk to ehm, like me mates and people like that who do manufacturing jobs, they say "How can you work in an office? It's got to be boring". They think working in an office is sitting down and doing paper work, you know, a lot of it is, but it's just, I would think, as enjoyable as what they're doing. Ehm I think that's got a lot to do with it, how people actually see the job that they're going for.. The way I see it is people saying "oh there's no way I could answer a phone, there's no way I could talk to people, there's no way I could write letters", it's just a *self belief* in themselves and also just thinking what the actual job is. I don't think they realise what the jobs are. (BI 18)

The first point to note here is the reference to the absence of communications skills on the part of factory workers, skills which were seen in the last chapter as being vital for office work. The second point to note is the association of the lack of these social and technical skills with the lack of an additional social skill - "self belief", with its strong association with confidence, with manufacturing workers assumed not to possess the right amount of confidence in their own abilities to "get on", to succeed in a career. The third point to note is the implications for superiority: this worker is not only detailing a difference between himself and his friends but is arguing that he possess's the *additional* characteristic of "*self belief*" which will enable him to be successful in an office job. This careerist attitude to ambition was also shared by other respondents:

> Q: Would it be more difficult to return to work after having children in manufacturing or in an office?
> I think it would be easier to go back to manufacturing if you were in that job anyway. I know it's a real generalisation but I would imagine it to be *more menial work* whereas if I came back to a *career* I'd have to give it a lot of effort. It depends on what your priorities are. I don't think work is as important to them as far as job satisfaction, it's more of *a means to an end*. (BI 7)

> Q: How would you picture your average manufacturing worker?
> Well the first thing that springs to mind if you think about a manufacturing, a factory floor job yeah, is somebody whose, if you like, the salt of the earth, the kind of person who is quite happy to do a *manual* job, ehm, perhaps, I don't know really, somebody whose quite willing to, who perhaps doesn't want to try anything else except do a *manual* job and like they're prepared to do that. Perhaps they're not really interested in *going to night school*. Perhaps *they're quite content* to do the same job they're doing for a long, long, time. Throughout the rest of their life. (BI 14)

> I often connect working in a factory when I was about, it was a *quick option*, it was an *easy option*. If you left school at 16 probably didn't have much *qualifications* to get anything else or *didn't want to prove themselves* and decided to do something, what I would say *simple* but like, sort of heavy work, quite tiring work at the end of the day, long hours, not much money. (BI 15)

The first of the above quotations illustrates that it is both factory work and factory workers which are seen as inferior to office work. Factory work is described as "menial", a word which implies inferiority and factory workers are assumed to be more instrumental, to be more interested in the "ends" of money than the "means" of satisfying work (Lockwood, 1966; Goldthorpe et al, 1969; Beynon and Blackburn, 1972; Wedderburn and Crompton, 1972; Marshall et al, 1988; Rose, 1994). The second respondent shares this belief, arguing that a factory worker is someone who does not have a career orientated attitude to work (associated with a desire to gain qualifications). This respondent, therefore, in addition to linking factory work with manual work and office work with mental work (an association commonly made and discussed earlier), sees office workers as more ambitious than factory workers. Many of these values are also to be found in the third extract where the respondent saw factory work as being "a *quick option*, an *easy option*" for workers without qualifications or who "*didn't want to prove themselves*." Again this points not only to the fact that a positive attitude to ambition serves to differentiate office from factory workers but also that it places office workers in a "superior" position. This is evident from the fact that factory workers are perceived as opting for the "*quick*" and "*easy*" option of "*simple*" work and of avoiding the challenge of "proving" oneself in a working environment which offered the potential for promotion.

The desire for promotion was also articulated by workers at Bristol Insurance through the perceived association between office work and better "prospects", an association which becomes clearer from closer examination of the comments of respondents from Bristol Insurance. The first set is from a Post and Control Clerk and relates to her discussion of a previous temporary job in the manufacturing sector while the second extract is from a young male clerk whose job mainly involved dealing with the post from insurance brokers and is in reply to a question on what put him off manufacturing work.

> Q: What sort of skills did you use?
> I worked there for a few weeks, it was a company that made rainwear for golfers and, ehm, you know it was basically packing and folding things up and putting them in plastic bags and putting the poppers on coats and things like that. I wouldn't say it was skilled at all, that particular job. Obviously there are some factory jobs that you need more skills for. I would say eye hand co-ordination rather than *using ehm, your, you know, your mind*. [Had most of the people been there a long time?] Yeah most of them. [Do you much prefer working here then?] Yeah I do. More secure. *Better prospects*, I think there're much *better prospects* working in an office than working in a factory. Better pay. (BI 16)

> Q: Why didn't you want to go into manufacturing?
> I didn't fancy working with my hands, I mean, ehm, I don't know whether it is skill, like we were talking earlier on, but I just didn't feel I could accomplish anything with my hands, obviously with experience I might have done, but I just felt like a nice cosy job in an office. (laugh) The way dad was talking as well, it just seems there was *more prospects* there, more chances of *promotion* in an office. (BI 18)

There is, again, the common association of factory work with manual work but, linked to this, a belief that workers who are attracted to (or at least willing to put up with) such work are not ambitious, are not interested in *"prospects"*. The emphasis of meaning associated with this term is again on movement, of an expectation that one's position will improve in the future and, in the context in which this word is used, the belief that the existence of such opportunities differentiates office from factory work.

The data in this section illustrate that office workers not only recognise a hierarchically structured labour market, with office work above factory work, but that the possession of a positive attitude to career ambition is seen as a defining feature of office work and one of the main reasons why office work (and consequently workers) may be viewed as "superior" to factory work (and workers). Thus offices and factories are divided not only by the fact that office work offers the potential for ambition, but also that office workers see this as a defining aspect of their personalities. Thus the feelings of difference and "superiority" are seen to be connected not simply to the type of job, but the personalities and values of the people who fill these jobs, with the implication that people who prefer the challenge of a career are "superior "to those who have chosen (or are at least willing to put up with) manual work which offers no "prospects" and only instrumental goals. The crucial discriminator here between office and factory workers is seen to be not the actual likelihood of promotion (which as Crompton and Jones [1984] argue is less for women) but the recognition of, and identification with, a bureaucratic hierarchy which, as Lane (1984b) points out, places clerical workers on a bureaucratic career ladder and "hence fundamentally distinguishes their market prospects from those of manual workers" (Lane, 1988b: 67). Office workers, then, recognise a hierarchically structured labour market which places them and their work above factory workers. What is more, office workers are seen to value the potential for mobility within this structure and recognise that this separate their work and them from factory work and workers.

Bristol Laminated

This section turns to Bristol Laminated data and analyses comments relating to perceptions of a hierarchically structured working community where it is found that office work is seen as "above" factory work. This hierarchical conceptualisation, similar to that of the Bristol Insurance respondents, points to the strength of industrial segmentation and the consequent implications for industrial mobility and labour market flexibility.

Turning firstly to the summary picture, table 6.7 illustrates that 6 out of the 10 respondents interviewed made 7 references to stratifying concepts.

Table 6.7
Bristol Laminated, references to stratification

	References to hierarchy	References to qualitative differences	Total
Managers		bl 6	1
Workers	bl 3; bl 4; bl 5; bl 9	bl 4; bl 10	5
Response total	4	3	*7*/6

Note: response total (in italics) may be more than number of respondents due to multiple replies

Closer analysis of this data illustrates the meanings attached to these concepts of hierarchy and demonstrates the strength of feeling lying behind this belief in the stratified nature of the labour market. The first three quotations, from one respondent, are from discussions around the topic of factory workers moving to offices:

> I think the British public, if you like, are sort of two camps, either *you're office worker or you're manual worker*. (BL 3)

> I'll tell you now, office work's a doddle compared to factory work. It's easier physically, can't be any harder mentally because if you're working on a machine you're always thinking what's going on and yet I see the average office person seeing themselves *above* a factory floor person. (BL 3)

> To be honest I think there's a lot of talent out on the factory floors but it's never tapped in the proper way. As I said to you when we started off, office *people up there* (pointing up in the air) *factory workers down there*, there ain't no way they're going to drop down to your level and there's no way they're going to see you go up to their level. (BL 3)

These quotes offer clear examples of a hierarchical conceptualisation of the labour market, with there being as association between the type of work a person does and the status this confers on this person. These status/class implications were also evident from other responses:

> Q: What general differences do you see between office and factory workers? I think years and years ago office staff thought they were *better* than *working class type people*. [Is this view still around?] Probably with the older people, yeah. (BL 4)

Well, it depends on the individual doesn't it, some individuals might feel *inferior*. There are people who think if you work in an office you're *upper class*, you're not really but they think you are. (BL 9)

The first quotation offers another example of how perceptions of hierarchy are seen as socially sensitive. This respondent uses the technique (also used by Bristol Insurance respondents) of projecting such a belief initially to the past ("years ago") and then, when pressed on the contemporary relevance of this sensitive opinion, suggests that it is only held by "the older people". Perceptions of the superiority of office work are more explicit in the second quote, where it is argued that some factory workers "might feel *inferior*" to office workers. This perception of the "*inferiority*" of factory workers is given added importance because it mirrors the perception of one of the respondents from Bristol Insurance who commented that factory workers may feel uncomfortable "sitting amongst people who, they might have thought were, who would regard them as *inferior*" (BI 2). The second response also highlights the complexity surrounding issues of ranking and consequently of class. This complexity was noted in an earlier discussion of the comments of a worker from Bristol Insurance who argued that, although it was a common view amongst office workers that they were "*worth more*" than factory workers this was a "fallacy, because people work hard wherever you are." (BI 14). The respondent from Bristol Laminated comments that: "There are people who think if you work in an office you're *upper class*, you're not really but they think you are." The source of complexity is again the ambiguity surrounding issues of ranking and class (Williams, 1988). If upper class is taken to mean people of rank or nobility then clearly working in an office does "not really" make one "*upper class*". If, however, one takes account of the social status which is often associated with office work then it is possible to understand why this office worker believes that: "There are people who think if you work in an office you're *upper class*."

It is clear, then, that respondents at Bristol Laminated recognised an occupational hierarchy, where, commonly, office work is considered in some ways "above" factory work. It is important to note, however, that contrary to the articulated beliefs of some at Bristol Insurance, no worker at Bristol Laminated talked of their *own* inferiority, but perceived that the popular perception was that office work placed office workers in a "superior" position to factory work and workers. Some of the data from Bristol Insurance respondents suggested that the differences which led to these perceptions of hierarchy were influenced by certain cultural traits and, again, these differences and the consequences they have for social status, were recognised by respondents at Bristol Laminated. For example, the following comments (used in an earlier chapter to indicate different approaches to qualitative interviewing) were given during a discussion of perceived differences between factories and offices:

I'm a blue collar worker, I'm not a white collar worker. I'm not the type of person what could get a job in a office. [Why not?] For the simple fact... that it's not in me, I would get bored out of my brain. More so than I do at the moment. [What's boring about it?] The *pressures* on me are the *pressures* I can handle but the *pressures* of being in a situation with my type of education and also *losing it* (your temper) a little bit you would be a little bit embarrassed. And also the *way I am* and the *way I talk* and the *type of person I am*, I would find it hard to get on and work with people who're better educated and who *talk differently*. You don't put me down 'cause I'm as good as anyone else but I'd find that I'd get a little bit, how can you say, *a little bit uppity*. (BL 10)

The emphasis of meaning here is on difference. This difference is initially described in terms of relative boredom (again reflecting images of office work as sedentary), however, when pressed, the description is expanded to include feelings of inadequacy and difference which may lead to an explosive situation. This worker talks of office work demanding certain requirements, both technical requirements which are evident through references to education and qualifications and social requirements, evident through references to "the *way I am* and the *way I talk* and the *type of person I am*." The cultural traits chosen to describe difference are similar to earlier comments offered by a respondent from Bristol Insurance who gave similar reasons as to why factory workers would feel uncomfortable in an office environment: "*their image* wouldn't fit. *The way they talk, the way they act, their manners, their dress and all the rest of it*". As was noted earlier, these cultural traits are descriptions of status groups (Collins, 1971), and this commonality of perceptions provides further evidence for the depth of difference and the consequent breadth of the barrier between these two working communities.

Turning briefly to comments relating to career orientated ambition, this was found to be less important to Bristol Laminated respondents than to Bristol Insurance respondents. The summary position is shown in table 6.8 with 5 respondents making 5 references to ambition.

Table 6.8
Bristol Laminated, references to ambition

	References to ambition	Total
Managers	bl 6	1
Workers	bl 3; bl 4; bl 9; bl 10	4
Response total	5	*5/5*

Note: response total (in italics) may be more than number of respondents due to multiple replies

Some respondents were seen to link "ambition" and promotion with offices and, when this was done, "ambition" was viewed negatively, while other respondents articulated their own "ambition" through a desire to "get on". What did emerge, however, was that the important role which association with ambition played in Bristol Insurance (in the sense that being ambitious was connected to office work and consequently was part of the package which made office work and workers superior to factory work and workers) was not strongly evident in the data from Bristol Laminated. A more detailed analysis of a selection of responses illustrate the different views and beliefs which were attached to this term. The first extract is from a worker who worked in an office when he first left school:

> Q: What made you leave the office?
> Ehm people mainly, *eh* I found office people were all, *eh* how could I put it, were *goody two shoes* and we want *promotion* and so *back stabbing* it wasn't my style at all. (BL 3)

The emphasis here is on the degree of difference in environments, with this worker feeling uncomfortable in what is described as an environment characterised by people who were "*goody two shoes*" and continually seeking "*promotion*". The two pre-delicate hitches and the phrase "how could I put it" give the impression this respondent would have preferred a more explicit and personal description of his feelings but, perhaps because of the presence of a tape recorder, chose the phrase "*goody two shoes*" to describe office workers. The underlying meaning is still quite clear, of describing a group of people who were motivated by personal progression through a career, a working environment this respondent found so distasteful he left the office. This negative view of career ambition was not, however, universal amongst respondents at Bristol Laminated. For example, one worker gave the following reply to a question on whether office work is better than factory work:

> It's awkward to say, really, it depends on you, how far do you want to go. I mean my boy's 22 but he's still *taking exams*... if your parents work at it *you can go a long way*." (BL 9)

What is important from this quotation is the clear association between education, ambition and offices. Similar to respondents from Bristol Insurance, this worker clearly links opportunity for promotion with working in offices and views this as a factor separating factories and offices. The importance of such an association (between office work and careerist ambition) was also evident from the comments from a production manager at Bristol Laminated, who saw the possession of a particular "attitude" to work as a discriminator between factory and office work and workers:

> Q: Would the people working with machines now feel at ease in, say, an insurance office?
> The vast majority, no... if they've worked on the shop floor for any length of time they tend to develop a *sort of attitude*, it sounds awful but it's *an approach* to the job where it's very much I'm here from this time to that time

and then I shut off and hand it over to somebody else. I'm a sort of innocent bystander, I can't do very much to change the way things happen and why should I concern myself too much about trying to do that anyway, I'm just here for the money. (BL 6)

The emphasis here is on the identification of an instrumental "attitude" amongst factory workers, who are assumed to be motivated by money as opposed to any other objectives. This perception of factory workers possessing an instrumentalist "attitude" is similar to that of respondents at Bristol Insurance (BI 7, BI 14 and BI 15) and is supported by other studies (Lockwood, 1966; Goldthorpe et al, 1969; Beynon and Blackburn, 1972; Wedderburn and Crompton, 1972; Marshall et al, 1988; Rose, 1994). Marshall et al, (1988) found that under both the Registrar General's classification system and Goldthorpe's classification system manual workers were more likely to view their work as "just a means of earning a living".[39] The keyword used to describe the attitude which distinguishes factory floor workers is "*attitude*" and, I would suggest, the emphasis of meaning is on a pattern of settled behaviour, or approach to work which, in the context in which the word is used, is characterised by non-careerist values. A fuller understanding of the values which this manager attaches to work (and implicitly to a set of values which go beyond work) is evident from comments made on the transition one employee made from the shopfloor to the office. This process involved not only a change of job function but also change of attitude, where the worker began to acquire a different set of values and to fully appreciate the tasks of office work in general and management in particular:

Just talking about the bloke that I did take off the machines to go and work in an office, it took him a long time to adjust, not necessarily working days from shift or sitting at a desk instead of by a machine, but the sort of *attitude twist* from the management's useless, it doesn't know how to run the place, and all I can do is criticise, to well maybe there is a different side to the story, it is a lot more complex, and yes, there is something I can do to help, and perhaps I can stay a little bit longer at the end of the day to finish a job instead of just dumping it... we had some rows in the early days where I told him he had an *attitude problem* and he took it very hard to start with, but the more he thought about it and the more he came into contact with other people on the

---

[39]In a more detailed analysis of their data Marshall et al found that the conventional belief that those in "working class" occupations were more likely to have a pecuniary attitude to work was oversimplified and that "...where proletarians do treat work simply as a source of income, more commonly they do so either because they lack sufficient skills to secure an interesting job, or because they are trapped in labour markets offering only a restricted range of opportunities." Thus the adoption of an instrumentalist approach may be through a combination of necessity and choice. (Marshall et al, 1988: 210)

staff and their approach to work, the more he understood what I was trying to get at, and he has changed quite considerably. (BL 6)

This quote refers to a machine operator who was moved to the office and is now a junior member of management. It therefore refers to two separate, but linked, processes, a move from manual worker to junior manager and a move from factory to office. As a consequence it is difficult to isolate which changes in values are due to joining junior management and which to moving to office work, but I would suggest that general points relating to movement from factory to office do emerge. Firstly, this worker is now recognised as one of the "staff", a term whose common uses and meanings include both reference to authority and, more broadly, a general description of office workers. This description of office workers as "staff" and the implications of being in a different category were also found by Wedderburn and Crompton (1972) and Prandy et al (1982). The former set of researchers, in their study of chemical workers in the North East, found that workers (especially tradesmen) were "... in favour of giving what has been called "staff status" to all employees..." (Wedderburn and Crompton, 1972: 105). Returning to the comments of the production manager, the extract describes how, in the process of joining the "staff", this worker underwent a "sort of *attitude twist*" which resulted in a change of thinking: "there is something I can do to help and perhaps I can stay a little bit longer at the end of the day". This belief in one's job as being more than a set number of hours was common amongst both management and clerical graded workers at Bristol Insurance and the tension involved in this process of change is illustrated by the chosen verb "twist" whose common uses and meanings emphasise the tensions involved in this process of change. It is a process which involves a vigorous alteration of previously held values and beliefs and it's use is illustrative of the similarity in views between this manager and respondents from Bristol Insurance and demonstrates the strength of segmentation in attitudes and motivations between the factory floor and office even within the same establishment. After the change in attitude however, it is alleged this worker associated more with the career approach to work of the "people on the *staff*" and "understood" the different set of values and motivations. As was mentioned earlier, one has to be careful in analysing such evidence because it concerns a movement both from factory floor to office *and* from worker to management. Nevertheless, I would argue there are certain similarities between the values which have been created by this process of change and the values which are evident from both management and clerical staff at Bristol Insurance. These changed values, in particular associating work with a bureaucratic career ladder, provide further evidence of perceived differences between factory and office work.

While data from Bristol Laminated were seen to support findings from Bristol Insurance which linked offices with careerist ambitions, other comments from Bristol Laminated respondents illustrated that some at did possess ambition, or a desire to "get on":

Q: What sort of skills do you would you say you brought along to Bristol Laminated?
(laugh then long pause) Good question, I think I've got *the right attitude* for working if that's any good. And obviously I'm a family man, *I want to get on*... (BL 4)

Q: What barriers do you see between factory and office work?
I'm still *ambitious*, believe it or not, *I still want to get on*. But a lot of people on my level worry, and this is the only problem, when we set to worry, and I'll be honest with you, is, ehm, is our *education* from the past, we haven't took full benefit of it... (BL 10)

These quotations illustrate that the view held by many of the respondents at Bristol Insurance and the production manager at Bristol Laminated, that factory workers lack "ambition", is too simple, and that certain factory workers do have "ambition", which is articulated through a desire to "*get on*". Unlike the comments from Bristol Insurance, however, not only do fewer respondents mention ambition but there is less emphasis on the existence of a bureaucratic career ladder as a *defining characteristic* of their type of work. There is also a hint that the major motivator is instrumental. For example, the emphasis in the first quote cited above (from BL 4) there is an association between "getting on" and being a "family man", with the suggestion that one needs an increased wage to raise a family.

In summary, the data analysed in this section have shown that respondents from Bristol Laminated share a similar hierarchical conceptualisation of the labour market to that of respondents from Bristol Insurance, with office work seen as being above factory work. There was seen to be a difference, however, in the perceptions of movement *within* such an occupational structure, with respondents from Bristol Insurance placing emphasis on possession of a positive attitude to career ambition which served not only to divide the workers but place office workers above factory workers. Those at Bristol Laminated, however, did not see ambition as critical to them or their work and most commonly linked ambition in a negative fashion with offices. It was also argued that while both sets of respondents recognised an occupational hierarchy, with office work and workers above factory work workers, it was not the case that Bristol Laminated respondents saw this as implying that they were "inferior" in any way, rather such a distinction was seen to be held by the broader community whose values (influenced by perceptions of status) shaped the occupational reality within which they operated.

6.4 Conclusion

This chapter has highlighted a number of key differences which emerged from the data and which reflect on the extent to which the labour market is flexible and the extent to which respondents hold "conventional" attitudes which were assumed to accompany Paddy Ashdown's "conventional" jobs within "conventional" firms

(Guardian, 19th September, 1994). The broad picture which emerged from the data was of a segmented workforce, with office work being above factory work in an occupational hierarchy and with respondents defining their labour market segment in an (at times aggressively) defensive manner. This picture of a structured labour market consisting of fundamentally different working environments (and workers) was seen to be based around a number of key differences. The first of these was the emergence of a mental/manual split, with office work characterised by mental demands and skills and factory work by manual skills. It was argued here that there was evidence which pointed to perceptions being influenced by gender, with factory work being characterised by male attributes (such as requiring physical strength) and a masculine outlook (described as "macho"). Furthermore, it was argued that this mental/manual split contained references not just to difference but to hierarchy, with office workers seeing the "mental" demands of their work placing them above factory work and workers. The second part of the chapter concentrated on direct references to occupational structure and to ambition. Bristol Insurance respondents were seen to recognise an occupational hierarchy which placed them and their work above factory work and workers. One of the articulated differences which carried overtones of superiority was the perception that office work offered the possibility of mobility through a bureaucratic career ladder. Office respondents, therefore, not only placed themselves and their work above factory work and workers but saw careerist ambition as a *defining characteristic* of their work and a fundamental component of its superiority. Factory respondents also acknowledged the existence of a hierarchy of occupations which placed them and their work below office work and workers. However, the "inferior" position which such a hierarchy placed them in was not accepted uncritically, with factory workers defending the difficult demands of their work by reference to the in-depth level of knowledge and skills required to do their work and linking any inferences to "inferiority" to the importance of the status of an occupation within broader society.

Turning to how these findings reflect on the work of others and the overall theoretical perspective of the research, several points can be made. Firstly, the evidence shows the prevailing importance of a "traditional" mental/manual split. Braverman, writing in 1974 argued that such a dichotomy was no longer applicable:

> In the beginning, the office was the site of mental labour and the shop the site of manual labour... the traditional distinctions between "manual" and "white collar" labour, which are so thoughtlessly and widely used in the literature on this subject, represent echoes of a past situation which has virtually ceased to have any meaning in the modern world of work. (Braverman, 1974: 315, 325-326)

The contemporary relevance of such an attitude is evident from Ainley's conclusion that:

> ... changes in the skills exercised at work have been shown to be influential upon class divisions, particularly the old distinction between manual and

mental work that has now been considerably erased. (Ainley, 1993: 43)

This assumption of the disappearance of "traditional" attitudes and demarcations is common, yet the case study data from Bristol Insurance and Bristol Laminated provides strong support for the continued prevalence of such "traditional" differences, with even the most routine workers from Bristol Insurance perceiving their work as "mental" and comparing it with the "manual" work of the factory.

Secondly, the conclusion of Braverman (1974) and others (Crompton and Jones, 1984)[40] that clerical work (like manual work) has been increasingly proleterianised and that: "the 'class situation' of the clerical worker now resembles that of the manual 'proletariat'" (Crompton and Jones, 1984: 1) is also affected by my data. For even if (using the technologically deterministic definition of the "deskilling" hypothesis) the tasks conducted by clerical workers are becoming increasingly proleterianised, the office workers themselves are seen to possess characteristics (such as qualifications) and values (such as positive attitudes to careerist ambition) which lead these workers to believe they and their work inhabit a different (and higher) occupational class position to those in manual factory work. Thus even if the *work* is increasingly mundane and routine (and therefore "proleterianised") the *workers* still recognise differences in the status of occupations, differences which carry inferences for the "class" position of these workers.

Thirdly, these data have important repercussions for our understanding of the non-competitive structure of the labour market. For in their perceptions of each other and of potential barriers these respondents are seen to be very defensive, holding strongly held views and values which serve to create non-competitive work groups. These differences, across a number of areas (strength, literacy, physical mobility, occupational hierarchy) add up to quite separate work cultures, where differences are articulated in a defensive manner which may illustrate not only that respondents are aware of barriers to mobility but are so fearful of change that they deliberately participate in the creation and propagation of these barriers. The next, and final, chapter, summarises the main findings and, in the light of these, explores future labour market prospects.

---

[40]As was noted earlier these authors did recognise a relationship between ambition and class - Crompton and Jones (1984: 80).

7 Conclusions: Prospects for the future

7.1 Introduction

The context within which the research for this work took place was one of industrial restructuring, a process which is over 20 years old and which, from the 1980s, has been accompanied by a changing political environment, with the 1979 Thatcher government ushering in an ideology which sought to role back the frontiers of the state and increase personal freedom and "choice". As was argued in chapters one and two this government mixed neo-classical labour market theory, new right thinking and monetarist economic theory to construct and implement a number of supply side economic policies. Perhaps nowhere was the impact of this combination of economic theory and political ideology felt more powerfully than in the labour market, where various deregulatory acts, initiatives and policies were introduced in order to make the labour market more flexible and responsive to changing market demands. While the consequent focus of much of the academic debate on flexibility concentrated on changes in methods of production (flexible specialisation) and changes in the organisation of labour within the firm (flexible firm) an important additional aspect of flexibility was seen to be the potential for mobility between industries and occupations. As was noted in chapter one the government argued in White Papers' and Employment Department publications that if Britain was to have a flexible labour market which could respond quickly to changes in demand then workers would have to be prepared and able to move to where the new work was and to learn the skills required in the expanding industries and occupations. It was this underdeveloped "mobility" aspect of flexibility which formed the main interest of this research, in particular the potential for mobility between jobs.

The investigation of mobility was carried out via case study work involving two firms on the opposite sides of industrial restructuring, and the data produced from these firms was used to demonstrate the extent to which the views and values of case study respondents represent a barrier to increased mobility. This final chapter seeks to draw together the themes emerging from the earlier empirical and theoretical material and is split into three sections. The first section summarises the substantive empirical material and examines where the case study data has produced innovative findings, the second investigates the broader theoretical picture and the third turns to policy and considers how the findings inform potential policy formulation.

7.2 Analytical material

The case study material was gathered from a large factory (Bristol Laminated) and a large office (Bristol Insurance) in Bristol. As was argued in chapter three the local labour market of Bristol has undergone a similar process of industrial restructuring to that of the country as a whole - for example in the ten years from 1981 to 1991 G.B. saw manufacturing employment fall by a quarter and service sector jobs increase by a fifth while Bristol experienced a drop in manufacturing of a third and a similarly sized increase in service sector employment to that of G.B. as a whole. It was felt, therefore, that by investigating the potential for mobility in two case study firms located within the Bristol labour market the study was being undertaken in a local economy which strongly reflected national macroeconomic patterns.

The first of the empirical chapters, chapter four, investigated methods of recruitment, and it was shown that (broadly speaking) informal methods were more common in Bristol Laminated and formal methods in Bristol Insurance. This section also investigated why such informal networks should be used and it was found that such channels offered advantages both to management and to workers. Both saw the potential to increase control in the workplace, with managers using networks as rewards and workers using networks to get jobs (or pass quality information which may improve employment opportunities) for friends and relatives. The last section of this chapter investigated why each sector should concentrate on formal (Bristol Insurance) and informal (Bristol Laminated) methods and it was argued that the main reason for this was the effectiveness of each method in satisfying the managerial recruitment criteria of suitability and acceptability. Finally, it was argued that the evidence which emerged from the data on recruitment illustrated an important difference between these two work groups, with respondents not only concentrating and highlighting different recruitment channels but, even when both use informal channels, these were different in kind and in nature. Thus it could be the case that anyone laid off in manufacturing would seek a job through the "wrong" channel and even if such an individual had access to a white collar informal channel they would conceptualise and use it in a different way.

The most important new finding in this chapter was the role played by family and friendship networks in office recruitment. It was found that by passing on information about the company's reputation informal methods played a low level but important role in the recruitment process in Bristol Insurance. Most case study work has concentrated on the function of family and friendship networks in the recruitment process of factories and my finding of a more subtle role for such methods in Bristol Insurance points to the need for further case study work in this area.

Chapter five moved on to investigate skill and it was found that the concept of skill is seen and used in dramatically different ways, so much so that talk of a "skills gap" which may be filled by retraining is oversimplistic. The primary results from the office respondents of Bristol Insurance and the factory respondents of Bristol Laminated showed that they saw themselves as possessing, and their work as requiring, quite different skills. The respondents from Bristol Laminated consistently articulated a skill conceptualisation which was close to a task centred notion of skill, with their own skills being closely linked with (often heavy) machinery. Conversely, the respondents from Bristol Insurance saw themselves as possessing social skills, such as being effective communicators, and emphasised the importance of holding qualifications. It was also argued that the whole area of skill conceptualisation was saturated by perceptions of gender. So, for example, the men of Bristol Laminated often associated their work and skill not only through familiarity with machinery but with certain physical properties, such as strength and fitness. This "gendering" of skills was also evident in the responses from Bristol Insurance respondents, some of whom linked abilities to certain traits which were assumed to be "female", such as patience and tact. This points to another practical difficulty, for if it is the case that skill conceptualisations are influenced by "traditional" values relating to craft and by notions of gender, then any simple "reskilling" course (such as putting ex-factory workers on a telephone techniques course) is not going to work. The people (perhaps especially men) who go on such courses would not see it as giving them "real" skills and the managers who would be likely to employ such workers may be strongly influenced by perceptions of the attitudes and abilities these workers have inherited from the factory.

The innovative findings emerging from this chapter were the existence and importance of office based tacit skills, abilities such as patience and tact, whose acquisition may perhaps be influenced by experiences outside the workplace and whose gendered nature leads them to be seen as "common sense" abilities which, consequently, do not receive recognition or reward. Again, case study investigation into tacit skills has concentrated mainly on blue collar work and so this could prove another fruitful area of future work, into the nature and extent of such office based tacit skills and into possible methods of measurement and adequate remuneration. In addition, the existence and extent of office based tacit skills could act to create boundaries to managerial control. Management may, in a sense, be caught between two unpleasant choices - either such skills are somehow recognised, which may well mean an increase in the workers "skill" base and a consequent increase in reward, or such abilities remain unacknowledged and therefore an important part of a job's skills remains "inside" each worker, making the process of increasing management control over the complete production process more difficult.

The final analytical chapter related to the pictures and perceptions respondents held of each other and of each others work. These differences illustrated a certain conservatism and defensiveness, with Bristol Insurance workers seeing themselves and their work as "mental" and viewing factory work and workers as "manual" and with Bristol Laminated respondents viewing office work as sedentary and as requiring qualifications. The comments were, again, seen to be influenced by gender perceptions, with factory workers linking the manual and movement aspects of their work to being masculine, and, furthermore, there were suggestions that the factory environment itself was characterised by certain norms and practices, such as manners of address (often associated with swearing), which were more suited to and suitable for men.

The most important addition to the literature to emerge from the analysis of this chapter related to the strength of perceptions of a mental/manual split and the attached deeply held recognition of occupational hierarchy. Both Braverman (1974) and Crompton and Jones (1986) have argued that the contours between office and factory work have become progressively softened with the process of increased proletarianisation spreading to office work and workers. Yet my case study evidence argues strongly against this, with notions of status and class heavily influencing perceptions of a relatively rigid occupational hierarchy, with office work and workers above factory work and workers. It could be the case, therefore, that allegations of the demise of such "traditional" class divides have been somewhat premature and that what Mill ([1848], 1976) described as "social rank" is still important in shaping labour markets.

7.3 Theoretical reflections

The picture emerging from the analytical material was of non-competing industrial groups, a finding which supports the theoretical position of the segmented labour market theorists and the earlier classical economists, and which has important repercussions for the potential for increasing labour market flexibility through industrial mobility. As was argued in chapter three, Government statistics show that some people do move between jobs - with 16% of job changes involving a shift from manufacturing to services and 12% a move from manual to non-manual occupations (Employment Gazette, 1991) - yet my empirical work has demonstrated how difficult it may be to increase this industrial and occupational mobility. As was argued earlier, the government has used neo-classical labour market theory, new right theorising and monetarist economics to argue for the creation of a flexible labour market. Yet, I would suggest, the increased mobility aspect of this flexibility is going to be a particularly challenging task because the model of the labour market used in this conceptualisation tends to play down the non-economic phenomena which my empirical work has shown to be central to the formation and working of labour markets.

The case study data from Bristol Insurance and Bristol Laminated allowed access to the forces underlying the (limited) statistical material on industrial and occupational mobility and, by so doing, showed some of the limitations of neo-classical labour market theory to describe and model labour markets. Neo-classical theory argues that labour markets should be controlled by economic phenomena, with the price mechanism, if allowed to work freely, bringing about labour market equilibrium. This model of the labour market sees any non-economic phenomena, such as historical, social and institutional forces as exogenous, as being outside the remit of labour market economics, yet my data and analysis has shown that such forces play a significant role in shaping labour markets and, therefore, must be seen as endogenous to the modelling and conceptualisation of labour markets.

These findings support the theoretical model of labour markets conceptualised by the segmented labour market theorists and their classical predecessors who argued that non-economic phenomena, such as perceptions of class or status, should be placed, not as by neo-classical theory, in the background, but rather that such forces should be in the foreground of labour market theorising. By making such historical, institutional and social forces endogenous to labour market formation it is possible to gain a deeper understanding of the functioning of labour markets and to assess the potential for labour markets to become more "flexible", in the sense of the likelihood of increased mobility between jobs. The views and values of respondents from Bristol Laminated and Bristol Insurance illustrated the difficulties facing attempts to increase such mobility, for not only are there practical barriers to mobility such as reading and writing (which may be addressed through education and training) but, perhaps more importantly, there are significant *cultural* differences. As one respondent commented: "I'm a blue collar worker, I'm not a white collar worker... the way I am and the way I talk and the type of person I am I would find it hard to get on and work with people who're better educated and who talk differently" (BL 10). Respondents, then, saw themselves not just as being different in an objective sense (such as possessing different literacy skills) but as being different in a subjective sense, of being part of distinct working communities, both at the local and immediate level of their place of work and at the more general level of sharing a set of common values and beliefs with others in a similar position in the hierarchy of occupations. It is these cultural differences, shaped by social, historical and institutional forces, which create what Cairnes ([1874], 1974) described as non-competing industrial groups.

This research, therefore, has shown that non-economic phenomena are integral to the nature and functioning of labour markets and, if labour markets and barriers to mobility are to be more fully understood, these non-economic phenomena must be seen as endogenous to our model of labour markets. Such a conclusion is at odds with the prevailing orthodoxy of labour markets where such phenomena are seen as, at best, marginal and, at worst, completely separate from the functioning of an "efficient" labour market. My findings suggest that the labour market, while being influenced, is not dominated by economistic price signals, and that non-economic phenomena, such as perceptions of status relating to occupations, are important to the conceptualisation and creation of separate labour markets. The task ahead is to build such an inclusive view of non-economic phenomena into our model of the labour market and, by so doing, move beyond the simple mainstream economistic policies of continually deregulating labour markets, and on to the more positive possibility of negotiating the development of programmes and policies which take account of the plurality of social, cultural and political forces operating on labour markets.

7.4 Labour market policy

A first step to developing such policies may be to look more closely at why respondents hold such different views and, more importantly, why these views are so often articulated in a defensively conservative fashion. I would suggest that one of the most important motivating factors underlying this defensive attitude is fear of unemployment and a consequent desire to increase present employment security. This is perhaps most obvious from the comments made by Bristol Laminated respondents in their discussions on skill, where they touched upon the importance of the political/social process in continuing to define printers jobs as skilled although much of their work was now completely mechanised. Thus it could be the case that workers in different sectors respond defensively to increase their employment security. This tendency to defensiveness may increase in response to the employment insecurity which has accompanied recent policies of labour market deregulation and flexibility. As Hutton (1995) has argued, the changes which have increased these feelings of insecurity move beyond the labour market:

> Individuals are compelled to look out for themselves. Businessmen seem fixated on their personal remuneration; politicians seem incapable of reaching out beyond their own tribal loyalties. Jobs can be lost quickly and never found again; lifetime savings can be stolen; home buyers can be trapped by debt in houses worth less than the price paid for them. There is a general sense of fear and beleagurement. (Hutton, 1995: 9, 10)

I would argue that the defensive nature of many of the comments from my case study respondents are influenced by this climate of insecurity, where jobs are continually under threat and where, in a system where earnings related supplements in unemployment benefits have been abolished,[41] unemployment would lead to severe economic and social dislocation. This is not to argue that flexibility and instability are recent phenomena, as Pollert (1988b) has written:

> Concern with both forms of flexibility is not new. It is the flexibility of human labour which creates the elastic commodity of labour power and allows its extension and intensification in the extraction of surplus value. Capital has always required flexibility of labour; the struggle over its control has structured management development, the capitalist labour process, and forms of labour organisation. (Pollert, 1988b: 45)

---

[41]For more on the effects of changes in social security entitlements see Deakin and Wilkinson (1991: 10-17).

The suggestion, therefore, is not that the cultural conservatism and aggressive defensiveness emerging from my data is a new response to a new phenomena[42] but that it provides contemporary evidence of employee reaction when faced with the (growing) threat of unemployment and/or loss of earnings. Under such uncertain conditions and with such limited real choices it is perhaps possible to understand the defensive nature of respondents views and values.

The focus of any positive alternatives, therefore, must, at least in the longer term, be on shifting the context of employment from insecurity to security. This is not to argue, of course, that a situation of steady employment would remove all barriers and cultural differences. As I noted earlier in this chapter many of these attitudes (perhaps in my study most particularly related to gender) are the consequence of deep and powerful social forces which will require sustained debate and negotiation to change, but rather it is to suggest that each of these inequalities exists within a more general debilitating atmosphere of economic insecurity and that, especially if there is to be more honest and thoughtful consideration of the myriad of labour market inequalities, the initial focus should be on minimising this insecurity. The emphasis, as SLM and institutionalist theorists have argued, should be on demand side policies to stimulate employment, with a boost to public employment, minimum wages and positive discrimination. Given the present hegemony of capital and dominance of transnational corporations, what one author has described as "nomadic capitalism" (Williams, 1989: 124), any such shift is obviously going to be difficult and demanding, but in many ways, this should make the search for positive alternatives a more pressing priority.

The task ahead, as SLM and classical authors have written, is to re-connect the economic with the social, to recognise that the labour market is not like any other market and that such non-economic phenomena as habit, custom and ideas of equity and fairness must be taken into account when formulating labour market policy. I would argue that the responses of those interviewed in Bristol Insurance and Bristol Laminated may offer some optimism that such moves are possible, for although the views articulated by my case study respondents were defensive, they demonstrate not a passive but an *active* workforce. The aim must be to tap and transform this human agency and energy, to offer the conditions for genuine flexibility in work, that is flexibility in work time and work patterns which reflect the needs of the community, where changes are controlled not by cynical competition but confident co-operation and where decisions are made in a context not of destabilising insecurity but of empowering social and economic security.

---

[42]For more on the historical incidence of flexibility see Thompson (1993).

Appendices

Appendix 1 (a)

Bristol Laminated, jobs of respondents and broad categories				
Respondent	Gender	Approx age	Job title	Broad grade
Bristol Lam 1	Female	45/50	Senior personnel officer	Manager
Bristol Lam 2	Male	50/55	Second op on a polythene extruder	Manual
Bristol Lam 3	Male	50/55	Timekeeper	Manual
Bristol Lam 4	Male	30/35	Labour pool worker	Manual
Bristol Lam 5	Male	50/55	Material handler	Manual
Bristol Lam 6	Female	35/40	Production manager	Manager
Bristol Lam 7	Male	45/50	Timekeeper	Manual
Bristol Lam 8	Male	30/35	Waste department worker	Manual
Bristol Lam 9	Male	50/55	First operative on emulsion coater	Manual
Bristol Lam 10	Male	30/35	Lacquer mix operative	Manual

Appendix 1 (b)

Bristol Insurance, jobs of respondents and broad categories				
Respondent	Gender	Approx age	Job title	Broad grade
Bristol Ins 1	Male	50/55	Remunerations and benefits manager	Manager
Bristol Ins 2	Male	35/40	Pensions marketing manager	Manager
Bristol Ins 3	Male	30/35	Assistant pensions marketing manager	Manager
Bristol Ins 4	Female	20/25	Marketing assistant	Supervisor*
Bristol Ins 5	Male	35/40	Assistant manager in investment mktg	Manager
Bristol Ins 6	Female	30/35	Life marketing manager	Manager
Bristol Ins 7	Female	25/30	Marketing assistant	Supervisor*
Bristol Ins 8	Male	40/45	Corporate comms manager	Manager
Bristol Ins 9	Female	35/40	Assistant corporate comms manager	Manager
Bristol Ins 10	Female	35/40	Public relations co-ordinator	Manager
Bristol Ins 11	Male	40/45	Marketing manager	Manager
Bristol Ins 12	Female	25/30	Marketing researcher	Supervisor*
Bristol Ins 13	Female	25/30	Unit leader in customer accounts	Supervisor
Bristol Ins 14	Female	40/45	Clerk in customer accounts	Clerk
Bristol Ins 15	Female	20/25	Unit leader	Supervisor
Bristol Ins 16	Female	20/25	Postal clerk	Clerk
Bristol Ins 17	Female	40/45	Clerk in commission accounts	Clerk
Bristol Ins 18	Male	20/25	Broking Clerk	Clerk

Note: The three jobs listed here are somewhat problematic as they do not easily fit into any of the categories, not being managers but differentiated from clerks in terms of pay, promotion potential and status. In order to reflect this these jobs have been classed as "supervisory".

Appendix 2

More detailed person and job description:

(a) Bristol Insurance

1. Remunerations and benefits manager.
2. Pensions marketing manager. Runs a small team, most of time spent planning and developing.
3. Assistant pensions marketing manager.
4. Marketing assistant. Deals with management accounts and analysis of survey results.
5. Assistant manager in investment marketing. Involved in the planning and marketing of new insurance products.
6. Life marketing manager. Responsible for life product range.
7. Marketing assistant. Involved in assessing and analysing projects based work.
8. Corporate communications manager.
9. Assistant corporate comms manager.
10. Public relations co-ordinator.
11. Marketing manager. Managed in-house research.
12. Marketing researcher. Conducted ad hoc research projects.
13. Unit leader in customer accounts. Contacts customers who are in arrears.
14. Clerk in customer accounts. Contacts customers who can't pay their bills and finds means of helping them to pay.
15. Unit leader. Works in accounts area, checking customer payments.
16. Postal clerk. Deals with all the post that comes into the department and helps with the general ledger.
17. Clerk in commission accounts. Works on the data preparation unit, which monitors payment statistics and ensures all entries into the computers are correct.
18. Broking Clerk. Mostly deals with post from brokers and answering phone call queries.

(b) Bristol Laminated

1. Senior personnel officer.
2. Second operator on a polythene extruder. This machine coats paper with a layer of hot polythene and laminates foil.
3. Timekeeper. Job involves "clocking" (recording the time) cards and locking the site.
4. Labour pool worker. This job involves covering for people who are off sick.
5. Material handler. Drives a fork lift truck.
6. Production manager. Manages the finishing department.
7. Timekeeper. Job involves "clocking" (recording the time) cards and locking the site.
8. Waste department worker. Collects and disposes of waste work from machines.
9. First operative on emulsion coater.
10. Lacquer mix operative. Prepares the lacquer for printers or polythene extruders.

Appendix 3

Aide-memoire

Introduction:

Hello, I'm George Callaghan and I'm presently doing some work on how difficult it may be for people to move between jobs.

1. To start with could you tell me what job you presently do ?

2. How is this job defined, you know does it have a title?

3. Skill.
   The next area I'm interested in is skill - you know, to find out if people think about skill in different ways:

Cover all or some of the following:
- What skills need for own job?
- How define general skills needed for their particular workplace?
- What about skills in general?
- What sort of jobs are considered skilled in this factory/office?
- How are they learned?
- What sort of skills do you think are needed for factory/office work?
- How are these skills learned?
- If there is any comments related to gender then follow this up.
- If relate skill to training ask how long it would take to be classed as "skilled" and what form the training would take.

4. Recruitment.
   Moving on to recruitment:

- Could you tell me how you found out about your job here? If from family/friends probe on:
  Who helped them
  The form this help took
  Whether this assistance was returned
  Any advantages of this method?
  Any disadvantages of this method?

- If management, what sort of recruitment channels would they use? Ever rely on family/friends, and if so, why?

- If they themselves had not experienced such networks were they aware of anyone else who had?

- Or indeed of any family connections?

- Or had they experienced such networks in the past?

5. Perceptions of work/workers:

- How would you describe your average manufacturing/office worker?

- If goes down skills avenue ask how acquired such skills.

- Can you think of anything that would stop people from, say a factory/office, coming to work in here?

- Be sensitive to any comments relating to gender differences and follow these up.

6. General areas:

- Ask about the social life, do people go out with friends from work?

- Ask about jobs of family.

Bibliography

Abbott, P. (1987), 'Women's social class identification: does husband's occupation make a difference?' *Sociology*, Vol. 21. No. 1. pp 91-103.
Abraham, K.G. (1991), 'Mismatch and labour mobility: some final remarks', in Padoa-Schioppa, F. (ed). (1991).
Acker, J. (1973), 'Women and social stratification: a case of intellectual sexism', in Huber, J. (ed). (1973).
Acker, J. (1980), 'Women and stratification: a review of recent literature'. *Contemporary Sociology*, No. 9. Jan. pp 25-39.
Acker, J. (1989), 'The problem with patriarchy'. *Sociology*, Vol.23 No.2. pp 235-240.
Advisory, Conciliation and Arbitration Service (ACAS). (1988). *Labour flexibility in Britain: the 1987 ACAS survey*. Advisory, Conciliation and Arbitration Service. Occasional paper 41. London.
Aglietta, M. (1979), *A theory of capitalist regulation*. Verso, London.
Ainley, P. (1993), *Class and skill, changing divisions of knowledge and labour*. Cassell, London.
Alford, B.W.E. (1976), 'The economic development of Bristol in the nineteenth century: an enigma?', in McGrath, P and Cannon, J. (eds). (1976).
Allan, G. (1991), 'Qualitative research', in Allan, G. and Skinner, C. (eds). (1991).
Allan, G. and Skinner, C. (eds). (1991), *Handbook for research students*. Falmer, London.
Allen, S. (1982), 'Gender, inequality and class formation', in Giddens, A. and Mackenzie, G. (eds). (1982).
Amin, (1991), 'Flexible specialisation and small firms in Italy: myths and realities', in Pollert, A.(ed). (1991).
Amsden, A.H. (ed). (1980), *The economics of women and work*. Penguin. Harmondsworth, Middlesex.
Annett, J. (1989), 'Training in transferable skills'. Department of Psychology. University of East Anglia. Employment Department Training Research and Development Series No. 50. Department of Employment, London.

Apostle, R. et al. (1985), 'Segmentation and labour force strategies'. *Canadian Journal of Sociology*. Vol. 10. No. 3. pp 50-63.

Armstrong, P. (1982), 'If it's only women's work it doesn't matter so much', in West, J. (ed). (1982).

Armstrong, P. (1988), 'Labour and monopoly capital', in Hyman, R. and Streek, W. (eds). (1988).

Artis, M.J. (ed). (1992), *The UK economy*. Weidenfield and Nicolson. London.

Ashenfelter, O.C. and Oates, W.E. (eds). (1977). *Essays in labour market analysis*. Israel University Press, Jerusalem.

Ashton, D.N. and Maguire M.J. (1984), 'Dual labour market theory and the organisation of local labour markets'. *International Journal of Social Economics*. Vol. 11. No. 7. pp 106-120.

Ashton, D.N. and Maguire M.J. (1986), 'Labour market segmentation and the structure of the youth labour market', Paper presented to the British Sociological Association. Annual Conference, Loughborough.

Ashton, D.N., Maguire M.J. and Garland, V. (1982), *Youth in the labour market*. Department of Employment Research Paper No. 34. Department of Employment, London.

Atkinson, J. (1984), 'Manpower strategies for flexible organizations'. *Personnel Management*. August, 1984. pp 28-31.

Atkinson, J. (1985a), IMS Report No. 89. Institute of Manpower Studies. University of Sussex. Falmer, Brighton.

Atkinson, J. (1985b), 'Flexibility: planning for an uncertain future'. *Manpower Policy andPractice*. Vol. 1. Summer. Institute of Manpower Studies. Brighton, Sussex.

Atkinson, J. and Gregory, D. (1986), 'A flexible future: Britain's dual labour force'. *Marxism Today*. April. pp 12-17.

Atkinson, J. and Meager, N. (1986), 'Is flexibility just a flash in the pan?' *Personnel Management*. September. pp 26-29.

Atkinson, J. et al. (1994), *Jobsearch: modelling behaviour and improving practice*. Institute of Manpower Studies. Report No. 260. Brighton, Sussex.

Averitt, R.T. (1968), *The dual economy: the dynamics of American industry structure*. Norton, New York.

Aydalot, P. (ed). (1986), *Milieux innovàteurs en Europe*. Gremi, Paris.

Babbage, C. (1832), *On the economy of machinery and manufacturers*. London.

Bagguley, P. et al. (1990), *Restructuring: place, class and gender*. Sage, London.

Bakke, E.W. (1940), *The unemployed worker: a study of the task of making a living without a job*. Yale University Press, New Haven.

Bakke, E.W. et al. (eds). (1954), *Labor mobility and economic opportunity*. Wiley, New York.

Barker, D.L. and Allen, S. (eds). (1976), *Dependence & exploitation in work and marriage*. Longmans, London.

Barrett, M. and McIntosh, M. (1980), 'The "family wage": some problems for socialists and feminists'. *Capital and Class*. No.11. Summer. pp 51-72.

Barron, R.D. and Norris, G.M. (1976), 'Sexual divisions and the dual labour market', in Barker, D.L. and Allen, S. (eds). (1976).

Beardsworth, A. et al. (1981), 'Employers strategies in relation to their demand for labour: some sociological hypotheses', in Windolf, P. (ed). (1981).

Beatson, M. (1995), 'Labour market flexibility'. Employment Department Research Series No. 48. Department of Employment, London.

Becattini, G. (1990), 'Italy, a case study', in Senberger, G.W. et al. (eds). (1990).

Becker, G. (1964), *Human capital.* Columbia University Press, New York.

Beechey, V. (1979), 'On patriarchy'. *Feminist Review.* No.3. pp 66-82.

Beechey, V. (1982), 'The sexual division of labour and the labour process: a critical assessment of Braverman', in Wood, S. (ed). (1982).

Beer, S.H. and Barringer, R.E. (eds). (1970), *The state and the poor.* Winthorp Press. Cambridge, Mass.

Bell, D. (1974), *The coming of post-industrial society.* Heinemann, London.

Bendix, R. and Lipset, S.M. (eds). (1967), *Class, status and power.* Routledge, London.

Benn, C. and Fairley, J. (1986), *Challenging the MSC.* Pluto Press, London.

Bennet, D. (1986), *Production design systems.* Butterworths, London.

Beynon, H. (1973), *Working for Ford.* Penguin. Harmondsworth, Middlesex.

Beynon, H. and Blackburn, R.M. (1972), *Perceptions of work, variations within a factory.* Cambridge University Press, Cambridge.

Blackburn, R.M. and Mann, M. (1979), *The working class in the labour market.* Macmillan, London.

Blau, P.M. (1963), *The dynamics of bureaucracy: a study of interpersonal relations in two government agencies.* University of Chicago Press, Chicago.

Blauner, R. (1964), *Alienation and freedom.* University of Chicago Press, Chicago.

Blaug, M. (1976), 'The empirical status of human capital theory: a slightly jaundiced survey'. *Journal of Economic Literature.* Vol. 14. No. 3. pp 827-55.

Blaug, M. (1983), *Economic theory in retrospect.* University of Cambridge Press, Cambridge.

Blustone, B. (1973), *Low wages and the working poor.* University of Michigan Press, Ann Arbor, Michigan.

Boddy, M., Lovering, J. and Basset, K. (1986), *Sunbelt city? A study of economic change in Britain's M4 growth corridor.* Clarendon Press, Oxford.

Boeke, J. (1953), *Economics and economic policy of dual societies as exemplified by Indonesia.* Institute of Pacific Relations, New York.

Bosanquet, N. and Doeringer, P.B. (1973), 'Is there a dual labour market in Great Britain?' *Economic Journal.* Vol. 83. June. pp 421-435.

Bott, E. (1971), *Family and social network* (2nd edn). Tavistock Publications, London.

Bowles, S. and Gintis, H. (1975), 'The problem with human capital theory - a Marxian critique'. *American Economic Review.* Vol. 65. No. 2. pp. 74-82.

Bowley, A.L. (1920), *The change in the distribution of national income 1880-1913.* Oxford.

Bradley, H. (1989), *Men's work, women's work.* Polity Press, Cambridge.

Braverman, H. (1974), *Labor and monopoly capital: the degradation of work in the twentieth century*. Monthly Review Press, New York.

Bresnen, M.J. (1988), 'Insights on site: research into construction project organisation', in Bryman, A. (ed). (1988b).

Bresnen, M.J. et al. (1985), 'The flexibility of recruitment in the construction industry: formalisation or re-casualisation'. *Sociology*. Vol 19. No.1. pp 108-124.

Brighton Labour Process Group. (1977), 'The capitalist labour process.' *Capital and Class*. No. 1. Spring. pp 3-26.

Brown, D.C. (1967), *The mobile professors*. American Council of Education. Washington. D.C.

Brown, R.K. (1985), 'Attitudes to work, occupational identity and industrial change', in Roberts, B., Finnegan, R, and Gallie, D. (eds). (1985).

Brusco, S. (1982), 'The Emilian model: productive decentralisation and social integration'. *Cambridge Journal of Economics*. Vol. 6. No. 2. pp. 167-84.

Bryman, A. (1988a), *Quantity and quality in social research*. Unwin Hyman, London.

Bryman, A. (ed). (1988b), *Doing research in organisations*. Routledge, London.

Buchanan, D., Boddy, D. and McCalman, J. (1988), 'Getting in, getting on, getting out, and getting back', in Bryman, A. (ed). (1988b).

Buchanan, R.A. (1967), *The industrial archaeology of Bristol*. Bristol University Branch of the Historical Association. Bristol.

Buchele, R. (1981), 'Sex discrimination and the U.S. labour market', in Wilkinson, F. (ed). (1988).

Bulmer, M. (1979), 'Concepts in the analysis of qualitative data'. *Sociological Review*. Vol. 27. No. 4. pp 651-679.

Bulmer, M. (1986), 'The value of qualitative methods', in Bulmer, M. et al. (eds). (1986).

Bulmer, M. et al. (eds). (1986), *Social science and social policy*. Allen & Unwin, London.

Burawoy, M. (1972), *Manufacturing consent: changes in the labour market under monopoly capitalism*. University of Chicago Press, Chicago.

Burchell, B. and Rubery, J. (1989), 'Segmented jobs and segmented workers: an empirical investigation.' Unpublished SCELI paper. Department of Applied Economics. University of Cambridge, Cambridge.

Burchell, B. et al. (1994), 'Management and employee perceptions of skill', in Penn, R. et al. (eds). (1994).

Burdett, K. and Mortensen, D.T. (1980), 'Search, layoffs, and labor market equilibrium'. Journal of Political Economy. Vol. 88. No. 4. pp 652-672.

Burgess, R. (ed). (1982), *Field research: a sourcebook and field manual*. Allen & Unwin, Hemel Hempstead.

Business Strategies Limited. (BSL), (1995), *Labour Market Flexibility and Financial Services*. BSL, London.

Cain, G.C. (1975), 'The challenge of dual and radical theories to orthodox theory'. *American Economic Review*. Vol. 65. No. 2. pp 16-22.

Cain, G.C. (1976), 'The challenge of segmented labour market theories to orthodox theory: a survey'. *Journal of Economic Literature*. Vol. 14. No. 4. pp 1215-1257.

Cain, G.C. (1991), 'Segmented labour markets', in Eatwell, J. et al. (eds). (1991).

Cairnes, J.E. [1874]. (1974), *Some Leading Principles of Political Economy*. Macmillan,London.

Calvert, P. (1982), *The concept of class*. Hutchinson, London.

Campbell, K.E. (1988), 'Gender differences in job-related networks'. *Work and Occupations*. Vol. 15. No. 2. pp 179-200.

Caplow, T. and McGee, R. (1958), *The academic marketplace*. Basic Books, New York.

Carter, M. (1982), 'Competition and segmentation in internal labour markets'. *Journal of Economic Issues*. Vol. 16. No. 4. pp 1063-77.

Catephores, G. (1990), 'Alienation', in Eatwell, J. et al. (eds). (1990).

Cave, C.H. (1899), *A history of banking in Bristol*. Bristol.

Cavendish, R. (1982), *On the line*. Routledge & Kegan Paul, London.

Chesire, P.C. (1979), 'Inner areas as spatial labour markets: a critique of the inner area studies'. *Urban Studies*. Vol. 16. pp 29-43.

Clark, G.L. (1983a), 'Fluctuations and rigididties in local labour markets. Part 1: theory and evidence'. *Enviroment and Planning A*. Vol. 15. No. 1. pp 165-185.

Clark, G.L. (1983b), *Interregional migration, national policy and social justice.*. Rowman & Allanheld, New Jersey.

Clutterbuck, D. and Hill, R. (1981), *The re-making of work, changing patterns of work and how to capitalise on them*. Grant McIntyre, London.

Cockburn, C. (1981), 'The material of male power.' *Feminist Review*. No. 9. pp 41-58.

Cockburn, C. (1983), *Brothers: male dominance and technological change*. Pluto Press, London.

Cockburn, C. (1986), 'Women and technology: opportunity is not enough', in Purcell, K. et al. (eds). (1986).

Cockburn, C. (1991), *It the way of women: men's resistance to sex equality in organisations*. Macmillan, London.

Cohen, S. (1960), *Labor in the United States*. Merrill.

Collins, R., (1971), 'Functional and conflict theories of educational stratification'. *American Sociological Review*. Vol. 36. No. 6. pp 1002-1019.

Collins, R. (1981), 'Micro-translation as a theory-building strategy', in Knorr-Cetina, K. and Cicourel, A.V. (eds). (1981).

Confederation of British Industry (CBI), (1985), 'Managing change: the organisation of work'. Confederation of British Industry, London.

Confederation of British Industry (CBI). (1995), 'A national minimum wage - the employers perspective' Confederation of British Industry, London.

Coombs, R. (1978), 'Labour and monopoly capital'. *New Left Review*. No. 107. Jan-Feb. pp 79-96.

Coontz, S. and Henderson, P. (eds). (1986), *Women's work, men's property: the origins of gender and class*. Verso, London.

Corcoran, M., Datcher, L. and Duncan, G.J. (1980a), 'Most workers find jobs through word of mouth'. *Monthly Labour Review*. Vol. 103. No. 8. pp 33-35.

Corcoran, M., Datcher, L. and Duncan, G.J. (1980b), 'Information and influence networks in labour markets', in Duncan, G.J. and Morgan, J.N. (eds). (1980).

Courtenay, G and Hedges, B. (1977), *A survey of employers' recruitment practices*. Social and Community Planning Research, London.

Coyle, A. (1982), 'Sex and skill in the organisation of the clothing industry', in West, J. (ed). (1982).

Coxon, A.P.M. and Davies, P.M. with Jones, C.L. (1986), *Images of social stratification, occupational structures and class*. Sage Publications, London.

Craig, C. et al. (1980), *Abolition and after: the paper box wages council*. Labour Studies Group Research Paper. No 12. Department of Employment, London.

Craig, C. et al. (1984), *Payment structures in smaller firms: women's employment in segmented labour markets*. Research Paper No. 48. Department of Employment, London.

Craig, C. et al. (1985), 'Economic, social and political factors in the operation of the labour market', in Roberts, B. et al. (eds). (1985).

Cressey, P. and MacInnes, J. (1980), 'Voting for Ford: industrial democracy and the control of labour'. Capital and Class. No. 11. pp 5-33.

Crompton, R. (1993), *Class and stratification: an introduction to current debates*. Polity Press, Cambridge.

Crompton, R. and Reid. S. (1982), 'The deskilling of clerical work', in Wood, S. (ed). (1982).

Crompton, R. and Jones, G. (1984), *White-collar proletariat: deskilling and gender in clerical work*. Macmillan, London.

Crompton, R. and Mann, M. (eds). (1986), *Gender and stratification*. Polity Press, Cambridge.

Crompton, R. and Jones, G. (1988), 'Researching white collar organizations: why sociologists should not stop doing case studies', in Bryman, A. (ed). (1988b).

Crossick, G.J. (1977), *The lower middle classes in Britain 1870-1914*. Croom Helm. London.

Crozier, M. (1971), *The world of the office worker*. University of Chicago, Chicago. (translated by David Landau).

Curran, M.M. (1985), *Stereotypes and selection: gender and family in the recruitment process*. HMSO, London.

Curran, M.M. (1988), 'Gender and recruitment: people and places in the labour market'. *Work, Employment & Society*. Vol. 2. No. 3. pp. 335-351.

Curry, J. (1993), 'The flexibility fetish'. *Capital and Class*. No. 50. pp 99-126.

Dawes, L. (1993), *Long-term unemployment and labour market flexibility*. Centre for Labour Market Studies, University of Leicester.

Day, G. (ed). (1982), *Diversity and decomposition in the labour market*. Gower Publishing Company. Aldershot, Hampshire.

Davies, M. (1979), 'Woman's place is at the typewriter: the feminisation of the clerical labour force', in Eisenstein, Z.R. (ed). (1979).

Davis, J. (1985), 'Rules not laws: outline of an ethnographic approach to economics', in Roberts, B. et al. (eds). (1985).
Deakin, S. (1986), 'Labour law and the developing employment relationship in the UK'. *Cambridge Journal of Economics*. Vol. 10. No.3. pp 225-246.
Deakin, S. and Wilkinson, F. (1991), *The economics of employment rights*. The Institute of Employment Rights, London.
Delphy, C. (1981), 'Women in stratification studies', in Roberts, H. (ed). (1981).
Delphy, C. (1984), *Close to home: a materialist analysis of women's oppression*. Hutchinson, London.
Dennis, G. (ed). (1994), *Key Data*. 1994-95 Edition. HMSO, London.
Department of Employment (1992), *Labour force survey*. No. 9. Department of Employment. London.
Department of Trade and Industry (1994), *Competitiveness helping business to win*. Cmnd. 2563. HMSO, London.
Dick, B. and Morgan, G. (1987), 'Family networks and employment in textiles'. *Work, Employment & Society*. Vol. 1. No. 2. pp 225-246.
Doeringer, P.B. and Piore, M.J. (1971), *Internal labour markets and manpower analysis*. D.C. Heath. Lexington, Mass.
Doeringer, P.B. et al. (1972), *Low income labor markets and urban manpower programs: a critical assessment*. U.S. Department of Labor. Research and Development findings No. 12.
Dore, R. (1988), 'Rigidities in the labour market'. *Government & Opposition*. Vol. 23. No. 4. pp 413-423.
Dorfman, N.S. (1983), 'Route 128: the development of a regional high technology economy'. *Research Policy*. Vol. 12. pp 299-316.
Duncan, G.J. and Morgan, J.N. (eds). (1980), *Five thousand American families: patterns of economic progress*. Vol 8. Michagan Institute for Social Research. Ann Arbor, Michagan.
Dunlop, J.T. (1957), *The theory of wage determination*. Macmillan, London.
Dunnell, K and Head, E. (1973), *Employers and employment services*. Office of Population Censuses and Surveys. HMSO, London.
Eatwell, J. et al. (eds), (1990), *Marxian economics*. Macmillan, London.
Eatwell, J. et al. (eds), (1991), *The new Palgrave dictionary of Economics*. Macmillan, London.
Eckaus, R.S., Safty, A.E. and Norman, V.D. (1974),'An appraisal of the calculations of rates of return to higher education', in Gordon, M.S (ed). (1974).
Eckstein, H. (1975), 'Case study and theory in political science', in Greenstein, F. and Polsby, N. (eds). (1975).
Edwards, R.C. (1979), *Contested terrain: the transformation of the workplace in the twentieth century*. Basic Books, New York.
Edwards, R.C. et al. (eds). (1975), *Labour market segmentation*. Lexington Press. Lexington. Massachusetts, USA.
Eisenstein, Z.R. (ed). (1979), *Capitalist patriarchy and the case for socialist feminism*. Monthly Review Press, New York.

Eisenstein, Z.R. (1981), *The radical future of liberal feminism.* Longman, New York.

Elger, T. (1982), 'Braverman, capital accumultion and deskilling', in Wood, S. (ed). (1982).

Elger, T. (1987), 'Flexible futures? New technology and the contemporary transformation of work'. *Work, Employment & Society.* Vol. 1. No. 4. pp 528-540.

Elger, T. (1991), 'The flexibility and the intensification of labour in UK manufacturing in the 1980s', in Pollert (ed). (1991).

Elias, P. and White, M. (1991), *Recruitment in local labour markets: employer and employee perspectives.* Institute of Employment Research and Policy Studies Institute. Research Paper No. 86. Department of Employment, London.

Employment Department. (1984), *Training for jobs.* Cmnd 9135. HMSO, London.

Employment Department (1985a), *Employment, the challenge for the nation.* Cmnd. 9474. HMSO, London.

Employment Department (1985b), *Lifting the burden.* Cmnd. 9571. HMSO, London.

Employment Department (1986), *Building businesses not barriers.* Cmnd. 1810. HMSO, London.

Employment Department (1988a), *Training for employment.* Cmnd. 316. HMSO, London.

Employment Department (1988b), *Employment for the 1990s.* Cmnd. 540. HMSO, London.

Employment Department (1991), *The best of both worlds: the benefits of a flexible approach to working arrangements.* Leaflet no. PL 916. Department of Employment, London.

Employment Department (1992), *People, jobs and opportunity.* Cmnd. 9794. HMSO, London.

Employment Department (1993a), *A guide to flexible working.* Leaflet no. PL 927. Department of Employment, London.

Employment Department Group (1993b), *Guide to the employment departament group.* Employment Department Group, London.

Employment Department Group (1994), *Employment Gazette Historical Supplement.* Vol. 102. No. 10. (October).

Employment Gazette (1991), *Labour mobility: evidence from the Labour Force Survey.* Vol. 99. No. 8. (August).

Erickson, R., Goldthorpe, J.H. and Portocarero, L. (1982), 'Social fluidity in industrial nations'. *British Journal of Sociology.* Vol. 33. No. 1. pp 1-34.

Eriksson, G. (1991), 'Human capital investments and labor mobility'. *Journal of Labor Economics.* Vol. 9. No. 3. pp 236-254.

Fallick, B.C. (1993), 'The industrial mobility of displaced workers'. *Journal of Labor Economics.* Vol. 11. No. 2. pp 302-323.

Financial Times 16th March. (1994), 'Flexible harmony marks G7 jobs talks'. pp 6.

Financial Times 15th March. (1995), 'Many retailers report fall in sales'. pp 1.

Financial Times 16th March. (1995), 'Voter confidence low says Clarke as recovery slows'. pp 1.
Finley, M.I. (1985), *The ancient economy*. Hogarth, London.
Finn, D. (1987), *Training without jobs*. Macmillan, London.
Firestone, S. (1974), *The dialectic of sex: the case for feminist revolution*. Morrow, New York.
Fischer, M.M. (ed). (1987), *Regional labour markets*. Elsevier, Amsterdam.
Fischer, M.M. and Nijkamp, P. (1987), 'Labour market theories: perspectives, problems and policy implications', in Fischer M.M (ed). (1987).
Flanagan, R. (1973), 'Segmented market theories and racial discrimination'. *Industrial Relations*. Vol. 12. No. 3. pp 253-73.
Fleisher, B.M. and Knieisner, T.J. (1984) *Labour economics: theory, evidence and policy*. Prentice-Hall International, London.
Fortune magazine. 'Women in business II'. August 1935. No. 12.
Franklin, B. (1818), 'Memoirs of the life and writings of Benjamin Franklin', in Musson, A.E. (1954).
Freeman, D. (1983), *Margaret Mead and Samoa: the making and unmaking of an anthropological myth*. Harvard Unversity Press. Cambridge, Mass.
Friedman, A. (1977), *Industry and labour: class struggle at work and monopoly capitalism*. Macmillan, London.
Friedman, A. (1978), 'Worker resistance and Marxist analysis of the capitalist labour process'. Paper given at Nuffield Deskilling Conference, Windsor.
Friedman, M. (1962), *Capitalism and freedom*. University of Chicago Press, Chicago.
Friedman, M. (1970), *The counter-revolution in monetary theory*. Institute of Economic Affairs. Occasional Paper No. 33. Institute of Economic Affairs, London.
Fuchs, V.R. (1968), *The service economy*. National Bureau of Economic Research, New York.
Gallie, D. (1978), *In search of the new working class: automation and social integration within the capitalist enterprise*. Cambridge University Press, Cambridge.
Gallie, D. (1985), 'Directions for the future', in Roberts, B. et al. (eds). (1985).
Gallie, D. (ed). (1988), *Employment in Britain*. Basil Blackwell, Oxford.
Gallie, D. (1991), 'Patterns of skill change: upskilling, deskilling or the polarization of skills?' *Work, Employment and Society*. Vol. 5. No. 3. pp 319-351.
Game, A. and Pringle, R. (1983), *Gender at work*. Allen & Unwin, Sydney.
Garnsey, E. (1978), 'Women's work and theories of class stratification'. *Sociology*. Vol. 12. No. 2. pp 223-43.
Garrahan, P. (1986), 'Nissan in the North East of England'. *Capital and Class*. No. 27. pp 5-13.
Gershuny, J.I. (1983), *Social innovation and the division of labour*. Oxford University Press, Oxford.

Giddens, A. (1973), *The class structure of the advanced societies*. Hutchinson, London.

Giddens, A. and Mackenzie, G. (eds). (1982), *Social class and the division of labour: essays in honour of Ilya Neustadt*. Cambridge University Press, Cambridge.

Gilmour, I. (1992), *Dancing with dogma: Britain under Thatcherism*. Simon & Schuster, London.

Gintis, H. J. (1971), 'Education, technology, and characteristics of worker productivity'. *American Economic Review*. Vol. 61. No. 2. pp 266-79.

Glaser, B and Strauss, A. (1967), *The discovery of grounded theory*. Aldine, Chicago. Illanois.

Glass, D.V. (ed). (1954), *Social mobility in Britain*. Routledge & Kegan Paul, London.

Glass, D.V. and Hall, J.R. (1954), 'A description of a sample inquiry into social mobility in Great Britain', in Glass, D.V. (ed). (1954).

Goldthorpe, J. H. (1983), 'Women and class analysis: a defense of the conventional view'. *Sociology*. Vol. 17. No. 4. pp 465-88.

Goldthorpe, J.H. and Hope, K. (1974), *The social grading of occupations: a new approach and scale*. Clarendon Press, Oxford.

Goldthorpe, J.H. and Payne, C. (1986), 'On the class mobility of women: results from different approaches to the analysis of recent British data'. *Sociology*. Vol. 20. No. 4. pp 531-556.

Goldthorpe, J.H., Llewellyn, C and Payne, C. (1980), *Social mobility and class structure in modern Britain*. Clarendon Press, Oxford. (2nd edition 1987).

Goldthorpe, J.H. et al. (1968b), *The affluent worker: industrial attitudes and behaviour*. Cambridge University Press, Cambridge.

Goldthorpe, J.H. et al. (1969), *The affluent worker in the class structure*. Cambridge University Press, Cambridge.

Gordon, D.M. (1972), *Theory of poverty and unemployment*. D.C. Heath. Lexington, Mass.

Gordon, D.M., Edwards, R. and Reich, M. (1982), *Segmented work, divided workers: the historical transformation of labor in the United States*. Cambridge University Press, Cambridge.

Gordon, M.S. (ed). (1974), *Higher education and the labour market*. McGraw Hill, New York.

Gorz, A. (1982), *Farewell to the working class*. Pluto Press, London.

Gramsci, A. (1948-1951]. (1991), *Selections from the prison notebooks*. Lawrence & Wishart, London.

Granovetter, M.S. (1973), 'The strength of weak ties'. *American Journal of Sociology*. Vol. 78. No. 6. pp 1360-1380.

Greenstein, F. and Polsby, N. (eds). (1975), *The handbook of political science: strategies of inquiry*. Vol. 7. Addison-Wesley, London.

Gregg, P. and Wadsworth, J. (1995), 'A short history of labour turnover, job tenure, and job security, 1975-93'. *Oxford Review of Economic Policy*. Vol. 11. No. 1. pp 73-90.

Grieco, M.S. (1987), *Keeping it in the family: social networks and employment chance.* Tavistock, London.
Griffin, G., Wood, S. and Knight, J. (1992), *The Bristol labour market.* Research Paper, No. 82. Department of Employment, London.
Guardian 8th March. (1994), 'Brown mocks pile 'em high jobs dogma'. pp 18.
Guardian 19th September. (1994), 'Minimum wage "would cut job flexibility"'. pp 6.
Guardian 15th March. (1995), 'Retail outlook getting darker'. pp 24.
Guardian 16th March. (1995), 'Depressed retailing figures show data at sixes and sevens.' pp 15.
Guardian 2nd May. (1995), 'Pound up as markets bet on rate rise'. pp 16.
Guardian 22nd May. (1995), 'Revolution that casts into political stone fear of losing our homes'. pp 19.
Hakim, C. (1987a), 'Homeworking in Britain'. *Employment Gazette.* Vol. 95. No. 2. pp 92-104.
Hakim, C. (1987b), 'Trends in the flexible workforce'. *Employment Gazette.* Vol. 95. No. 11. pp 549-560.
Hakim, C. (1990), 'Core and periphery in employers' workforce strategies: evidence from the 1987 E.L.U.S. survey'. *Work Employment & Society.* Vol. 4. No. 2. pp 157-188.
Hales, J. (1993), '1992 survey of employers' recruitment practices'. Social and Community Planning, London.
Hall, S. (1988), 'Brave new world'. *Marxism Today.* October. pp. 24-29.
Hall, S. and Jacques, M. (eds). (1989), *New times: the changing face of politics in the 1990s.* Lawrence & Wishart, London.
Hall, J. and Jones, D.C. (1950), 'The social grading of occupations'. *British Journal of Sociology.* Vol. 1. No. 1. pp 31-55.
Hammersley, M. and Atkinson, P. (1983), *Ethnography, principles in practice.* Tavistock, London.
Handy, C. (1984), *The future of work.* Blackwell, London.
Harrison, B, (1972), *Education, training, and the urban ghetto.* John Hopkins University Press. Baltimore, USA.
Hardwick, P., Khan, B. and Langmead, J. (1990), *An introduction of modern economics.* Longman, London.
Hart, O.D. (1983), 'Optimal labour contracts under asymetric information: an introduction'. *Review of Economic Studies* Vol. 50. No. 160. pp 3-35.
Hartmann, H. (1979), 'Capitalism, patriarchy and job segregation by sex', in Eisenstein, Z.R. (ed). (1979).
Hartmann, H. (1981), 'The unhappy marriage of Marxism and Feminism: towards a more progressive union', in Sargent, L. (ed). (1981).
Hayek, J. (1944), *The road to serfdom.* Phoenix Books, London.
Hayek, J. (1980), *1980s unemployment and the unions.* Hobart Paper No. 87. Institute of Economic Affairs, London.
Hayek, J. (1986), 'The moral imperative of the market', in Institute of Economic Affairs. (1986).

Hechter, M. (1978), 'Group formation and the cultural division of labour'. *American Journal of Sociology*. Vol. 84. No. 2. pp 293-318.

Hedges, B. (1983), *Survey of employers' recruitment practices (1982)*. Social and Community Planning Research, London.

Hedges, N. and Beynon, H. (1982), *Born to work*. Pluto Press, London.

Hegel, G.W.F. (1840), *Philosophie des Rechts*. Berlin.

Hendy, J. (1993), A *law unto themselves. Conservative employment laws: a national and international assessment*. (3rd edition), The Institute of Employment Rights. London.

Hepple, B. (1987), 'The crisis in EEC labour law'. *Industrial Law Journal*. Vol. 16. No. 2. June.

Hicks, J.R. (1932), 'Marginal productivity theory and the principle of variation' *Economica*. Vol. 12. No. 35. pp 79-88.

Hicks, J.R. (1963), *The theory of wages*. Macmillan, London.

Hill, S. (1976), *The dockers: class and tradition in London*. Heinemann, London.

Hirst, P. and Zeitlin, J. (1988), 'Crisis, what crisis?'. *New Statesman*. 18th March. pp 10-12.

Hirst, P. and Zeitlin, J. (1989), *Reversing industrial decline? Industrial structure and policy in Britain and her competitors*. Berg, Oxford.

HMSO (1966), *Census 1961*: Occupation tables. London.

Hobsbawn, E.J. (1964), *Labouring men*. Weidenfield and Nicolson, London.

Hobsbawn, E.J. (1990), *Industry and empire*. Penguin, London.

Hodge, R.W., Treiman, D.J. and Rossi, P.H. (1967), 'A comparative study of occupational prestige', in Bendix and Lipset (eds). (1967).

Hooks, B. (1984), *Feminist theory: from margin to centre*. South End Press. Boston, USA.

Horrell, S., Rubery, J. and Burchell, B. (1990), 'Gender and skills'. *Work, Employment & Society*. Vol. 4. No. 2. pp 189-216.

Huber, J. (ed). (1973), *Changing women in a changing society*. University of Chicago Press, Chicago.

Humphries, J. (1987), '"...The most free from objection..." The sexual division of labor and women's work in nineteenth-century England'. *The Journal of Economic History*. Vol xlvii. No. 4. Dec. pp 929-949.

Hunter, L., Senior, G.J. and Danson, M. (1988), *Information gaps in the local labour market*. Avebury, Aldershot.

Hutton, W. (1995), *The State we're in*. Jonathan Cape. London.

Hyman, R. (1988), 'Flexible specialisation: miracle or myth?' in Hyman, R. and Streek, W. (eds). (1988).

Hyman, R. and Streek, W. (eds). (1988), *New technology and industrial relations*. Basil Blackwell, Oxford.

Industrial Facts and Forecasting Research Ltd. (IFF). (1988), *Vacancies and recruitment study*. Research report prepared for the Department of Employment's Employment Service. IFF, London.

Institute of Directors. (IOD). (1985), *Labour market changes and opportunities: new patterns of work*. Institute of Directors, London.

Institute of Economic Affairs. (1986), *The unfinished agenda: Essays on the political economy of government policy in honour of Arthur Seldon*. Institute of Economic Affairs, London.

Institute of Manpower Studies. (IMS). (1984), 'Training for versatility'. *IMS News*. No. 59. June. Institute of Manpower Studies. Falmer, Brighton.

Institute of Manpower Studies. (IMS). (1985), *New forms of work organisation*. IMS commentary. No. 30. Institute of Manpower Studies. Falmer, Brighton.

James, S. and della Costa, M. (1973), *The power of women and the subversion of the community*. Falling Wall Press, Bristol.

Jeanes, R. (1966), *Building operatives work*. Building Research Station. HMSO, London.

Jencks, C. et al.(1972), *Inequality*. Basic Books, New York.

Jenkins, C. and Sherman, B. (1979), *The collapse of work*. Eyre Methuen, London.

Jenkins, R. (1982), *Managers, recruitment procedures and black workers*. SSRC Research Unit on Industrial Relations. Working paper No. 18.

Jenkins, R. (1983), *Lads, citizens and ordinary kids: working-class youth lifestyles in Belfast*. Routledge & Kegan Paul, London.

Jenkins, R. (1985), 'Black workers in the labour market: the price of recession', in Roberts, B. et al. (eds). (1985).

Jenkins, R. (1986), *Racism and recruitment: managers, organisations and equal opportunity in the labour market*. Cambridge University Press, Cambridge.

Jenkins, R. (1988), 'Discrimination and equal opportunity', in Gallie, D. (ed). (1988).

Jenkins, R. and Solomos, J. (eds). (1987), *Racism and equal opportunity policies in the 1980s*. Cambridge University Press, Cambridge.

Jenkins, R. et al. (1983), 'Information in the labour market: the impact of recession'. *Sociology*. Vol. 7. No. 2. pp 260-267.

Jenson, J. (1989), 'The talents of women, the skills of men: flexible specialisation and women', in Wood, S. (ed). (1989).

Johnson, C. (1991), *The economy under Mrs Thatcher 1979-1990*. Penguin, London.

Joll, C. et al. (eds). (1983), *Developments in labour market analysis*. Allen & Unwin, London.

Jones, C. (1991), 'Qualitative interviewing', in Allan, G. and Skinner, C. (eds). (1991).

Joseph, K. (1979), *Monetarism is not enough*.

Joyce, P. (1980), *Work, society and politics*. Wheatsheaf, Brighton.

Kahn, H. (1964), *The reprecussions of redundancy*. Allen & Unwin, London.

Kaufman, R. et al. (1981), 'Defrocking dualism: A new approach to defining industrial sectors'. *Social Science Research*. Vol. 10. No. 1. pp 1-31.

Keeble, D. (1987), 'Entrepeneurship, high technology and regional development in the United Kingdom: the case of the Cambridge phenomenon'. Department of Geography, University of Cambridge, Cambridge. (Mimeographed).

Keenan, J.M. and Thom, A.A. (1988), 'The future through the keyhole: some thoughts on employment patterns'. *Personnel Review*. Vol. 7. No. 1 pp 20-24.

Kelley, M.R. (1989), 'Alternative forms of work organisation under programmable automation', in Wood, S. (ed). (1989).

Kelly, P.M. (1980), *White-collar proletariat: the industrial behaviour of British civil servants*. Routledge & Kegan, London.

Keohane, N.O. et al. (eds). (1982), *Feminist theory: a critique of ideology*. Harvester Press, Brighton.

Kerr, C. (1954), 'The Balkanisation of labor markets', in Bakke, E.W. et al. (eds). (1954).

Kiker, B.F. (1968), *Human capital: in retrospect*. Bureau of Business and Economic Research. University of South Carolina. Columbia.

King, J.E. (1990), *Labour economics*. Macmillan, London.

Kirosingh, M. (1989), 'Changed working practices'. *Employment Gazette*. Vol. 97. No. 8. pp 422-429.

Knight, D. et al. (eds). (1985), *Job redesign: critical perspectives on the labour process*. Gower Press, Aldershot.

Knight, K.G. and Wilson, R.A. (1974), 'Labour hoarding, employment and unemployment in British manufacturing industry'. *Applied Economics*. Vol. 6. No. 4. pp 303-310.

Knorr-Cetina, K. (1981a), *The manufacture of knowledge: an essay on the constructivist and contextual nature of science*. Pergamon Press, Oxford.

Knorr-Cetina, K. (1981b), 'The micro-sociological challenge of macro-sociology: towards a reconstruction of social theory and methodology', in Knorr-Cetina, K. and Cicourel, A.V. (eds). (1981).

Knorr-Cetina, K. and Cicourel, A.V. (eds). (1981), *Advances in social theory and methodology: toward an integration of micro- and macro- sociologies*. Routledge & Kegan Paul, London.

Kreckel, R. (1980), 'Unequal opportunity structure and labour market segmentation'. *Sociology* Vol. 15. No. 1. pp 56-78.

Krelle, W. and Shorrocks, A. (eds). (1978), *Personal income distribution*. Elsevier, North-Holland. Amsterdam.

Kuhn, A. and Wolpe, A. (eds). (1978), *Feminism and materialism: women and modes of production*. Routledge & Kegan Paul, London.

Kumar, K. (1978), *Prophecy and progress*. Penguin. Harmondsworth, Middlesex.

Kusterer, K. (1978), *Know how on the Job*. Westview Press. Boulder, California.

Labour Market Quarterly. (LMQ). (1984), Feb. HMSO, London.

Lane, C. (1988a), 'Flexible specialisation in Britain and Germany.' *Work, Employment & Society*. Vol. 2. No. 2. pp 141-168.

Lane, C. (1988b), 'New technology and clerical work', in Gallie, D. (ed). (1988).

Lawson, N. (1992), *The view from No. 11: Memoirs of a Tory radical*. Transworld, London.

Lazonick, W. (1979), 'Industrial relations and technical change: the case of the self-acting mule'. *Cambridge Journal of Economics*. Vol. 3. No. 3. pp 231-262.

Lee, C.H. (1986), *The British economy since 1700 - a macroeconomic perspective.* Cambridge University Press, Cambridge.

Lee, D. (1982), 'Beyond deskilling: skill, craft and class', in Wood (ed). (1982).

Lee, G and Loveridge, R. (eds). (1987), *The manufacture of disadvantage: stigma and social closure.* Open University Press, Milton Keynes.

Lee, G. and Wrench, J. (1981), *In search of a skill.* Commission for Racial Equality, London.

Lee, G. and Wrench, J. (1987), 'Training and organisational change: the target racism', in Jenkins, R. and Solomos, J. (eds). (1987).

Lee, R.M. (1985), 'Redundancy, labour markets and informal relations'. *Sociological Review.* Vol. 33. No. 3. pp 469-494.

Leete, R. and Fox, J. (1977), 'Registrar General's social classes: origin's and uses'. *Population Trends.* No. 8. Summer. pp 1-7.

Leigh, D. (1976), 'Occupational advancement in the late 1960s: an indirect test of the dual labour market hyothesis'. *Journal of Human Resources.* Vol. 11. No. 2. pp 151-71.

Lewis, O. (1951), *Life in a Mexican village: Tepoztlan restudied.* University of Illinois Press. Urbana, Illinois.

Lewis, R. (1987), 'Reforming labour law: choices and constraints'. *Employee Relations.* Vol. 9. No. 4. pp 28-31.

Lindert, P.H. and Williamson, J.G. (1983), 'English workers' living standards during the industrial revolution: a new look'. *Economic History Review.* Vol. 36. No. 1. pp 1-25.

Lipietz, A. (1987), *Mirages and miracles.* Verso, London.

Littler, C.R. (1982), *The development of the labour process in capitalist societies.* Heinemannn, London.

Littler, C.R. (1985), 'Taylorism, Fordism and job design.' In Knight, D. et al. (eds). (1985).

Lockwood, D. (1958), *The blackcoated worker.* Allen & Unwin, London (2nd edition 1989).

Lockwood, D. (1966), 'Sources of variation in working class images of society'. *Sociological Review.* Vol. 14. No. 3. pp 249-267.

Loveridge, R. (1987), 'Stigma - the manufacture of disadvantage', and 'social accomodations and technological transformations - the case of gender', in Lee, G and Loveridge, R. (eds). (1987).

Loveridge, R. and Mok. A.L. (1979), *Theories of labour market segmentaion.* Nijhoff, Boston and London.

Lovering, J. (1991), *Bridging the gap: skills, training and barriers to employment in Bristol.* School of Advanced Urban Studies. (SAUS). University of Bristol, Bristol.

Lucas, R.E.B. (1972) *Working conditions, wage-rates, and human capital: a hedonic study.* Ph.D dissertation. Massachusetts Institute of Technology. Massachusetts, USA.

Lummis, T. (1987), *Listening to history.* Hutchinson, London.

MacDonald, G.M. (1980), 'Person-specific information in the labor market'. *Journal of Political Economy*. Vol. 88. No. 3. pp 578-597.

MacDonald, G.M. (1988), 'Job mobility in market equilibrium'. *Review of Economic Studies*. Vol. 55. No. 181. pp 153-168.

MacKay, D.I. et al. (1971), Labour markets under different employment conditions. Allen & Unwin, London.

MacKenzie, G. (1977), 'The political economy of the American working class'. *British Journal of Sociology*. Vol. 28. No. 2. pp 244-52.

MacKinnon, C.A. (1979), *Sexual harassment of working women*. Yale University Press, New Haven.

MacKinnon, C.A. (1982), 'Feminism, Marxism, method and the state: an agenda for theory', in Keohane, N.O. et al. (eds). (1982).

McCormick, K. (1985), *The flexible firm and employment adjustment: fact and fable in the Japanese case*. Unit for Comparative Research on Industrial Relations. University of Sussex, Sussex. Mimeographs.

McDonough, R. and Harrison, R. (1978), 'Patriarchy and relations of production', in Kuhn, A. and Wolpe, A.M. (eds). (1978).

McGrath, P and Cannon, J. (eds). (1976), *Essays in Bristol and Gloucestershire History*. Western Printing Services, Bristol.

McKenzie, F. (undated), 'Feminism and Socialism', in *Scarlet Women collective*. Scarlet Women No. 5. North Shields Tyne and Wear.

McNabb, R. and Ryan, P. (1990), 'Segmented labour markets', in Sapsford, D. and Tzannatos, Z. (eds). (1990).

Mandel, E. (1978), *Late capitalism*. New Left Books, London.

Manwaring, T. (1984), 'The extended internal labour market'. *Cambridge Journal of Economics*. Vol. 8. No. 2. pp 161-187.

Manwaring, T. and Wood, S. (1985), 'The ghost in the labour process'.in Knight, K.G. and Wilson, R.A. (eds). (1985).

Marin, A. and Psacharopolous, G. (1982), 'Confiramtions and contradictions: the reward for risk in the labour market: evidence from the United Kingdom and a reconciliation with other studies'. *Journal of Political Economy*. Vol. 90. No. 4. pp 827-871.

Marginson, P. (1991), 'Change and continuity in the employment structure of large companies', in Pollert, A. (ed). (1991).

Martin F.M. (1954), 'Some subjective aspects of social stratification', in Glass, D.V. (ed). (1954).

Martin, R. (1988), 'Technological change and manual work', in Gallie, D. (ed). (1988).

Marsden, D. (1982), *Workless: an exploration of the social contract between society and the worker*. Croom Helm, London.

Marshall, A. [1890]. (1970), *The principles of economics*. Macmillan, London.

Marshall, G. et al. (1988), *Social class in modern Britain*. Hutchinson, London.

Marx, K. (1867]. (1976), *Capital* Vol. 1. Penguin. Harmondsworth, Middlesex.

Marxism Today. (1988), 'New Times'. October. pp 3-7.

Mayhew, K. and Rosewell, B. (1979), 'Labour market segmentation in Britain'. *Oxford Bulletin of Economics and Statistics*. Vol. 41. No. 2. pp 81-107.

Mead, M. (1928), *Coming of age in Samoa: a pyschological study of primitive youth for Western civilisation*. William Morrow, New York.

Melnik, A. and Saks, D.H. (1977), 'Information and adaptive job search behaviour: an empirical analysis', in Ashenfelter, O.C. and Oates, W.E. (eds). (1977).

Milkman, R. (1983), 'Female factory labour and industrial structure: control and conflict over "women's place" in auto and electrical manufacturing'. Politics and Society. Vol. 9. No. 3. pp 379-407.

Mill, J.S. (1848]. (1976), *The principles of political economy*. Senator Press, New York.

Miller, H. (1960), 'Annual and lifetime income in relation to education'. *American Economic Revew*. Vol. 50. No. 5. pp 962-86.

Millet, K. (1977), *Sexual politics*. Virago, London.

Mincer, J. (1958), 'Investment in human capital and personal income distribution.' *Journal of Political Economy*. Vol. 66. August. pp 281-302.

Mincer, J. (1970), 'The distribution of labour income: a survey with special reference to the human capital approach'. *Journal of Economic Literature* Vol. 8. No. 1. pp 1-26.

Mincer, J. (1974), *Schooling experience and earnings*. Columbia University Press, New York.

Mitchell, B.R. and Deane, P. (1962), *Abstract of British historical statistics*. Cambridge University Press, Cambridge.

Mitchell, J. (1975), *Psychoanalysis and feminism*. Penguin. Harmondsworth, Middlesex.

Mitchell, J.C. (1983), 'Case and situation analysis'. *Sociological Review*. Vol. 31. No.2. pp 187-211.

More, C. (1980), *Skill and the English working class, 1870-1914*. Croom Helm, London.

More, C. (1982), 'Skill and the survival of apprenticeship', in Wood, S. (ed). (1982).

Morgan, D.H.J. (1992), *Discovering men*. Routledge, London.

Morgan, G and Hooper, D. (1982), 'Labour in the woollen and worsted industry: a critical analysis of dual labour market theory', in Day, G. (ed). (1982).

Morgan, K. and Sayer, A. (1988), *Microcircuits of capital, 'sunrise' industry and uneven development*. Polity Press, Cambridge.

Morris, L. and Irwin, S. (1992), 'Employment histories and the concept of the underclass'. *Sociology*. Vol. 26. No.3. pp 401-420.

Murgatroyd, L. (1982), *Gender and occupational stratification*. Lancaster Regionalism Group Working Paper No.6. Lancaster Regionalism Group, Lancaster.

Murray, F. (1987), 'Flexible specialisation in the "third Italy"'. *Capital and Class*. No. 33. Winter. pp. 84-95.

Murray, R. (ed). (1988), *Technology strategies and local economic intervention.* Spokesman, Nottingham.
Murray, R. (1989a), 'Benetton Britain', in Hall, S. and Jacques, M. (eds). (1989).
Murray, R. (1989b), 'Fordism and post-fordism', in Hall, S. and Jacques, M. (eds). (1989).
Musson, A.E. (1954), *The typographical association, origins and history up to 1949.* Oxford University Press, Oxford.
Myers, C. A. and Shultz, G. (1951), *The dynamics of labor markets.* Prentice Hall, New York.
Napier, B. (1993), *CCT, market testing and employment rights; the effects of TUPE and the acquired rights directive.* The Institute of Employment Rights. London.
National Economic Development Office (NEDO). (1986), *Changing working patterns: how companies achieve flexibility to meet new needs.* NEDO. London.
Nichols, T. (1986), *The British worker question.* Routledge & Kegan Paul, London.
Noble, D. (1979), 'Social change in machine design: the case of automatically controlled machine tools', in Zimbalist, A. (ed). (1979).
Noble, D. (1984), *Forces of production.* A. Knopf, New York.
North, G.C. and Hatt, P.K. (1947), 'Jobs and occupations: a popular evaluation'. *Opinion News.* Vol. 9. pp 3-13.
Oakley, A. (1974), *The sociology of housework.* Martin Robertson, London.
O'Brien, M. (1981), *The politics of reproduction.* Routledge & Kegan Paul, London.
Office of Population Censuses and Surveys (OPCS). (1970), *Classifications of occupations 1970.* HMSO, London.
Organisation for Economic Co-operation and Development (OECD). (1989), *Labour market flexibility: trends in enterprises.* OECD, Paris.
Organisation for Economic Co-operation and Development (OECD). (1994), *Outlook.* No. 55. OECD, Paris.
Oster, J. (1979), 'A factor-analytic test of the theory of the dual economy'. *Review of Economics and Statistics* Vol. 62. No. 1. pp 33-39.
Osterman, P. (1975), 'An empirical study of labor market segmentation'. *Industrial and Labor Relations Review.* Vol. 28. No. 4. pp 508-523.
Osterman, P. (1980), *Getting started: the youth labour market.* MIT Press, London.
Oxford English Dictionary (1989), *The concise Oxford dictionary of current English.* Sykes, J.B. (ed). Oxford University Press, Oxford.
Oxford Thesauraus. (1991), *The Oxford thesaurus.* Urdang. L. (ed). BCA in arrangement with Oxford University Press, England.
P.A. Cambridge Economic Consultants, (1990), *Labour market assessment and review of training and enterprise provision.* PACEC, Cambridge.
Padoa-Schioppa, F. (ed). (1991), *Mismatch and labour mobility.* Cambridge University Press, Cambridge.
Palloix, C. (1976), 'The labour process from Fordism to Neo-Fordism'. Conference of Socialist Economists. (CSE). Pamphlet 1. pp 46-67.

Parkin, F. (1972), *Class inequality and political order: social stratification in capitalist and communist countries.* Holt, Reinhart and Winson, New York.
Parliamentary Papers. (1842), Vol. 16. pp 262-263.
Parnes, H.S. (1954), *Research on labour mobility.* Social Science Research Council, New York.
Parsons, T. (1954), *Essays in sociological theory.* Free Press, London.
Parsons, T. and Bales, R.F. (1956), *Family, socialisation and interaction process.* Routledge, London.
Patrick, J. (1973), *A Glasgow gang observed.* Eyre Methuen, London.
Peacock, A.T. and Wiseman, J. (1961), *The growth of public expenditure in the United Kingdom.* Princeton University Press, Princeton.
Penn, R.D. (1983), 'Trade union organisation and skill in the cotton and engineering industries in Britain, 1850-1960.' *Social History.* Vol. 8. No. 1. January. pp 37-55.
Penn, R.D. (1985), *Skilled workers in the class structure.* Cambridge University Press, Cambridge.
Penn, R.D. (1990), *Class, power and technology: skilled workers in Britain and America.* Polity Press, Cambridge.
Penn, R.D. and Francis, B. (1994), 'Towards a phenomenology of skill', in Penn, R. et al. (eds). (1994).
Penn, R.D. and Scattergood, H. (1985), 'Deskilling or enskilling? An empirical investigation of recent theories of the labour process'. *British Journal of Sociology.* Vol. 36. No. 4. pp 611-630.
Penn, R.D. et al. (1992), 'Technical change and the division of labour in Rochdale and Aberdeen: evidence from the social change and economic life initiative'. *British Journal of Sociology.* Vol. 43. No. 4. pp 657-680.
Penn, R.D. et al. (eds). (1994), *Skill and occupational change.* Oxford University Press, Oxford.
Perrin, J.C. (1986), 'Le phenomene Sophia-Antipolis dans son environmment regional', in Aydalot, P. (ed). (1986).
Phillips, A. and Taylor, B. (1980), 'Sex and skill: notes towards a feminist economics'. *Feminist Review.* Vol. 6. pp 79-88.
Piore, M.J. (1970), 'Jobs and training', in Beer, S.H and Barringer, R.E. (eds). (1970).
Piore, M.J. (1975), 'Notes for a theory of labour market stratification', in Edwards, R.C. et al. (eds). (1975).
Piore, M.J. (1986a), 'Perspectives on labour market flexibility'. *Industrial Relations.* Vol. 25. No. 2. Spring.
Piore, M.J. (1986b), 'The decline of mass production and the challenge to union survival'.*Industrial Relations Journal.* Vol. 19. No. 3. pp 207-213.
Piore, M.J. and Sabel, C.F. (1984), *The second industrial divide: possibilities for prosperity.* Basic Books, New York.
Planque, B. (1986), 'La zone d' Aix-Marseille', in Aydalot, P. (ed). (1986).
Polanyi, M. and Prosch, H. (1975), *Meaning.* University of Chicago Press, Chicago.

Pollert, A. (1981), *Girls, wives, factory lives*. Macmillan, London.
Pollert, A. (1987), *The "flexible firm": a model in search of reality (or a policy in search of a practice)?* Warwick papers in Industrial Relations No. 19. Industrial Relations Research Unit. University of Warwick, Coventry.
Pollert, A. (1988a), 'The 'flexible firm': fixation or fact?' *Work, Employment & Society*. Vol. 2. No. 3. pp 281-316.
Pollert, A. (1988b), 'Dismantling flexibility'. *Capital and Class*. No. 34. Spring. pp 42-75.
Pollert, A. (1990), 'Conceptions of British employment re-structuring in the 1980s', in Varcoe, I. et al. (eds). (1990).
Pollert, A. (ed). (1991), *Farewell to flexibility*. Basil Blackwell, London.
Porter, J.A. (1965), *The vertical mosaic: an analysis of social class and power in Canada*. Toronto U.P., Toronto.
Potter, T. (1987), *A temporary phenomenon: flexible labour, temporary workers and the trade union response*. West Midlands Low Pay Unit, Birmingham.
Prandy, K. (1991), 'The revised Cambridge scale of occupations'. *Sociology*. Vol. 24. No. 4. pp 629-56.
Prandy, K., Stewart, A. and Blackburn, R.M. (1982), *White-collar work*. Macmillan, London.
Purcell, K, (1982), 'Female manual workers, fatalism and the reinforcement of inequalities', in Robbins, D. et al (eds). (1982).
Purcell, K. et al. (eds). (1986), *The changing experience of employment*. Macmillan, London.
Psacharopoulos, G. (1977), *Market duality and income distribution: the case of the UK*. Centre for Labour Economics. Discussion paper No. 5. reproduced in Krelle, W. and Shorrocks, A. (eds). (1978).
Psacharopoulos, G. and Hinchliffe, H. (1974), 'College quality as a screening device?' *Journal of Human Resources*. Vol. 9. No. 4. pp 556-58.
Redfield, R. (1930), *Tepoztlan: a Mexican village*. University of Chicago Press, Chicago.
Redfield, R. (1955), *The little community*. University of Chicago Press, Chicago.
Redstockings. (1970), 'Redstockings manifesto', in Tanner. L.B. (ed). (1970).
Rees, A. (1966), 'Information networks in labour markets'. *American Economic Review*. Vol. LVI. No.2. pp 559-566.
Reiss, A.J. (1961), *Occupations and social status*. Free Press, New York.
Renold, H. (1928), 'The nature and present position of skill in industry'. *Economic Journal*. Vol. 38. pp 593-604.
Reynolds, L.G. (1951), *The structure of labour markets*. Harper & Row, New York.
Robbins, D. et al. (eds). (1982), *Rethinking inequality*. Gower, Farnborough.
Roberts, B. et al. (eds). (1985), *New approaches to economic life*. Manchester University Press, Manchester.
Roberts, H. (ed). (1981), *Doing feminist research*. Routledge, London.
Rose, H. (1991), 'Case studies', in Allan, G. and Skinner, C. (eds). (1991).

Rose, M. (1994), 'Skill and Samuel Smiles: Chaning the British work ethic', in Penn, R. et al. (eds). (1994).

Rottenberg, S. (1956), 'On choice in labour markets'. *Industrial Labour Relations Review*. Vol. 9. No. 2. pp 183-199.

Routh, G. (1980), *Occupation and pay in Great Britain 1906-79*. Macmillan, London.

Rowbotham, S. (1979), 'The trouble with 'patriarchy''. *New Statesman*. December. pp 21-28.

Roy, D.F. (1960), '"Banana time", job satisfaction and informal interaction'. *Human Organisation*. Vol. 18. No.4. pp 156-68.

Rubery, J. (1978), 'Structured labour markets, worker organisation and low pay'. *Cambridge Journal of Economics*. Vol. 2. No. 1. pp 17-36.

Rubery, J. and Wilkinson, F. (1981), 'Work and segmented labour markets', in Wilkinson, F. (ed). (1981).

Rubery, J. and Wilkinson, F. (1994), *Employer strategy and the labour market*. Oxford University Press. Oxford.

Rubery, J., Tarling, R. and Wilkinson, F. (1987), 'Flexibility, marketing and the organisation of production'. *Labour and Society*. January. Vol. 12. No. 1. pp 131-151.

Rumberger, R. W. and Carnoy, M. (1980), 'Segmentation in the US labour market: its effects on the mobility and earnings of whites and blacks'. *Cambridge Journal of Economics*. Vol. 4. No. 2. pp 117-132.

Runciman, W.G. (1966), *Relative deprivation and social justice*. Routledge & Kegan Paul, London.

Sabel, C. and Zeitlin, J. (1985), 'Historical alternatives to mass production'. *Past and Present*. No. 108. pp 133-176.

Salop, S.C. (1973), 'Systematic job search and unemployment'. *Review of Economic Studies*. Vol. 40. pp 191-201.

Samuel, R. (1977), 'The workshop of the world: steam power and hand technology in mid-Victorian Britain'. *History Workshop*. Issue. 3. Spring. pp 6-72.

Sapsford, D. and Tzannatos, Z. (eds). (1990), *Current issues in labour market economics*. Macmillan, London.

Sargent, L. (ed). (1981), *Women and revolution: the unhappy marriage of Marxism and Feminism*. Pluto Press, London.

Sayer, A. (1989), 'Postfordism in question'. *International Journal of Urban and Regional Research*. Vol. 13. No. 4. pp 666-695.

SCELI (1992), Unpublished material from Social Change in Economic Life Initiative. Department of Applied Economics. University of Cambridge, Cambridge.

School of Advanced Urban Studies (SAUS). (1990), *Bristol skills and training survey: an analysis of problems faced by groups disadvantaged in the Bristol labour market with respect to access to training and employment*. SAUS. Bristol University, Bristol.

Schultz, T. (1961), 'Investment in human capital'. *American Economic Review*. Vol. 51. No. 1. pp 1-17.

Schumacher, E.F. (1973), *Small is beautiful.* Blond and Briggs. London.
Schumpeter, J.A. (1972), *History of economic analysis.* Oxford University Press, Oxford.
Schutz, A. (1964), *Collected papers II: studies in social theory.* Martinus Nijoff. The Hague, Netherlands.
Scott, A. (1986), 'High technology industry and territorial development: the rise of the orange country complex, 1955-1984'. *Urban Geography.* Vol. 7. No. 1. pp 3-45.
Scott, A. (1988), 'Flexible production systems and regional development: the rise of new industrial spaces in North America and Western Europe'. *International Journal of Urban and Regional Research.* Vol. 12. No. 2. pp 171-86.
Scott, A. and Angel, D. (1987), 'The US semi-conductor industry: a locational analysis'. *Environment and Planning A.* Vol. 19. No. 7. pp 875-912.
Scott, W.H. et al. (1956), *Technical change and industrial relations.* Liverpool University Press, Liverpool.
Seccombe, W. (1974), 'The housewife and her labour under capitalism'. *New Left Review.* No. 83. Jan-Feb. pp 3-24.
Seccombe, W. (1975), 'Domestic labour - reply to critics'. *New Left Review.* No. 94. Nov-Dec. pp 85-96.
Senberger, G.W. et al. (eds). (1990), 'The re-emergence of small enterprises: industrial restructuring in industrialised countries'. International Labour Organisation, Geneva.
Shaiken, H., Herzenberg, S. and Kuhn, S. (1986), 'The work process under flexible production'. *Industrial Relations.* (US). Vol. 23. No. 2. pp 167 -183.
Sheppard, H.L. and Belitsky, A. (1966), *The job hunt: job seeking behaviour of unemployed workers in the local economy.* John Hopkins, Baltimore.
Sked, A. and Cook, C. (1993), *Post - War Britain: A political history.* Penguin, London.
Skills and Enterprise Network Publication. (1993), *Labour market and skill trends, 1994/1995.* Skills and Enterprise Network. Department of Employment, London.
Sloane, P.J. et al. (1993), 'Labour market segmentation: a local labour market analysis using alternative approaches'. *Applied Economics.* Vol. 25. No. 5. pp 569-581.
Sloman, J. (1991), *Economics.* Harvester Wheatsheaf, Hemel Hempstead.
Smith, A. (1776]. (1892), *The wealth of nations.* Routledge, London.
Smith, C. (1989), 'Flexible specialisation, automation & mass production'. *Work, Employment & Society.* Vol. 3. No. 2. pp 203-220.
Smith, C. (1991), 'From 1960s automation to flexible specialisation: a deja vu of technological panaceas', in Pollert, A. (ed). (1991).
Smith, D.J. (1977), *Racial disadvantage in Britain.* Pelican. Harmondsworth, Middlesex.
Solow, R. (1990), *The labour market as a social institution.* Blackwell, Oxford.
Spriegel, W.R. and Myers, C.E. (1953), *The writings of the Gilbreths.* Homewood, Illinois.
Stanworth, M. (1984), 'Women and class analysis: a reply to John Goldthorpe'.

Stanworth, M. (1984), 'Women and class analysis: a reply to John Goldthorpe'. *Sociology*. Vol. 18. No. 2. pp 159-170.
Stark, D. (1980), 'Class struggle and the transformation of the labour process'. *Theory and Society*. Vol. 9. No. 1. pp 89-130.
Stedman-Jones, G. (1975), 'Class struggle and the Industrial Revolution'. *New Left Review*. No. 90. March-April. pp 35-69.
Steiger, T.L. (1993), 'Construction skill and skill construction'. *Work, Employment & Society*. Vol. 7. No. 4. pp 535-560.
Stevenson, R.C. (1920), 'The fertility of various social classes in England and Wales from the middle of the nineteenth century'. *Journal of the Royal Statistical Society*. Vol. 83. Part. 3. (May). pp 401-432.
Stewart, A., Prandy K. and Blackburn, R.M. (1980), *Social stratifications & occupations*. Macmillan, London.
Stigler, G.J. (1941), Production and distribution theories. Macmillan, London.
Stigler, G.J. (1962), 'Information in labour markets'. *Journal of Political Economy*. Vol. 70. No. 5. Part. 2 (Supplement). pp 94-105.
Stone, L., (1975), 'The origins of job structures in the steel industry', in Edwards, R.C. et al. (eds). (1975).
Storper, M. and Scott, A.J. (1988), 'The geographical foundations and social regulation of flexible production complexes', in Wolch, J. and Dear, M. (eds). (1988).
Sturdy, A., Knights, D. and Willmott, H. (eds). (1992), *Skill and consent: contemporary studies in the labour process*. Routledge, London.
Sutcliffe, J. (1816), *A treatise on canals and reservoirs*. Hartley, Rochdale.
Tanner, L.B. (ed). (1970), *Voices from women's liberation*. Signet, New York.
Taylor, F.W. [1895]. (1947), *Scientific management*. Harper & Row, New York.
Tebbit, N. (1988), *Upwardly mobile*. Weidenfield & Nicolson, London.
Thatcher, M. (1993), *The Downing Street years*. Harper Collins, London.
Thomas, R. and Elias, P. (1989), 'Development of the standard occupational classification'. *Population Trends*. No. 55. Spring. pp 16-21.
Thompson, E.P. (1980), *The making of the English working class*. Penguin. Harmondsworth, Middlesex.
Thompson, E.P. (1993), *Customs in common*. Penguin. Harmondsworth, Middlesex.
Thompson, P. (1988), 'Playing at being skilled men: factory culture and pride in work skills among Coventry car workers'. *Social History*. Vol. 13. No. 1. pp 45-70.
Thompson, P. (1989), *The nature of work: an introduction to debates on the labour process*. (2nd edition). Macmillan, London.
Tolliday, S. and Zeitlin, J. (1987), *The automobile industry and its workers: between Fordism and flexibility*. Polity Press, Cambridge.
Topel, R.H. and Ward, M.P. (1992), 'Job mobility and the careers of young men'. *The Quarterly Journal of Economics*. Vol. 107. Issue. 2. pp 439-479.
Training Agency. (1989), *Training and enterprise: priorities for action 1990/91 labour market supplement for Avon*. Training Agency, Bristol.

Trotter, R. de B. (1901), *Galloway Gossip: the Stewartry*. Courier & Herald Press, Dumfries.

Tunstall, J. (1969), *The fishermen*. MacGibbon & Kee, London.

Turner, B.A. (1981), 'Some practical aspects of qualitative data analysis: one way of organising the cognitive processes associated with the generation of grounded theory'. *Quality and Quantity*. Vol. 15. No. 3. pp 225-247.

Turner, B.A. (1983), 'The use of grounded theory for the qualitative analysis of organizational behaviour'. *Journal of Management Studies*. Vol. 20. No. 3. pp 333-348.

Turner, B.A. (1988), 'Connoisseurship in the study of organizational cultures', in Bryman, A. (ed). (1988b).

Turner, B.S. (1988), *Status*. Open University Press, Milton Keynes.

Turner, H.A. (1962), *Trade union growth, structure and policy*. Allen & Unwin, London.

Urry, J. (1988), 'Disorganised capitalism'. *Marxism Today*. October. pp 30-33.

Vanek, J. (1980), 'Time spent in housework', in Amsden, A.H. (ed). (1980).

Varcoe, I. et al. (eds). (1990), *Decyphering science and technology*. Macmillan, London.

Villa, P. (1986), *The structuring on labour markets: a comparative analysis of the steel and construction industry in Italy*. Clarendon, London.

Walby, S. (1986a), 'Gender and class stratification: towards a new approach', in Crompton, R. and Mann, M. (eds). (1986).

Walby, S. (1986b), *Patriarchy at work*. Polity Press, Cambridge.

Walby, S. (1989), 'Theorising patriarchy'. *Sociology*. Vol. 23. No. 2. pp 213-234.

Walters, A. (1986), *Britain's economic renaissance*. Oxford University Press, Oxford.

Watson, G. (1994), 'The flexible workforce and patterns of working hours in the UK'. *Employment Gazette*. Vol. 102. No. 7. pp 239-247.

Weber, M. (1947), *The theory of social and economic organisation*. Free Press, New York.

Weber, M. (1968), *Economy and society*. Bedminster Press, New York.

Wedderburn, D. (1964), *White collar redundancy: a case study*. Cambridge University Press, Cambridge.

Wedderburn, D. (1965), *Redundancy and the railwaymen*. Cambridge University Press, Cambridge.

Wedderburn, D. and Crompton, R. (1972), *Workers' attitudes and technology*. Cambridge University Press, Cambridge.

Wells, C. (1909), *A short history of the port of Bristol*. Bristol.

West, J. (ed). (1982), *Work, women and the labour market*. Routledge & Kegan Paul, London.

Westergaard, J.R. and Resler, H. (1975), *Class in a capitalist society: a study of contemporary Britain*. Heinemann, London.

Whipp, R. (1985), 'Labour markets and communities: an historical view'. *Sociological Review*. Vol. 33. No. 4. pp 768-91.

Whyte, N.F. (1955), *Money and motivation*. Harper, New York.

Whyte, W.F. (1982), 'Interviewing in field research', in Burgess, R. (ed). (1982).
Wilkinson, F. (ed). (1981), *The dynamics of labour market segmentation*. Athlone Press, London.
Williams, K. et al. (1987), 'The end of mass production'. *Economy and Society*. Vol. 16. No. 3. pp 405-439.
Williams, R. (1988), *Keywords*. Fontana, London.
Williams, R. (1989), *Resources of hope*. Verso. London.
Willis, P. (1977), *Learning to labour*. Saxon House. Westmead, England.
Wilson, F. and Buchanan, D. (1988), 'The effect of new technology in the engineering industry: cases of control and constraint'. *Work, Employment & Society*. Vol. 2. No. 3. pp 12-30.
Windolf, P. (ed). (1981), *Allocation and selection in the labour market*. Wissenschaftzentrum, Berlin.
Wolch, J. and Dear, M. (eds). (1988), *Territory and social reproduction*. Allen & Unwin, London.
Wolf, A., Kelson, M. and Silver, R. (1990), *Learning in context: patterns of skills transfer and training implications*. Institute of Education. University of London. Employment Department Training Research and Development Series. No. 58. Employment Department, London.
Wood, S. (ed). (1982), *The degradation of work? Skill, deskilling and the labour process*. Hutchinson, London.
Wood, S. (1986), 'Recruitment systems and the recession'. *British Journal of Industrial Relations*. Vol. 24. No. 3 pp 103-120.
Wood, S. (ed). (1989), *The transformation of work? Skill, flexibility and the labour process*. Unwin Hyman, London.
Wood, S. and Kelly, J. (1982), 'Taylorism, responsible autonomy and management strategies', in Wood, S. (ed). (1982),
Wright, E.O. (1979), *Class, crisis and the state*. Verso, London.
Wright, T. (1868), *The great unwashed*. London.
Yin, R.K. (1984), *Case study research: design and methods*. Sage. Beverly Hills, California.
Young, I. (1981), 'Beyond the unhappy marriage: a critique of the dual systems theory', in Sargent, L. (ed). (1981).
Young, M. and Wilmott, P. (1957), *Family and kinship in East London*. Routledge & Kegan Paul, London.
Zagorski, K. (1987), 'Labour mobility between industries'. *Work and Occupations*. Vol. 13. No. 4. Nov 1986. pp 562-575.
Zeitlin, J. (1979), 'Craft control and the division of labour: engineers and compositors in Britain, 1890-1930'. *Cambridge Journal of Economics*. Vol. 3. No. 3. pp 263-74.
Zeitlin, J. (1988), 'The Third Italy: inter-firm co-operation and technological innovation', in Murray, R. (ed). (1988).
Zimbalist, A. (ed). (1979), *Case studies on the labour process*. Monthly Review Press, New York.

Index

Abbott, P. 167
Abraham, K.G. 13
Aglietta, M. 5
Ainley, P. 94,186
Alford, B.W.E. 25
Allan, G. 28,29,31,37
Ambition 38,77,153,165,173-178, 181-182,184-187
Amin, F. 5
Apostle, R. 18
Armstrong, P. 92,95,98,115,126
Ashton, D.N. 18,83
Atkinson, J. 3,4,17,33,35,37,41,44, 48,67,85,96,140
Atkinson, P. 33,35,37
Averitt, R.T. 17
Barron, R.D. 18
Beardsworth, A. 50
Beatson, M. 1,3,6,25,144
Becker, G. 92,101,120
Beechey, V. 94,98,126
Belitsky, A. 43
Bell, D. 92
Benn, C. 7,89
Beynon, H. 38,45,67,69,77,84,97, 150,151,152,176,183
Blackburn, R.M. 38,84,97,119,131, 132,151,152,172,176,183,184
Blau, P.M. 173
Blaug, M. 19
Blauner, R. 150
Boddy, M. 25
Boeke, J. 17
Bosanquet, N. 18
Bowles, S. 83,96,97,119,140,154
Bradley, H. 98,127
Braverman, H. 84,89,90,91,92,101, 106,117,129,186,187,192
Bresnen, M.J. 28,33,45,68,77
Bristol's economy 21,25-26
Brown, D.C. 44
Bryman, A. 28,29,30
Buchanan, D. 34,92
Buchele, R. 17
Burchell, B. 18,94,95,98,114-117,126
Burgess, R. 37
Cain, G.C. 16,19
Cairnes, J.E. 15,16,193
Campbell, K.E. 48,96
Caplow, T. 44
Carter, M. 19
Case studies 7,31-32,48
CBI 12,140
Cockburn, C. 38,92,94,95,98,99,109, 115,117,126,127,129,130,131,147
Collins, R. 27,97,153,154,166,171, 181
Coombs, R. 99
Corcoran, M. 44, 81
Courtenay, G. 48,68
Coxon, A.P.M. 62,154,166
Coyle, A. 95

Craig, C. 95,98
Cressey, P. 94,117
Crompton, R. 28,35,38,85,92,95, 98,117,126,173,176,178,183, 184,187,192
Crozier, M. 152,154,171,173
Curran, M.M. 38,48,81,115,116,126
Curry, J. 4,5,97,140
Davies, M. 115
Davies, P.M. 62,154,166
Dawes, L. 48,67,154
Deakin, S. 3,4,193
Dennis, G. 93
Department of Employment 115
Deskilling 89-96,109,114,117,187
Dick, B. 45,46,65,67,68,69,70,77, 78,81,81,85,116
Doeringer, P.B. 15,17,18
Dunlop, J.T. 16,17
Dunnell, K. 86
Eckstein, H. 31
Edwards, R.C. 96,109
Elger, T. 4,5
Elias, P. 166,171
Employment Department 1,2,4,6,12, 24,95,144,189
Employment Department Group 9,95, 144
Employment Gazette 24,192
Erickson, R. 166
Extended internal labour markets 46-47,81
Fairley, J. 7,89
Family and friendship networks 42, 47,51,53,56-61,67,68,70-72,74, 75,76,78-80,81,82,85,86,87,190
Finn, D. 7,89
Flanagan, R. 17
Flexible firm 3-6,13,17,93,96,189
Flexible labour markets 1,13
Flexible specialisation 3-6,13,93,189
Fordism 5
Francis, B. 99,100,104-106
Freeman, D. 29
Friedman, A. 96
Friedman, M. 14
Fuchs, V.R. 92
Gallie, D. 31
Game, A. 147
Gender: manual work 33,146-147,155, 164,186,191
Gender: recruitment 38,81
Gilmour, I. 14
Gintis, H. 83,96,97,119,140,154
Glaser, B. 28,37
Glass, D.V. 166
Goldthorpe, J.H. 166,173,176,183
Gordon, D.M. 17,84,96,140
Gramsci, A. 94
Granovetter, M.S. 47
Grieco, M. 44-47,65-75,77,78,81,116
Griffin, G. 26
Guardian 143
Hakim, C 143
Hales, J. 41,48
Hall, J.166
Hammersley, M. 33,35,37
Hardwick, P. 12
Hatt, P.K. 166
Hayek, J. 13,14
Head, E. 86
Hedges, B. 48,52,60,68
Hedges, N. 41,45,67,69,77,83
Hendy, J. 3,4
Hicks, J.R. 9,10
Hill, S. 45,47,67,70,84,97
Hirst, P. 5
HMSO 165,171
Hope, K. 166
Horrell, S. 95,98,115,116,126
Human capital 15,90,92-93,100,101, 102,105,111,112,119,120
Humphries, J. 127,130
Hutton, W. 194
Hyman, R. 5
IFF 41,48-50,52,60
Internal labour markets 18,19,46,96
Irwin, S. 48
Jenkins, R. 38,44,48,68-71,73-75, 77,80,81,119

Jenson, J. 98,115-117,127
Johnson, C. 3
Jones, C. 34-36
Jones, G. 28,35,38,85,92,95,98, 126,173,178,187,192
Joseph, K. 13
Kahn, H. 44
Keenan, J.M. 140
Kelley, M.R. 5
Kelly, J. 96
Kerr, C. 16
Kinship networks 38,45-47,53,67,71, 75,80,81,82,86
Knorr-Cetina, K. 27,28,30
Kumar, K. 92
Kusterer, K. 94,123,137
Labour Market Quarterly 48,52,60
Lane, C. 117,173,178
Lawson, N. 3,14
Lazonick, W. 83,98,99,115,126,147
Lee, G. 68,69,74,77,81,97
Lee, R.M. 45,68
Lewis, O. 29
Lipietz, A. 5
Littler, C.R. 99
Lockwood, D. 176,183
Lummis, T. 34
MacDonald, G.M. 13
MacInnes, J. 94,117
MacKay, D.I. 132
MacKenzie, G. 99
Maguire, M.J. 18, 83
Mann, M. 97,119,131,132
Manufacturing industry 21-23
Manwaring, T. 45-47,51,62,65,61-75, 77,78,81,82,94,96,115,116
Marginson, P. 4
Marsden, D. 44,65,70
Marshall, A. 42
Marshall, G. 153,154,166,173,176, 183
Martin, R. 99
Marx, K. 90
McCormick, K. 140
McGee, R. 44
McNabb, R. 15,18
Mead, M. 29
Meritocracy 38,58-60,72,77,85
Milkman, R. 117,127
Mill, J.S. 15,16,191
Mitchell, J. 28,31,32
Mobility: industrial 6,20,21,24-25, 33,87,90,141,160,165,170,172, 178,192
Mobility: labour 6,24
Mobility: occupational 6-7,13,24-25, 27,41,87,89,140,192
More, C. 97-99,105,106,109,129
Morgan, D.H.J. 146,147,150,159
Morgan, G. 45,46,65,67,68,69,70, 77,78,81,81,85,116,119
Morris, L. 48
Murray, F. 4,93
Murray, R. 5
Myers, C.A. 43
Neo-classical theory 2,5,9,11-14,15, 16,17,19,20,189
Nichols, T. 97,109,140
Noble, D. 92
Non-competing groups 7,16-17,19,20, 28,31,39,41,87,89,141,143,144, 187,192,193
Norris, G.M. 18
North, G.C. 166
Occupational hierarchy 104,163,165, 167-173,180,185,186,187,192
OECD 2
OPCS 166
Osterman, P. 17
Oxford English Dictionary 103,107
Oxford Thesaurus 103,107
Palloix, C. 5
Parliamentary Papers 130
Parnes, H.S. 43
Patrick, J. 35
Penn, R.D. 18,92-94,99,100,104-106, 109,120,123
Phillips, A. 95,98,99,115,116,126, 129,147
Piore, M.J. 4,5,17,93

Polanyi, M. 94
Pollert, A. 4,5,97,98,126,127,129, 140,147,148,151,194
Potter, T. 97,140
Prandy, K. 152,172,172,184
Pringle, R. 147
Prosch, H. 94
Psacharopoulos, G. 18
Purcell, K. 127
Qualitative methodology: criticism 28-31
Qualitative methodology: description 26-28
Recruitment: formal 38,68,75,85
Recruitment: informal 7,38,41-45,48, 51,67-70,83,84,85,86
Recruitment: tacit skills 81-83
Redfield, R. 29
Rees, A. 42,43,67,68,70,71,74
Reid, S. 117
Reiss, A.J. 166
Reynolds, H. 43,71
Rose, H. 28,31
Rose, M. 176,183
Roy, D.F. 151
Rubery, J. 2,5,17,71,84,95,98,99, 105,106,109,115,116
Ryan, P. 15,18
Sabel, C.F. 4,5,93
Sayer, A. 119
SCELI 41,48,49,52,60
Schultz, G. 43
Schutz, A. 28
Scientific management 91,96
Scott, W.H. 38,44,70
Sedentary work 149-151,157-159, 165,175,181,192
Segmented labour markets 9,15-19, 20,185,194,195
Service sector industry 21-23
Sheppard, H.L. 43
Shiftwork 164-165
Skills: communication 95,113-114, 117,120,134,136
Skills: gender 89,115,126-131,141
Skills: mismatch 26
Skills: political/social 95,97-99,103, 104,105,107,108,111-112,114,126, 131,136
Skills: qualifications 94,112,116,118-121,131,134,135
Skills: responsibility 100,102,104-105, 111
Skills: trade 103,105-107,108,110,111, 114,115,122,134,136,138
Skills and Enterprise Network 1,7,41, 89,143
Smith, A. 5,9,15
Solow, R. 17
Stark, D. 95,96,99
Status 15,20,98,108-109,139,153-155, 158,163,166,167-173,179-180,184, 187,192,193
Steiger, T.L. 94,97,99,105,116,124
Stevenson, R.C. 165,166
Stewart, A. 152,172,172,184
Stigler, G.J. 9
Strauss, A. 28,37
Supply side 2,12,15,18,189
Swearing 129,193
Tacit skills 69-71,78,80,86,93-95,116-117,123,126,132,137,191
Tarling, R. 5
Taylor, F.W. 91,129
Thatcher, M. 2
Thomas, R. 166,171
Thompson, E.P. 194
Thompson, P. 45,92,99,105,106,151, 162
Tolliday, S. 4
Topel, R.H. 13
Trade unions 3,15,84,98
Training Agency 26
Tunstall, J. 44
Turner, B.A. 28,166
Urry, J. 5
Walters, A. 14
Ward, M.P. 13
Watson, G. 6,144
Weber, M. 166

Wedderburn, D. 38,44,176,183,184
Whipp, R. 70,71
Whyte, W.F. 34
Wilkinson, F. 2,5,18,194
Williams, R. 5,168,170,175,180,190
Wilmott, P. 38,44,45
Wilson, F. 92
Wood, S. 26,45-51,62,65,61-75,77,
78,81,82,91,94-96,115,116
Working communities 28,31,168,
181,193
Wrench, J. 68,69,74,77,81,97
Yin, R.K. 31,32
Young, M. 38,44,45
Zeitlin, J. 4,5,93,96

Printed in the United States
by Baker & Taylor Publisher Services